Sri Lanka's Remittance Economy

Employing a multiscalar approach to migration outcomes, spanning individual households, local communities, the macroeconomy and global patterns of capital accumulation, this book demonstrates how cumulatively causal processes at structural, institutional and agency levels have forged a precariously remittance-dependent economy in Sri Lanka.

This book combines historical-structural analysis with qualitative research to contend that remittance inflows have reinforced patterns of uneven development in Sri Lanka. At the heart of this argument is a bold critique of remittance capital that inverts the migration–development nexus which has come to dominate international policymaking, with implications for Sri Lanka and other 'remittance economies' throughout the Global South. The author contends that temporary labour migration from Sri Lanka is a process of 'migration-underdevelopment', in which remittance inflows – ubiquitously considered a key source of capital for developing economies – are reinforcing of uneven development at multiple scales and produce unsustainable development outcomes.

Offering a uniquely systematic critique of remittances as a source of developmental capital for countries of origin, such as Sri Lanka, this book will be of interest to academics in the field of development studies, migration studies and Asian studies.

Matt Withers is a research fellow in the Department of Sociology at Macquarie University, Australia. His research is concerned with the political economy of temporary labour migration and the developmental implications of remittances both in Sri Lanka and throughout the Asia-Pacific region.

Routledge Series on Asian Migration

Series Editors: Yuk Wah Chan (City University of Hong Kong), Jonathan H. X. Lee (San Francisco State University, US) and Nicola Piper (The University of Sydney, Australia)

1 **Racism and Resistance among the Filipino Diaspora**
Kristine Aquino

2 **New Chinese Migrations**
Mobility, Home, and Inspirations
Edited by Yuk Wah Chan and Sin Yee Koh

3 **International Migrants in China's Global City**
The New Shanghailanders
James Farrer

4 **Asylum-Seeking Journeys in Asia**
Refugees in Hong Kong and Bangkok
Terence Chun Tat Shum

5 **Sri Lanka's Remittance Economy**
A Multiscalar Analysis of Migration-Underdevelopment
Matt Withers

NAMS
Network for Asian Migration Studies

Sri Lanka's Remittance Economy

A Multiscalar Analysis of Migration-Underdevelopment

Matt Withers

Routledge
Taylor & Francis Group
LONDON AND NEW YORK

First published 2019
by Routledge
2 Park Square, Milton Park, Abingdon, Oxon OX14 4RN

and by Routledge
605 Third Avenue, New York, NY 10017

First issued in paperback 2022

Routledge is an imprint of the Taylor & Francis Group, an informa business

Publisher's Note
The publisher has gone to great lengths to ensure the quality of this reprint but points out that some imperfections in the original copies may be apparent.

British Library Cataloguing-in-Publication Data
A catalogue record for this book is available from the British Library

Library of Congress Cataloging-in-Publication Data
Names: Withers, Matt, author.
Title: Sri Lanka's remittance economy : a multiscalar analysis of migration-underdevelopment / Matt Withers.
Description: Abingdon, Oxon ; New York, NY : Routledge, 2019. |
Series: Routledge series on Asian migration ; 5 | Includes index.
Identifiers: LCCN 2019005863| ISBN 9781138320048 (hardback) |
ISBN 9780429453557 (ebook) | ISBN 9780429843051 (epub)
Subjects: LCSH: Economic development–Sri Lanka. | Emigrant remittances–Sri Lanka. | Sri Lanka–Emigration and immigration–Economic aspects.
Classification: LCC HC424 .W58 2019 | DDC 332/.04246095493–dc23
LC record available at https://lccn.loc.gov/2019005863

ISBN 13: 978-1-138-32004-8 (hbk)
ISBN 13: 978-1-03-240150-8 (pbk)
ISBN 13: 978-0-429-45355-7 (ebk)

DOI: 10.4324/9780429453557

Typeset in Times New Roman
by Wearset Ltd, Boldon, Tyne and Wear

Contents

	List of illustrations	vi
	Acknowledgements	vii
	Introduction	1
1	The history of migration-development	14
2	The political economy of uneven development in Sri Lanka	33
3	In search of the 'good life': uneven development and forced migration	49
4	The cost of being exploited: fees, debts and the merchants of labour	74
5	Manufacturing success: status and the re-socialisation of migrant labour	95
6	Remittances and the financing of uneven development	120
7	The unequal 'wins' of temporary labour migration	145
	Conclusion: migration-underdevelopment	167
	Index	175

Illustrations

Figures

3.1	Map of fieldwork locations	53
4.1	Recruitment costs in Thavapuram, 2000–2013	76
4.2	Migrant incomes in Thavapuram, 2000–2013	77
4.3	Temporary labour migration recruitment networks in Sri Lanka	86
6.1	Remittance decision tree	123
6.2	Goods exports vs. remittances (percentage of GDP), 2000–2017	135
7.1	Unemployment vs. foreign employment, 1991–2015	149

Tables

3.1	Top remittance priority for women	62
3.2	Top remittance priority for men	62
3.3	Top remittance expenditure for women	65
3.4	Top remittance expenditure for men	65
3.5	Business expenditures by location	66
3.6	Employment benefits by location	68
3.7	Overall benefit by number of trips	69
3.8	Repeat migration	70
4.1	Method of arranging employment	76
4.2	Method of financing foreign employment	82
4.3	Length of debt repayments	83
5.1	Occupation before migration	96
5.2	Occupation during migration	98
5.3	Main hardship endured during migration	99
6.1	Largest shares of remittance expenditure	127
6.2	Ownership of consumer durables	131

Acknowledgements

Thanks are due to a great number of people who have offered support and lent guidance throughout the course of my research in Sri Lanka.

I would like to extend my appreciation foremost to my wonderful supervisors, Elizabeth Hill and Stuart Rosewarne, whose encouragement and criticism have been invaluable in shaping this book. I similarly offer my heartfelt thanks to colleagues and collaborators who have given me their time, advice and support: to Nicola Piper and Janaka Biyanwila, who I have had the privilege of working closely with, and to a much longer procession of individuals who have offered guidance and friendship along the way. Particular gratitude is reserved for Magdalena Cubas, Sohoon Yi, Beck Pearse, Rosie Hancock, Bill Dunn, Mike Beggs and Rianne Mahon.

A special mention must be made for the Centre for Poverty Analysis in Colombo, without whose assistance my research would simply not have been possible. I would like to thank Priyanthi Fernando for her readiness to accommodate me at CEPA, Mohamed Munas for his help with fieldwork arrangements, and to Vagisha Gunasekara for her friendship and willingness to answer my incessant questions. I'm likewise indebted to Mohamed Shamil, whose interpreting, liaising and motorcycle handling skills were indispensable.

Recognition is also due to the Women's Centre of Sri Lanka and their numerous field contacts who generously facilitated the initial interviews and 'got the ball rolling', and to the Women and Media Collective and International Centre for Ethnic Studies for their assistance along the way.

Thanks too for friends who've offered moral support and compliant ears, as well as the occasional spot of proofing: Arun Devasia, Dave Goldschmidt, Ryan Cain, Annemari de Silva, Tehani Ariyaratne and others I won't mention for fear of accruing too great a tab of unreturned favours. Lastly, I'm very grateful to my family, who have endured the ups and downs and comings and goings of the last few years: to my parents, Alex and Jon, my brothers, Richard and Sam, and to my partner Ezreena who's borne more of the turbulence than most.

Introduction

International labour migration in the Asian century

An estimated 244 million international migrants cross borders each year, for reasons that may involve any combination of structural pressures, institutional pulls or deeply personal decisions (UNDESA 2016). The movement of people is constrained by coalescing political economic imbalances at local, national and regional scales that allow for frameworks of migration governance preferencing wealthier actors. Institutions, both formal and informal, take shape around particular migration pathways and attempt to preserve these corridors and the interests vested within them. Households, too, make decisions and pursue livelihood strategies according to a gamut of known, or partially known, opportunities and risks that can vary dramatically with personal circumstance. The movement of people *within* the territorial confines of established political borders, so-called internal migration, is driven by a similarly broad interplay of macro, meso and micro factors – only on a far greater scale (Skeldon 2017). The heterogeneity of these flows, whether internal or international, thwarts generalisation or adherence to any totalising theory of migration (Castles 2010; King 2012). What we do know of all human migrations, however, is that the compulsion to move is deeply associated with the need to work, whether as a primary or supporting reason for migration or as an attendant necessity of forced displacement (ILO 2015).

The sheer diversity of the world's migrant population defies neat distillation into the reductionist binary of 'refugee' and 'economic migrant' that, with all its pejorative weight, has littered the political and media landscape of the Global North in recent years. At the heart of this typological crisis is the question of *labour*. As Purkayastha (2018) has argued, all instances of migration exist along a continuum of choice and coercion. This continuum can be envisioned as a spectrum of broad migration types, spanning from internationally mobile highly waged workers at one end, to those violently displaced or trafficked at the other. But any attempt at simple categorisation is quickly muddied by consideration of the labour practices and policy frameworks that mediate the internal and international movements of migrant workers, and of the unfurling processes of uneven development that shape and reshape structural disparities between different locales of the world economy. That a migrant may cross borders in pursuit of work does not in itself connote the unimpinged exercise of free agency. Yet this is an assumption that has become self-evident in policy, in the media and also in mainstream migration scholarship – where notions of 'forced migration' are jealously guarded by those studying refugees and displaced populations, while the tired positivism of rational choice theory continues to inform dominant analyses of the factors driving international labour migration.

In one sense, this book is about challenging prevalent assumptions of 'economic migrants' at the cusp of an emerging 'Asian Century', in which the loci of core industrial production, finance capital and economic growth has begun shifting from Europe and North America to East and Southeast Asia. This shift has entailed the global distribution of capitalist production and reproduction being altered in some ways, but reinforced in others. In Sri Lanka, as throughout most of South Asia, low-waged temporary labour migration into regional hubs of growth and accumulation is a longstanding livelihood practice, internally and internationally. Patterns of uneven development, their roots extending far back into colonial and pre-colonial history, have hewn vast fault-lines of economic exclusion across the subcontinent and conditioned a common need to migrate seasonally or temporarily in search of work. This survival strategy prevails as a dominant feature of South Asian labour relations (Breman 2009). It is perhaps most notably manifest in the international migration of poorly paid domestic workers, construction workers and other, typically menial, forms of labour as an in-situ fix for the developmental aspirations of oil-rich Gulf Cooperation Council countries in West Asia. Commencing in the 1960s, and involving the temporary migration of millions of workers by the early 1970s, this South to West Asian migration corridor has overseen the largest coherent international movement of labour in history (Thiollet 2011). These workers have endured some of the most deplorable working conditions and rights abuses of the postcolonial era, not only performing '3D' jobs (i.e. the dirty, dangerous and demeaning) routinely earmarked for migrant workers but routinely employed in conditions unexaggeratedly akin to modern-day slavery (Degorge 2006). To consider the decision to work under such arrangements as constitutive of free choice is to neglect the totality of circumstances that constrain individual agency in this context.

Though still in its infancy, the political and economic reconfiguration of the world economy at the onset of the Asian Century is already having far-reaching consequences for 'advanced' and 'emerging' countries alike. As returns to labour have bourgeoned within countries like China, where real wages have nearly doubled during the past decade, so too have they tightened, stagnated or declined throughout the Global North (ILO 2019). These changes to the geography of production have been accompanied by unmistakable trends in the way immigration regimes interface with labour relations. Led by Canada and Australia, wealthy countries have stemmed family and humanitarian visa pathways while adopting a bifurcated approach to labour migration. Permanent immigration has been curtailed to attract 'highly skilled' workers deemed desirable to a post-industrial economy, while low-waged workers are increasingly confined to temporary visas (Castles 2013). This condition of temporariness further precarises more vulnerable migrant workers and abates conservative political unease about immigration amidst deteriorating conditions of employment and welfare. Meanwhile, non-inclusive growth has been rife throughout most of the Global South, with rural–urban divides intensifying as economic activity becomes concentrated in large cities and the viability of traditional livelihoods wane. Against this backdrop, centres of growth have demonstrably relied on the exploitation of temporary migrant labour to underscore capital accumulation and offset the costs of social reproduction. This applies whether workers be internal migrants whose long-term immigration prospects are tempered by formal or informal barriers (e.g. China's *hukou* system), or international migrants whose visas are either strictly contingent (e.g. West Asia's *kafala* system) or non-existent (e.g. irregular Indonesian domestic workers in Malaysia).

Widening inequality is proving a defining feature of the Asian Century and temporary labour migration is one of the most immediate expressions of this trend (Phillips 2017). In both the Global North and Global South, 'economic migrants' labouring on a temporary basis and with diminished rights form a growing share of the labour force. In this context, a closer examination of the established capital–labour relations that Sri Lanka's temporary migrants work within can offer an instructive framework for understanding the structural, institutional and personal drivers of contemporary labour migration as similar practices expand elsewhere in the world.

In another sense though, this book is more intimately concerned with the dominant assumption of migration-led development that is extrapolated from the application of rational choice theory to the motives of 'economic migrants'. This rational choice argument is a simple one: if migrants are believed to work abroad voluntarily, as a result of individual or household rational cost-benefit analysis, it follows that the weight of developmental outcomes must be beneficial (or else rationality itself is belied). The crux of this argument dates back to the modernisation and neoclassical foundations of migration-development theory, and despite significant and sustained counterclaims from critical migration scholarship during the 1970s and 1980s, has been re-established as axiomatic following the post-millennial 'rediscovery' of migration-led development (de Haas 2010). At the heart of contemporary fervour for the prospect of migration-development is the foreign income sent home by migrant workers – *remittances*. Whereas earlier waves of migration-development theory took shape around debates over wage equalisation, human capital formation and trajectories of developmental convergence/divergence, remittances are a relatively new source of academic and policy attention. This is not coincidental. Until the 1990s, the sum of remittance receipts flowing to developing countries was not particularly significant relative to other capital inflows. By the early 2000s, however, remittances had eclipsed official development assistance (ODA), and even foreign direct investment (FDI), for many developing economies (de Haas 2010). Taken in aggregate, remittances appear to entail a large transfer of capital that should not only benefit individual migrants and their households, but yield spillover effects that catalyse development outcomes for local communities and national economies. The intuitive sway of this logic – that income transfers promote development – has left even those critical of temporary labour migration schemes acknowledging the implicit developmental benefit of remittances as a given (Wucker 2004; Skeldon 2006; Faist 2008; Lenard and Straehle 2010; Martin 2012; Wickramasekara 2015).

It is the characterisation of remittances as a form of developmental capital that underscores the World Bank's now-ubiquitous 'triple win' thesis (World Bank 2006), which has been used to promote temporary or 'circular'[1] labour migration schemes involving workers from countries throughout the Global South. The triple win scenario posits that temporary labour migration is mutually beneficial for migrant workers, the (developing) countries they originate from and the (developed) countries they travel to – i.e. a 'win–win–win' scenario. Migrant workers are expected to benefit from improved wages, from the development of skills and from opportunities to invest their remittances upon returning home; migrant-sending countries are expected to benefit from a net increase in human capital via 'brain circulation' and the accumulation of foreign exchange earnings from remittance receipts; while migrant-receiving countries are expected to benefit from access to 'flexible' labour markets to address skill shortages and supplement production (World Bank 2006). The triple win thesis has unprecedented backing by key developmental institutions and has exerted profound influence over global, regional and national economic policymaking. The notion that temporary labour migration leads to development has become enshrined in the prescriptions of international development bodies (e.g. the World Bank and International Monetary Fund (IMF)), regional economic organisations (e.g. the Organisation for Economic Cooperation and Development (OECD) and the Asian Development Bank (ADB)) and sending-country governments who increasingly frame migrants as 'heroes' and 'agents of development' (Lee and Piper 2017).

Yet, while the 'wins' for migrant-receiving economies are readily apparent (i.e. access to a global reserve army of cheap and exploitable labour), the benefits for migrants and migrant-sending countries are far more ambiguous and lack empirical support. Remittances are thought to alleviate poverty, spur migrant entrepreneurship, create spillover effects for local communities and improve the creditworthiness of the migrant-sending country (World Bank 2006); in short, they are a priori expected to effect outcomes envisioned as conducive to market-driven development. However, primary research has instead tended to suggest that remittances, and temporary labour migration more generally, produce a variety of contextually specific outcomes for migrants and their countries of origin that are significantly tempered by individual circumstances and prevailing structural constraints on development. Although framed as mutually beneficial, the relative distribution of 'wins' associated with temporary labour migration seem decisively skewed towards migrant-receiving countries, while the assumed gains accruing to migrants and migrant-sending countries remain both under-theorised and empirically unsubstantiated. The irresponsibility of promoting temporary labour migration schemes on this basis is readily apparent. In West Asia, where violations of migrant workers' rights are unequivocal and widespread, the 'ends justify the means' logic of the triple win thesis has lent legitimacy and international policymaking support to the continued exploitation of migrant workers.

The acuteness of human suffering embedded in these exploitative labour practices was made clear at the very inception of my research in Sri Lanka. Fieldwork for this book commenced in Colombo during January 2013 and coincided with widespread public outrage concerning the treatment of Sri Lanka's migrant domestic workers in West Asia. A few days earlier, on 9 January, a young Sri Lankan domestic worker – Rizana Nafeek – had been beheaded in Saudi Arabia, charged with the murder of a four-month-old child that had died in her care several years earlier. Nafeek had been 17 at the time of the child's death, having migrated to Saudi Arabia on a forged passport doctored by recruitment agents to bypass age restrictions on foreign employment (Weerasooriya 2013). Her death tipped longstanding concern about the abuse of migrant women in West Asia into a public and media uproar accompanied by demands for greater protection of migrant domestic workers. Yet Nafeek's execution, proselytising of public opinion though it was, represents only the most violent extremity of a wide spectrum of human and labour rights violations that occur during temporary labour migration from South to West Asia. Just as fatalities amongst Nepalese migrant workers constructing stadiums for the FIFA World Cup in Qatar have brought transient international attention to the most grievous end of a malignant abuse of labour that stretches back to the 1960s, so too did Nafeek's death garner a wave of mediated indignation whose receding tide left the more commonplace abuses of migrant domestic workers unstirred. The International Labour Organisation (ILO) has catalogued historical and ongoing rights violations that occur in the vacuums of jurisdiction that temporary labour migration routinely operates within, including incidence of physical and sexual abuse, deception regarding wages and conditions, withholding pay and chronic overwork (ILO 2010). Such abuses occur alongside psychological and social traumas associated with migration that are less-readily quantifiable, such as experiences of isolation and familial separation (ILO 2010; Gündüz 2013).

There are numerous reasons why the hardships associated with temporary labour migration are overlooked and even tolerated, including the very 'invisibility' of migrant suffering and the prevalence of similar hardships within migrant-sending countries. Perhaps most influential, though, is the persistent economic justification for temporary labour migration: the belief that it brings about economic development. Considering the gravity of this assumption, there is a pressing need to interrogate the supposed 'wins' accruing to migrant workers and their countries of origin. Sri Lanka's uneven and unsustained economic development, despite large and steady outflows of temporary labour migrants to West Asia and commensurate inflows of remittances, demands a more critical examination of the assumed causality between migration and development.

This book provides such an analysis. By tracing the dynamics of migration-underdevelopment in Sri Lanka, in which remittances play a central role at multiple scales, it unpicks key aspects of the triple win thesis and postulates an alternative explanation for the proliferation of fragile remittance economies across the Global South as the world economy reorients towards Asia.

Sri Lanka: temporary labour migration and remittance capital

Some prefacing is necessary to situate Sri Lanka's relationship with temporary labour migration.

Temporary labour migration has quietly become the cornerstone of Sri Lanka's economy. Although the South Asian island is more frequently associated with tea, tourism and garment manufacturing, in 2017 the combined net foreign exchange earnings of its three largest industries were eclipsed by workers' remittances amounting to US$7.16 billion (CBSL 2018). Equivalent to 63 per cent of total goods exports and 8.25 per cent of gross domestic product (GDP) for the same year (CBSL 2018), the prominence of these remittance inflows is proportionate to the volume of domestic and low-waged workers leaving Sri Lanka to work abroad, overwhelmingly in the oil-economies of West Asia's Persian Gulf. The last available data indicates that there were 1,932,245 Sri Lankans in foreign employment as of 2010, approximately 10 per cent of the country's total population and equivalent to roughly 25 per cent of the domestic workforce (SLBFE 2012). Given that annual departures have increased year-on-year till 2014 before declining slightly in 2015 and 2016 (SLBFE 2016), and that large irregular migration flows remain unaccounted for (ILO 2018), these figures can be considered conservative estimates of the true extent of Sri Lanka's migrant workforce.

For Sri Lanka's working poor, this statistical snapshot reflects a more intimate socio-economic reality: the prevalence of temporary labour migration as a dominant livelihood and survival strategy. Since sweeping economic reforms in 1977 liberalised Sri Lanka's migration policy, foreign employment in West Asia has become an increasingly common means of earning an income in lieu of decent local work and, for the most developmentally marginalised communities, almost a rite of passage. The conditions and commonness of temporary labour migration cuts asymmetrically across Sri Lanka's gender, ethnic and class divisions. Throughout the first two decades of migration to West Asia, the clear majority of workers were female domestic workers, typically of poor Sinhalese background (Eelens, Mook, and Schampers 1992; Kottegoda 2004). By 1997 women accounted for 75 per cent of all Sri Lanka's temporary labour migrants (SLBFE 2012).

This trend is consistent with the broader feminisation of Sri Lanka's export sector following the 1977 reforms, which oversaw the establishment of Export Processing Zones (EPZs) within which young Sinhalese women were employed as cheap labour for a then-nascent garments industry (Biyanwila 2011). As traditional male livelihoods in fishing and agriculture waned amidst rapid inflation and economies of scale, women were increasingly positioned as the new breadwinners of the rural economy, either through internal migration to work in the garments industry or through international migration as domestic workers (Kottegoda 2004). These migrant domestic workers were, by and large, Sinhalese. Sri Lankan Muslim[2] women made up a comparatively small segment, though had the highest proportional involvement; Tamil women from the north and east of Sri Lanka meanwhile faced a radically different political economic landscape and had little formal participation while the civil war endured (Kottegoda 2004). Along with male migrants, women were (and still remain) almost uniformly drawn from Sri Lanka's working class – 'unskilled' workers, 'low-skilled' workers and 'housemaids' comprised 95 per cent of migrants in 1994 (the earliest available skill data) (SLBFE 2012) and still account for 89 per cent as of 2016 (SLBFE 2016).

Since 2004, male migrant departures have been on the rise, reaching parity with female departures in 2008 and as of 2016 accounting for 65 per cent of annual outflows (SLBFE 2016). Despite this pronounced change in the gender composition of temporary labour migration, the common sentiment that Sri Lanka has become a 'country of housemaids' endures (Waldman 2005). Although the economic significance of temporary labour migration is rarely discussed in policy or media, there is a palpable sense of public concern for the treatment of female migrant workers and the consequences for families left behind. This concern is, however, often articulated as patriarchal unease about migrant domestic workers eschewing maternal responsibilities by 'abandoning' their children or 'breaking up' families via foreign employment (Cooray 2017). In 2013, the Sri Lankan government responded to these concerns about the 'social cost' of migration by introducing a government circular known as the Family Background Report (FBR). The FBR increased the minimum age requirement for women migrant domestic workers according to the country of destination,[3] but more notably imposed an outright ban on the migration of women with children under the age of five and established screening procedures to ensure those with children over the age of five had allocated a 'suitable' (i.e. female) guardian in their stead (Abeyasekera and Jayasundere 2015; ILO 2018). While the FBR has shaped the gender composition of official migrant departures in recent years, notwithstanding evidence of increased irregular migration (Weeraratne 2016), the government has stopped short of enacting a genuine curtailment of domestic worker migration.

The problem is that Sri Lanka can no longer afford *not* to send domestic workers: the country's growing dependency on remittances has become an elephant in a room otherwise populated by bold proclamations of developmental promise. The acrimonious end to civil war in 2009 has been framed as a watershed moment for Sri Lanka's economic development, expected to deliver the stability necessary to attract galvanising investment and tourism. Rajapaksa's post-war developmental manifesto, *Sri Lanka – The Emerging Wonder of Asia*, left no room for ambiguity in this regard:

> Sri Lanka's growth targets for the 2010–2016 period appear well within reach. The 26-year conflict is over. Necessary infrastructure is in place. The global economy is on the recovery path … Sri Lanka's investment climate for the private sector has been affected adversely in the past by conflict related uncertainties, legal disputes and infrastructure limitations. However, there are indications that the climate in Sri Lanka is rapidly improving.
>
> (DNP 2010, 5)

The macroeconomic prospectus laid out in *Sri Lanka – The Emerging Wonder of Asia* evokes a popular local motif of seeing Sri Lanka as a nascent Singapore, a 'dynamic global hub' in waiting (DNP 2010). Yet this vision, in its haste to appropriate and transpose fashionable tropes of development parlance – to erect a 'modern market economy', driven by 'knowledge-based enterprise', 'globally competitive industry' and 'vibrant capital markets' – makes little acknowledgement of Sri Lanka's reliance on remittances to maintain its current macroeconomic stability. Neither migrant workers nor their earnings are mentioned throughout the 318 pages of the manifesto, save for a lone bullet point projecting a near doubling of remittance inflows to US$7 billion by 2016 and a single sentence avowing greater protection for migrant domestic workers from sexual exploitation (DNP 2010). The macroeconomic importance of remittances is instead only alluded to, as an uncredited foreign exchange buffer that allows for 'a competitive, yet stable exchange rate … supported by a surplus in the Balance of Payments' (DNP 2010, 6).

In more recent years, Sri Lanka's post-war optimism has begun to lull, with GDP growth and exports falling short of projected figures, and tourism emerging as the most prominent growth industry (CBSL 2018). Export earnings, in particular, remain decisively flat. Meanwhile, the anticipated doubling of remittances had already occurred by 2014, without garnering much recognition. Although remittance inflows have plateaued since 2014, correlated with slumping oil prices and the introduction of the FBR, the government had hoped to secure an annual US$10 billion in remittance receipts by the end of 2016 (IPS 2014). The need for increasing remittances, as evident under the current Sirisena government as it was under Rajapaksa, is underscored by burgeoning external debt from 'muscular' post-war infrastructural development constructed using readily-available Chinese loans and labour (Safi 2018).

In light of its persistent trade deficit, Sri Lanka had – under Rajapaksa – relied on growing remittances to buffer its current account and maintain a relatively stable exchange rate needed to repay maturing development loans. During Sirisena's presidency, the incumbent government has refrained from interventionist currency management,[4] causing the rupee to depreciate in volatile fashion, hitting record lows against the US dollar and creating politically destabilising price shocks (Reuters 2018). If the rupee continues its depreciation, the central bank will no doubt have to resume selling foreign exchange reserves to defend the currency and ward off inflation of Sri Lanka's external debt, thus reaffirming the economy's tacit reliance on remittance earnings. The fragility of this scenario is made more acute by the fact that remittance inflows have stagnated in recent years, gravitating around the US$7 billion mark since 2014, in keeping with declining departure figures and economic downturns in migrant-receiving economies (CBSL 2018). While increasing receipts from tourism go some way towards offsetting diminished foreign exchange earnings, the tourism industry remains a smaller source of revenue and employment than temporary labour migration and is no less susceptible to the vicissitudes of the global economy (WTTC 2018).

The Nation, a popular English-language weekly, sums up this concern:

> The comparatively slower growth in Sri Lanka's consistently largest foreign exchange earner, worker remittances, in 2015 till to-date is a major concern given the fact that other predominant revenue streams, such as exports, tourism and Foreign Direct Investments (FDI) have also not performed to expectations … if the current trend continued, Sri Lanka would be under severe fiscal pressure owing to the lack of proper revenue mechanisms to match the gap between current expenditure and revenue.
>
> (Razak and Wamanan 2015)

Thus, while the government faces persistent moral pressure to stem domestic worker migration, there appears to be an overriding imperative to encourage further temporary labour migration as a means of securing remittance inflows. For Sri Lanka's economically marginalised, this developmental strategy means a deepening reliance on performing notoriously exploitative and precarious work for questionable financial returns to their households and communities. Meanwhile, the immediate threat of a macroeconomic bottleneck is telling of a more profound structural contradiction at the heart of Sri Lanka's 'remittance economy'. With ever-greater remittances needed to buttress its current account, Sri Lanka appears intractably reliant on redoubling temporary labour migration to West Asia in lieu of substantive economic development at home. This contradiction, itself entwined with uneven development that has forced marginalised populations into foreign employment to finance further projects of uneven development, is the central topic of this book.

A brief overview of theory, methodology and chapters

This book examines whether the transfer and consumption of remittances constitutes a valuable source of developmental capital for Sri Lanka. It responds to the problems posed by the dominant triple win framing of migration-development, as well as the limitations of existing critical perspectives, by exploring the economic outcomes of Sri Lankan temporary labour migration at various scales. In emphasising contextually specific interlinkages between individual migrants, their communities, the Sri Lankan economy and global patterns of capital accumulation, I reject the binary representation of structure and agency. By drawing attention to the internal complexities of Sri Lanka's uneven development, I instead identify a multiscalar series of cumulatively causal processes that have etched a path dependence on temporary labour migration for individual households and the macroeconomy alike. Central to this analysis is a systematic critique of remittances – both as atomised income transfers and as aggregated foreign exchange earnings – in relation to existing conditions of underdevelopment.

The very notion of 'development' speaks to a variety of analytical levels, from individual livelihoods, to the dynamics of local economies, to broader disparities in wealth between core and peripheral regions of the world economy. My research responds to the need for a systematic analysis of remittances at multiple scales of economic development by adopting a Marxian analysis that situates migrant agency in tension with local institutions and countrywide uneven development processes, which in turn interface with global patterns of capital accumulation (Chapter 1). This theoretical orientation underscores the importance of analysing the spatio-temporal complexities of uneven development in Sri Lanka, and the manner in which strategies of capital accumulation have retained elements of continuity from colonialism to post-colonialism and into the fabric of the current economy (Chapter 2).

The resultant interplay of theory and historical analysis oversees the development of four conceptual themes, each addressing a different scale of migration: *remittance capital* (international), *forced migration* (countrywide), *place* (local community) and *status* (individual). Each of these themes are apertures opening onto differing facets of Sri Lanka's path dependency on temporary labour migration. The latter three themes – *forced migration*, *place* and *status* – were explored through my empirical research and frame the three chapters that discuss fieldwork findings (Chapters 3, 4 and 5). *Remittance capital*, on the other hand, speaks to the macroeconomic implications of temporary labour migration for Sri Lanka and is extrapolated from fieldwork findings, but also triangulated with other studies and secondary data. This discussion of *remittance capital* is partitioned into an analysis of the macroeconomic implications of remittance-driven development within Sri Lanka (Chapter 6) and relative to other regions of the world economy (Chapter 7).

Throughout the course of these chapters, the book makes three specific contributions to the migration-development debate. By espousing a multiscalar migration framework that emphasises the geographic and institutional intermediaries that shape (and are shaped by) individuals and capital, it makes an important theoretical contribution to reconciling the way agency and structure are conceptualised in migration studies (Bakewell 2010). Further, it stresses the disparate experiences of migration *within* migrant-sending countries that are too often homogenised by structure-centric or agency-centric approaches – either as uniformly exploited by capital or populated by bland rational actors. Historically and geographically specific economies of gender, ethnicity and class differentiate who migrates and under what circumstances, but also reveal complex migration cultures that can become path dependent in their own right – these are themes that are interwoven throughout the analytical arc of the study. Most importantly, though, the book offers a systematic analysis of *remittance capital* hitherto missing from the historical-structuralist critique of migration development. This conceptualisation of remittances coherently maps the interplay of household remittance transfers with countrywide economic development and global patterns of underdevelopment to unpick overlapping cumulatively causal processes that ingrain new forms of dependency within emergent remittance economies like Sri Lanka.

Notes

1 'Circular' denotes the inevitability of migrant workers returning and better satisfies aspects of the migration-development narrative, such as 'brain circulation' and remittance inflows.
2 Sri Lankan Muslims are considered ethnically distinct, and identify as Moors descendant from Arabic traders; a much smaller population of Muslims identify as Sri Lankan Malays, tracing their origins to Malaysia (DCS 2012).
3 Twenty-five years for women working in Saudi Arabia; 23 years for women working elsewhere in West Asia; and 21 years for women working in all other countries (ILO 2018).
4 A stance reinforced by loan conditionalities following an IMF bailout in 2016 (Reuters 2016).

References

Abeyasekera, Asha L., and Ramani Jayasundere. 2015. 'Migrant Mothers, Family Breakdown, and the Modern State: An Analysis of State Policies Regulating Women Migrating Overseas for Domestic Work in Sri Lanka'. *The South Asianist* 4 (1): 1–24.

Bakewell, Oliver. 2010. 'Some Reflections on Structure and Agency in Migration Theory'. *Journal of Ethnic and Migration Studies* 36 (10): 1689–1708.

Biyanwila, Janaka. 2011. *The Labour Movement in the Global South: Trade Unions in Sri Lanka*. London: Routledge.

Breman, Jan. 2009. 'The Great Transformation in the Setting of Asia'. Rotterdam: International Institute of Social Studies.

Castles, Stephen. 2010. 'Understanding Global Migration: A Social Transformation Perspective'. *Journal of Ethnic and Migration Studies* 36 (10): 1565–86.

Castles, Stephen. 2013. 'The Forces Driving Global Migration'. *Journal of Intercultural Studies* 34 (2): 122–40.

Central Bank of Sri Lanka (CBSL). 2018. 'Economic and Social Statistics of Sri Lanka 2018'. Colombo: Central Bank of Sri Lanka.

Cooray, Devoushi. 2017. 'The Care Drain and Its Effects on the Families Left Behind: A Case Study of Sri Lanka'. *Comparative Sociology* 16 (3): 369–92.

Degorge, Barbara. 2006. 'Modern Day Slavery in the United Arab Emirates'. *The European Legacy* 11 (6): 657–66.

Department of Census and Statistics (DCS), ed. 2012. *Census of Population and Housing 2012*. Colombo: Department of Census and Statistics.

Department of National Planning (DNP). 2010. 'Sri Lanka – The Emerging Wonder of Asia'. Colombo: Ministry of Finance and Planning.

Eelens, Frank, T. Mook, and Toon Schampers. 1992. 'Introduction'. In *Labour Migration to the Middle East: From Sri Lanka to the Gulf*, 1–27. London: Kegan Paul International.

Faist, Thomas. 2008. 'Migrants as Transnational Development Agents: An Inquiry into the Newest Round of the Migration–Development Nexus'. *Population, Space and Place* 14 (1): 21–42.

Gündüz, Zuhal. 2013. 'The Feminisation of Migration: Care and New Emotional Imperialism'. *Monthly Review* 65 (7): 32–43.

Haas, Hein de. 2010. 'Migration and Development: A Theoretical Perspective'. *International Migration Review* 44 (1): 227–64.

Institute of Policy Studies (IPS). 2014. 'Summary Report: International Conference on Policies for Mainstreaming Migration into Development in Sri Lanka, 14 August 2014'. Colombo: Institute of Policy Studies of Sri Lanka.

International Labour Office (ILO). 2010. *International Labour Migration: A Rights-Based Approach*. Geneva: International Labour Office.

International Labour Office (ILO). 2015. *ILO Global Estimates of Migrant Workers: Results and Methodology*. Geneva: International Labour Office.

International Labour Organisation (ILO). 2018. 'Sri Lankan Female Migrant Workers and the Family Background Report'. Colombo, Sri Lanka: International Labour Organisation (ILO).

International Labour Office (ILO). 2019. 'Global Wage Report 2018/19: What Lies Behind Gender Pay Gaps'. Geneva: International Labour Organisation (ILO).

King, Russell. 2012. 'Theories and Typologies of Migration: An Overview and a Primer'. Willy Brandt Series of Working Papers in International Migration and Ethnic Relations. Malmö: Malmö University.

Kottegoda, Sepali. 2004. *Negotiating Household Politics: Women's Strategies in Urban Sri Lanka*. Colombo: Social Scientists' Association.

Lee, Sohoon, and Nicola Piper. 2017. 'Migrant Domestic Workers as "Agents" of Development in Asia: An Institutional Analysis of Temporality'. *European Journal of East Asian Studies* 16 (2): 220–47. https://doi.org/10.1163/15700615-01602003.

Lenard, Patti Tamara, and Christine Straehle. 2010. 'Temporary Labour Migration: Exploitation, Tool of Development, or Both?' *Policy and Society* 29 (4): 283–94.

Martin, Philip. 2012. 'Reducing Migration Costs and Maximizing Human Development'. In *Global Perspectives on Migration and Development: GFMD Puerto Vallarta and Beyond*, edited by Irena Omelaniuk, 27–52. Global Migration Issues 1. Dordrecht: Springer.

Phillips, Nicola. 2017. 'Power and Inequality in the Global Political Economy'. *International Affairs* 93 (2): 429–44.

Purkayastha, Bandana. 2018. 'Migration, Migrants, and Human Security'. *Current Sociology* 66 (2): 167–91.

Razak, Azhar, and Arthur Wamanan. 2015. 'Sri Lanka's Slowing Remittance Growth a Cause for Concern'. *The Nation*, 9 May 2015. http://nation.lk/online/2015/09/05/revenue-dilemma.html.

Reuters. 2016. 'IMF Agrees $1.5 Billion Bailout for Sri Lanka to Avert Balance Of …', 29 April 2016. www.reuters.com/article/us-imf-sri-lanka-idUSKCN0XQ063.

Reuters. 2018. 'Sri Lankan Rupee at Record Low on Importer Dollar Demand', 24 August 2018. www.reuters.com/article/sri-lanka-forex-idUSL3N1VF460.

Safi, Michael. 2018. 'Sri Lanka's "New Dubai": Will Chinese-Built City Suck the Life out of Colombo?' *Guardian*, 2 August 2018. www.theguardian.com/cities/2018/aug/02/sri-lanka-new-dubai-chinese-city-colombo.

Skeldon, Ronald. 2006. 'Interlinkages between Internal and International Migration and Development in the Asian Region'. *Population, Space and Place* 12 (1): 15–30.

Skeldon, Ronald. 2017. 'International Migration, Internal Migration, Mobility and Urbanization: Towards More Integrated Approaches'. Expert Group Meeting Paper UN/POP/EGM/2017/7. New York: United Nations Department of Economic and Social Affairs.

Sri Lanka Bureau of Foreign Employment (SLBFE). 2012. *Annual Statistical Report of Foreign Employment 2011*. Colombo: Sri Lanka Bureau of Foreign Employment.

Sri Lanka Bureau of Foreign Employment (SLBFE). 2016. 'Different Perspectives of Departure Details'. Colombo: Sri Lanka Bureau of Foreign Employment.

Thiollet, Helene. 2011. 'Migration as Diplomacy: Labor Migrants, Refugees, and Arab Regional Politics in the Oil-Rich Countries'. *International Labor and Working-Class History* 79 (1): 103–21.

United Nations Department of Economic and Social Affairs (UNDESA), Population Division. 2016. 'International Migration Report 2015'. ST/ESA/SER.A/384. New York: United Nations Department of Economic and Social Affairs.

Waldman, Amy. 2005. 'Sri Lankan Maids Pay Dearly for Perilous Jobs Overseas'. *New York Times*, 5 August 2005.

Weeraratne, Bilesha. 2016. 'Protecting the Welfare of Children and Its Causal Effect on Limiting Mother's Labour Migration'. *International Migration* 54 (5): 59–75.

Weerasooriya, Nayomini. 2013. 'A Requiem for Rizana ...' *Daily Mirror*, 10 January 2013.

Wickramasekara, Piyasiri. 2015. 'Migration Regimes and Their Linkages for Family Unity, Integrity and Development'. In *The Palgrave Handbook of International Labour Migration: Law and Policy Perspectives*, edited by Marion Panizzon, Gottfried Zürcher, and Elisa Fornalé, 146–80. London: Palgrave Macmillan.

World Bank. 2006. *Global Economic Prospects: Economic Implications of Remittances and Migration*. Washington, DC: World Bank.

World Travel and Tourism Council (WTTC). 2018. 'Travel and Tourism: Economic Impact 2018, Sri Lanka'. London: World Travel and Tourism Council.

Wucker, Michele. 2004. 'Remittances: The Perpetual Migration Machine'. *World Policy Journal* 21 (2): 37–46.

1 The history of migration-development

The migration–development nexus is anything but a new concern (de Haas 2012). Resurgent academic and policy enthusiasm regarding the relationship between temporary labour migration and economic development has overshadowed a longer and more ideologically fraught migration-development debate. Perhaps the most influential recent interpretation has been Hein de Haas's argument that the migration-development debate has 'swung back and forth like a pendulum' (de Haas 2012, 8) from 'optimism' to 'pessimism' and back again. De Haas claims this pendulum has shifted between generalisably positive and negative appraisals of migration's contribution to development without ever truly settling on the nuanced 'middle ground' demanded by the metaphor. Within this narrative, 'optimism' is synonymous with neoclassical agency-centric modelling that shaped the emergence of development economics in the 1950s and 1960s and the neoliberal resuscitation of these ideals in policy and practice. 'Pessimism', meanwhile, is associated with the broad array of neo-Marxist and dependency critiques of systemic labour migration articulated throughout the 1970s and 1980s that are together housed under the banner of historical-structuralism.[1] De Haas suggests these opposing positions constitute countervailing extremes of the pendulum swing, cancelling each other out as equally unreasonable and pointing to a more nuanced 'middle ground' in the New Economics of Labour Migration (NELM) developed throughout the 1980s and 1990s.

This chapter examines the overarching narrative of the migration-development literature with historical and ideological sensitivity, retracing the movements of de Haas's pendulum while exposing the weaknesses of the metaphor and the 'middle ground' it promotes. The chapter follows de Haas's ideas intimately, both because of their prominence in shaping conventional interpretations of the migration-development debate and because of the obstacles they pose to the formation of critical migration theory. The chapter contests the pretences under which historical-structuralist perspectives have been dismissed and instead locates their diminishing credence within broader ideological delegitimisation under the hegemony of a neoliberal development paradigm ensconced in Washington and post-Washington agendas. Further, it draws attention to the subtle repackaging of neoclassical assumptions embedded in the NELM, critiquing the body of work as a superficial concession to structural concerns that shelters the ontological kernel of neoclassical economics within a more 'nuanced' and reputable guise.

Having followed the debate to its present manifestation in policy enthusiasm for migration as a mutually beneficial triple win, the chapter then identifies legitimate shortcomings to historical-structuralism in order to outline a new theoretical direction. Here the necessity of analysing class-relations and institutional characteristics to produce a multiscalar understanding of the factors shaping migration-development outcomes is foregrounded. Central to this approach is the identification of four theoretical concepts – *remittance capital*, *forced migration*, *place* and *status* – that address cumulatively causal processes at differing scales of analysis that together instil path dependence on temporary labour migration.

The migration-development debate

Todaro, along with Harris in 1970, developed the standard neoclassical theory of migration, in which migration emerges from rational, utility-maximising decision-making at the individual level and is aggregated to offer macro-level explanations (Harris and Todaro 1970). Specifically, it is hypothesised that migration results from the rational calculation of expected earning differentials between rural and urban employment (or, internationally, between sending and receiving economies). Todaro thus offers a simple behavioural model of micro-level migration decisions that supports the macro-level assumption that migration facilitates an optimal resource allocation of human labour between labour-abundant and labour-scarce regions (Abreu 2012). The model presumes an accompanying flow of capital in the opposite direction (i.e. from capital-abundant to capital-scarce regions), chasing higher rates of return. Thus, with migration reallocating labour and investment reallocating capital, there is a presumed process of factor price equalization leading to economic convergence between regions. Here migration is unambiguously a central driver of development and, eventually, global economic equilibrium.

The neoclassical model of migration-development is parochial in its identification of factor price equalisation as the mechanism of developmental convergence, providing no room to conceptualise remittances or non-migrant gains (de Haas 2010). Contributions from development theory, then characterised by the paradigm of modernisation, thus complemented the neoclassical framework by fleshing out accompanying benefits of migration grounded in the transfer of remittances – both monetary and social. Migrants were portrayed as agents of development, capable of accumulating skills and savings through foreign employment, along with sufficient entrepreneurial savvy to commit these assets to productive ends in countries of origin. Such transfers of wealth and expertise were expected to catalyse investment in sending communities, creating employment and producing multiplier effects within the local economy to precondition 'developmental takeoff' and industrialisation (Beijer 1970). The ensuing belief that widespread migration would entail the mutually beneficial delivery of rapid economic growth in migrant-sending and migrant-receiving countries thus led to an adoption of pro-immigration policies across the developed and developing world alike (Wickramasekara 2011).

By the time the neoclassical model of migration matured in the 1970s, a radically opposed 'historical-structuralist' tradition was emerging out of fragmented contributions within the neo-Marxist dependency and world-systems literature. Accompanying a proliferation of economic heterodoxy across the social sciences, and particularly within development studies, historical-structuralists framed migration as an exploitative process bounded by the historically shaped macro-structures of global capitalism deemed to entrench 'the development of underdevelopment' (Gunder Frank 1966). The perspective offers no unified theory of migration's relationship with processes of capitalist development, but instead houses a number of critical observations within a broader philosophical consensus that migration is an issue of *structure* above *agency*. This distinction is articulated methodologically, in rejecting deductive formalism in favour of an inductive historical approach, and ontologically in dismissing the equilibrium principle as entirely inconsistent with the cumulative causation of inequalities reproduced by global capitalist expansion.

It is possible to distinguish two prominent branches of theory within the diverse contributions of the historical-structuralist tradition: those concerned with the structure of migrant-receiving economies and those addressing the structures of migrant-sending regions (Abreu 2012). Notable contributions to the former (Castles and Kosack 1973; Nikolinakos 1975; Piore 1980; Cohen 1987; Sassen 1988) have emphasised the social and economic demand for cheap and exploitable migrant labour inputs within core economies of the globe, structuring migration patterns as a means of sustaining a reserve army of labour to perform the dirty, dangerous and demeaning work that local workers would rather not perform. Meanwhile, drawing on dependency critiques and world-systems analysis, a number of authors (Portes and Walton 1981; Petras 1981; Castells 1999; Morawska 1990) have sought to explain the structural determinants of migration from the labour-sending regions of the global periphery, emphasising the geopolitical configuration of the world economy and associated mechanisms by which capital in core regions seeks to extract surplus value from the labour (and other resources) of peripheral regions.

Piore, in his development of dual labour market theory, outlines a particularly comprehensive analysis of the conditions within developed industrial economies that structurally necessitate the presence of immigrant labour (Piore 1980). Capital, Piore argues, constitutes a fixed factor of production. If demand wanes, it is not capital that ceases to be invested, but labour that is laid off as a variable input. Similarly, there exists a bifurcated labour market of capital-intensive primary workers – who are similarly 'fixed' with stable, well-remunerated and socially protected jobs – and a vulnerable labour-intensive secondary sector. This secondary sector constitutes the variable factor of production and, as such, is required by capital to be cheap to employ and easy to expend, thus being characterised by precarity. Piore further posits that demand for local secondary labour (i.e. within the secondary sector) cannot be sufficiently influenced by wage adjustment, as socially conditioned and institutionalised correlations between status and pay determine that wage increases for menial employment threaten to rupture the established hierarchy and provoke corresponding wage hikes throughout the economy. Similarly, maintaining motivation amongst local secondary workers is deemed problematic given the lack of status (being relational) gained from working at the bottom of the employment hierarchy. International labour migration allows capital to address both of these issues, by providing a secondary sector workforce willing to accept low wages (thus maintaining the existing wage-status order) and not primarily motivated by the cultivation of status in the local economy (as temporary migrants are assumed to experience status relative to their home communities) (Piore 1980). Moreover, the presence of migrants socially conditioned as a priori inferior is deemed to create a motivating sense of status amongst local secondary workers. Piore accordingly argues that international migration is not simply a cost–benefit decision made by the individual migrant, but rather a structural necessity of the advanced industrial economy. The relevance of this argument is extended into the realm of the post-industrial economy by Sassen (1988, 1991), wherein bifurcated labour markets are recast in relation to the polarisation of modern service economies in global cities.

On the labour-sending side of historical-structuralism, contributions are derived from neo-Marxist theories of development, specifically Frank's dependency theory and later Wallerstein's more holistic model of world-systems analysis. Through this lens the relevant units of analysis are not individuals or countries, but core and peripheral regions of production within the world economy and the mechanisms through which this global division of labour is sustained (Morawska 2012). Alongside existing emphasis on systems of trade and capital investment, migration has been framed as a structural process of *unequal exchange* through which core economies exploit the periphery and extract surplus value to entrench historical and geographic patterns of development and underdevelopment (King 2012). From this perspective, the penetration of capitalist relations into the (often non-capitalist) global periphery effects disruptions and dislocations within the traditional economy, uprooting populations and catalysing migration. Uneven peripheral development arises from a concentration of foreign and local capital in urban metropoles, progressively undermining traditional livelihoods and necessitating internal or international labour migration to core regions as a survival strategy. In this sense, the expansion of global capitalism both produces migrants through the reshaping of local economies and reaccommodates them under the exploitative duress of core accumulation processes in urban and foreign milieus.

A swinging pendulum?

Neoclassical and historical-structuralist perspectives, as archetypal yet diametrically opposed foundations to the migration-development debate, have been popularly portrayed as 'optimistic' and 'pessimistic' binaries bookending the extremes of migration theory (de Haas 2012). For de Haas, they represent opposing swings of a theoretical pendulum that has oscillated from one extreme to the other – from neoclassical optimism, to historical-structural pessimism, to neoliberal 'neo-optimism' and a potential 'neo-pessimistic' backswing – without coming to rest on a nuanced 'middle ground' (2012). Unpacking this metaphor helps explain both the waning legitimacy of historical-structuralism over time, but also the subtle repackaging of neoclassical theories as an ostensible 'middle ground'.

De Haas rightly identifies neoclassical migration models, and related claims of 'trickle-down' development via remittance investment, consumption multipliers and human capital gains, as optimistic (2012). His criticism of the neoclassical position is anchored in its adherence to the linearity of modernisation theory and the presumption of positive developmental outcomes, including North–South convergence from factor price equalization – none of which is demonstrated in empirical analyses (de Haas 2010). Although flagging the tendency for neoclassical models to neglect extra-economic factors shaping migrant decision-making (de Haas 2010), there is little critique of the assumptions of rational choice theory or the primacy of income differentials in determining the 'push' and 'pull' forces from which migration supposedly arises. For de Haas, it is a failure to sufficiently consider the contextual factors and complex social relations surrounding migration that accounts for the undue optimism of neoclassical theory, not the internal logic of the model itself.

The opposite is true of his critique of 'pessimistic' historical-structuralist theories, whose deficiency is deemed to be ontological: an alleged disregard for migrants' agency and social contributions by predetermining that migration is unilaterally negative (de Haas 2012). In making this claim, de Haas portrays historical-structuralist theories as having a rigidity beyond what is articulated within the theories themselves. Structures of capital are ascribed a law-like determinacy quite at odds with the historical inductive methodology that informs such approaches. Simplified as such, the historical-structuralist stance appears to make very definitive claims to migration outcomes – for example, brain and brawn drains, increasing inequality, non-productive remittance use and inflation (de Haas 2007) – that stand to be invalidated by heterogeneous empirical evidence. Thus 'pessimistic' historical-structuralist theories come to represent an equally axiomatic pole to the 'optimistic' neoclassical approach and an opposing swing in the pendulum metaphor.

According to de Haas, 'the fundamental question is, therefore, not whether migration has either positive or negative developmental impacts, but why migration has contributed to development in some communities and much less, or even negatively, in others' (2007, 7). In answer, de Haas argues the need to centre the pendulum on a contextually nuanced approach that can better accommodate diverse empirical findings that underscore the complex realities of migration. In the NELM de Haas identifies an approach that purportedly avoids the 'simplistic opposition between optimistic and pessimistic views' (de Haas 2012, 15–16) by drawing attention to a diversity of development contexts, the relative constraints within each determining the potential for positive or negative outcomes from migration. Yet the conclusion that 'the extent to which migration can play a positive (or negative) role … fundamentally depends on more general development conditions' (de Haas 2012, 16) tends to corroborate, more than contest, historical-structuralist perspectives. Historical-structuralism does not contend that migration is a priori negative, but rather recognises that migration is interlinked with, and tends to compound, underdevelopment in peripheral regions of the global economy that are already disadvantaged by historical structures of capitalism. As a body of theory, it does nothing to obfuscate or diminish the contributions of migrants to their families and communities, but instead provides a coherent and historically sensitive backdrop in which to ground diverse lived realities and the processes of underdevelopment that shape them. From this perspective it is little surprise that de Haas observes relatively positive migration outcomes in Spain, South Korea, India, Taiwan and Turkey – semi-peripheral regions where capitalist expansion has historically been tempered by significant periods of protectionism and statist economic policy – and more negative experiences in Sub-Saharan and North African countries (De Haas 2012), where colonialism had barely subsided before debilitating Structural Adjustment Programmes (SAPs) began.

De Haas's oversimplification of historical-structuralism takes on a normative dimension when viewed alongside his tacit adherence to neoclassical ontology and identification of the NELM as a natural 'middle ground' in migration theory.

In the first instance, de Haas subtly invokes a neoliberal lexicon when privileging the role of individual economic actors, conflating development with 'attractive environments in which to invest' (2012, 16) and ahistorically identifying 'misguided macro-economic policies, socio-economic inequalities, authoritarianism, corruption and legal insecurity' (2012, 16) as the primary plights of the Global South. Consciously or not, his portrayal of developing contexts sits comfortably within the ideological parameters of the Washington Consensus and its circumscribed role for the state in providing a 'golden straightjacket' of legal-normative structures in which markets can operate unperturbed (Friedman 2000).

In the second instance, the NELM, emerging from the contributions of Stark and others in the 1980s (Stark 1984; Stark and Bloom 1985; Katz and Stark 1986; Lauby and Stark 1988; Stark and Taylor 1989), is not a substantially new theory. Rather, it is a more sophisticated repackaging of neoclassical migration theory (Abreu 2012). Self-styled as a reconciliation of structure and agency in the spirit of Giddens's structuration theory (Giddens 1984), the NELM contends that migration is a household strategy to diversify income streams in order to mitigate risk and overcome relative deprivation within a given community (Stark and Bloom 1985). It effectively shifts decision-making from an individual optimisation of income, to a household optimisation of risk, for example, by using migration to hedge against crop failures, price volatility and precarious employment conditions that threaten household income in lieu of sufficient social insurance (Abreu 2012). Migrant households, as with utility-maximising individuals, are assumed to be perfectly rational: it is only the incompleteness of *markets* and *information* that constrain decision-making and produce disparate outcomes (Abreu 2012). The NELM's information-theoretic character is, however, no concession to historical processes of development nor the continuing existence of structural constraints. Rational choice prevails as the fundamental mechanism through which migration supposedly occurs, albeit alongside a more empirically satisfying account of how and why such decisions are made and why remittances are of similar or greater importance to wage differentials.

De Haas's 'middle ground', then, is less an empirically nuanced resting point of a pendulum swinging between extremes of agency and structure than it is symptomatic of a normative re-centring of neoclassical economics within development theory and practice. That de Haas portrays this approach as neutral is particularly concerning. Quite aside from the entire pendulum metaphor constituting an *argumentum ad temperantiam*, wherein natural correctness is conferred upon the middle position between two arbitrary extremes, there is an implicit declaration that the contours of reasonable debate are too narrow to accommodate critiques of capitalist development. While de Haas echoes the concerns of Kapur (2003) and Castles (2006) regarding the post-millennial neoliberal 'rediscovery' of migration as a self-help developmental panacea, he himself limits the developmental role of the state to 'creating a fertile soil where the remittance seeds can be sown and can actually germinate and grow' (de Haas 2012, 20). By this he means, in no uncertain terms, the creation of investment conditions through which migrants can 'reap benefits from their inclusion in the capitalist economy' (de Haas 2012, 14).

The accompanying empirical evidence for positive capitalist development – improved incomes, living conditions, human capabilities and investment (de Haas 2012) – is undermined by several neglected considerations. To what extent is uneven capitalist development responsible for creating the conditions of underdevelopment from which such improvements were made? Is there potential for development policies that produce similar outcomes without recourse to migration? Can developmental improvements from migration be understood without consideration of relative gains produced within and between the economies involved? Such questions lie outside the purview of mainstream migration-development, which prefers to see migration as a means of 'protecting people from the destabilising and exclusionary effects of absent or ill-functioning markets' (de Haas 2012, 16) attributable to the 'bad governance' of the developing world and the bogeyman of non-market development. This is not to imply that there are not serious shortcomings with the existing historical-structuralist approach, but rather that mainstream migration-development scholars have found it easier to ideologically delegitimise these arguments than engage with their actual limitations.

The post-Washington rediscovery of migration-development

The revival of neoclassical migration theory in the NELM preceded a proliferation of empirical migration research (Clemens, Özden, and Rapoport 2014) alongside a relative lull in the theoretical advancement of migration scholarship (de Haan 1999). This is partly accounted for by the 'cultural turn' in migration studies, towards perspectives originating from anthropology and qualitative sociology that are more concerned with the migration experience than its causes or outcomes (King 2012). These empirical studies have tended to be misaligned with dominant theoretical frameworks and somewhat dislocated from broader debates in the migration-development literature (de Haas 2007). This turn is also accounted for by the waning credibility of historical-structuralism, and neo-Marxism in the social sciences more generally, following the Soviet Union's collapse and the ascension of neoliberal globalism as the dominant development paradigm (Stiglitz 2003; Chang 2003). The rise of the 'Washington Consensus'[2] (Williamson 1990) directed academic and policy attention towards issues of trade and economic governance that attributed little importance to migration or remittances, despite an increase in economic displacement arising from the adoption of neoliberal models of development (Delgado Wise 2009; Castles 2013). This theoretical lull ended with the 'rediscovery' of migration-development within an emerging post-Washington agenda taking shape at the turn of the millennium. The Washington Consensus had faced declining legitimacy on account of a growing catalogue of developmental failings under SAP proscriptions (Cornia 2004), necessitating the abandonment of hard-line neoliberal development in favour of a 'softer' approach (Onis and Senses 2005). Within this new doctrine, global and regional policymaking institutions enthusiastically recast temporary or 'circular' migration programs, and particularly remittances, as a 'new' mechanism for market-led development via private capital flows and investment.

By the turn of the millennium, global remittances to developing countries began significantly outstripping ODA and rivalling FDI as the main source of foreign capital (World Bank 2011). The economic literature on remittances exploded with optimistic appraisals of the potential for remittances to galvanise 'human capital formation, investments, poverty and macro-economic stability' (Agunias 2006, 5) within the bounds of market-led, self-help development (Kapur 2003). The dominant theoretical interpretation behind this wave of policy attention is that temporary labour migration constitutes a mutually beneficial triple win scenario, an idea first put forward by the World Bank (2006) and since syndicated by a number of North American and European migration policy think tanks and financial institutions (Wickramasekara 2011). The argument contends that temporary contract or 'circular' migration benefits all parties involved by providing migrant-receiving countries with access to foreign labour, migrant-sending countries with remittances and human capital development, and migrants themselves with greater wages and financial stability (World Bank 2006). It therefore promotes 'managed temporary labour migration' between sending and receiving economies to regularise, legalise and capitalise migration (Piper 2010). The relative disparity of the 'wins' involved are not considered. The ready supply of cheap and exploitable workers clearly coincides with the interest of foreign capitalists (Binford 2003), yet the developmental outcomes for migrant-sending countries and migrants themselves are far more tenuous and lack empirical substantiation (Wickramasekara 2011).

The post-Washington migration-development narrative is striking for its growing policy-level acceptance[3] and, with notable exceptions (Delgado Wise 2009; Delgado Wise and Covarrubias 2009; Castles 2010; Abreu 2012), an absence of attempts to outline comprehensive theoretical alternatives. The intergovernmental policy salience of managed temporary labour migration is understandable given the likelihood of such schemes generating wins for influential stakeholders (i.e. migrant-sending country elites, foreign employers and receiving economies in general) while curtailing social, personal and economic losses to the relatively disempowered (i.e. migrants and their families). The lack of alternative theory-building is more difficult to explain. There have, of course, been numerous critical responses to various aspects of current migration-development policy: the disregard of migrant rights, working conditions and abuse inherent to temporary labour migration programs (Piper 2010); the absence of empirical support for remittance-driven development in migrant-sending countries (Binford 2003); the outsourcing of developmental burdens to private individuals (Rankin 2001); the deepening and reinforcing of regional inequalities through transnational exploitation (Phillips 2009). Yet little has emerged by way of a systemic account of the observed inequalities and relative underdevelopment produced and reproduced through systems of temporary labour migration. Van Hear (2010) speaks of a diminishing appetite for overarching theories of migration amidst a diversity of migration experiences and outcomes, but contextually sensitive and empirically heterogeneous research need not preclude the possibility of analysing structures and systems too. Rather, such varied and contextually dependent outcomes can and should be understood as constituent of a spectrum of migration-development experiences that are nonetheless situated within complex structures of capitalism.

There is a real need for new, critical theories of temporary labour migration as such schemes proliferate globally as a new norm governing the international movement of low-wage workers. An important step in this direction can be achieved by reformulating the insights of historical-structuralism in a way that: (i) redresses an implicit reliance on unequal exchange as an explanatory mechanism of development and underdevelopment; (ii) unifies harmonious fragments of the existing approach with relevant institutional insights; and (iii) offers a conceptualisation of remittances as reproducing uneven development on local and global scales. The remainder of this chapter outlines the foundations of such an approach.

Migration-underdevelopment: a new theoretical approach

The question of 'development'

It is unhelpful to offer a theoretical understanding of the relationship between migration and development without first presupposing what 'development' itself constitutes. Of course, defining a term as equivocal as 'development' with any degree of specificity is not a straightforward task. There is a substantial literature concerned with such questions and, in light of a stubborn lack of consensus, this book makes no claims to a definitive interpretation. What it does contend is the existence of two broad (but not mutually exclusive) typologies of development: those of a capitalist character and those of a socially transformative character.

Through a Marxian lens, capitalist development refers to the spatio-temporal expansion of capitalist social relations – i.e. a societal mode of production predicated on the exploitation of commodity labour by capital – resulting in the development of productive forces and the further accumulation of capital (Brenner 1977). For Marx, the spread of capitalist social relations would bring with it the material wealth of capitalist economic development – that this has not occurred evenly points, as Brenner argues, to 'the particular, historically developed class structures through which these processes [of development] actually worked themselves out' (1977, 90). It is therefore the uneven expansion of capitalist relations at local and global levels, and specifically the extent to which pre-capitalist social relations are transformed or reinforced by historically specific class struggles, that are identified as pivotal in shaping relative disparities in capitalist economic development (Brenner 1977). Thus, macroeconomic development or underdevelopment typically refers to the relative penetration of capitalist class relations and the attendant accumulation of capital bounded within the geography of a given economy. Conversely, socially transformative development refers to a multitude of alternative developmental frameworks (normative or existing) that contest the inequalities reproduced under capitalism. Examples range from revolutionary socialism, to social democracy, economic autarky, anarchy and subsistence production. This distinction is important, as the migration-development debate frames the empirical implications of migration with implicit reference to capitalist development. Despite often existing within or alongside capitalist development (Mies and Shiva 1993; Gibson-Graham 2006), socially transformative development will therefore be ascribed a normative quality. For the purposes of theory, 'development' will hereafter be considered synonymous with capitalist development.

The question of development leads to the most substantial critique that needs to be made of historical-structuralist accounts of migration-development and the dependency and world-systems theories they generally derive from. Both sets of theory locate the fundamental mechanism of underdevelopment in some variation of Arghiri Emmanuel's concept of *unequal exchange*,[4] in which trade between peripheral and core regions transfers surplus-value to the effect of making core development contingent on the simultaneous underdevelopment of the periphery (Emmanuel 1972; Wallerstein 2004). By identifying the root cause of underdevelopment in relations of exchange, rather than production, theories of unequal exchange have attracted pronounced criticism for disregarding the social relations of production and offering an overly abstract simplification of capital accumulation (Brenner 1977; Petras 1981; De Silva 2013). These theoretical shortcomings have been reproduced in historical-structuralist approaches to migration-development (Abreu 2012). Specifically, there is a tendency to portray migration from the periphery, as *ex ante*, representing another avenue through which surplus-value is appropriated by the core (Papademetriou and Martin 1991), a position clearly underscored by brain- and brawn-drain arguments that evoke unidirectional transfers of resources. The inadequacy of these explanations is highlighted by the diversity of individual experiences and developmental outcomes produced by temporary labour migration within and between migrant-sending country contexts. Although an apparent paradox if migration is taken simply as a vehicle for surplus transferral, these observations become intuitive if the uneven and contextually nuanced expansion of capitalist social relations is taken into consideration. For example, uneven development within a migrant-sending country might undermine traditional livelihoods and catalyse exploitative migration in one region while simultaneously permitting more favourable migration circumstances in another, while creating profits for recruitment agents operating in a third.

A multiscalar migration theory

What is needed, then, is a conceptualisation of migration as it relates to processes of uneven development on global *and* local scales. The uneven expansion of capitalist relations on a global scale creates a clear precedent for temporary labour migration as a means of providing exploitable labour for the purposes of capital accumulation across spatially stratified networks of production. The transnational division of labour involves not only the outsourcing of production in pursuit of cheaper and more exploitable wage labour, but also systems of migration that have been established to provide an in-situ reserve army of labour for spatially fixed production and services such as care and construction. These movements of labour, rather than simply flowing in the opposite direction to capital (as proposed by factor price equalisation and unequal exchange alike), are shaped both by formal intergovernmental frameworks and informal migration networks. While there is a general 'pull' towards centres of capital accumulation in core economies, migration patterns are significantly tempered by cultural and institutional factors that together shape particular corridors of migration, as often South–South as they are South–North (Hujo and Piper 2010). At the local scale, migration from Sri Lanka is embedded in specific processes of uneven development formed under the historical and geographic expansion of capitalism and its intersection with existing economies of gender, ethnicity and class. The growth of capitalist social relations cannot be divorced from specific histories of colonialism and the endurance pre-capitalist modes of production that together shape and reinforce developmental asymmetries and class struggles. Economic marginalisation arising from these processes of uneven development are pivotal in shaping who migrates and under what circumstances, as well as who stands to gain from inward flows of remittances. Furthermore, the character of social, political, economic and cultural institutions across different communities significantly influences migration practices, experiences and outcomes.

To extend this Marxian rationale of uneven development into a multiscalar framework applicable to migration occurring between South Asia and West Asia, it is necessary to draw on a number of conceptual tools from existing historical-structuralist approaches and complementary insights from institutional economic theory. First, Piore's (1980) analysis of *status* in receiving economies needs to be bridged with a complementary account of migrants' own experiences of status in migrant-sending countries: both the denial of status rooted in the fictitious commodification of their labour (Polanyi 2001 [1944]) and its material reconstruction through the conspicuous consumption of remittances (Veblen 2009 [1899]). Second, an understanding of *place* – representative not only of the geographical manifestation of class and ethno-religious identity, but also the networks and institutions that bind their interactions with the broader economy – is required to adequately account for the heterogeneity of migrant practices within migrant-sending economies. Third, a theory of *forced migration* indebted to the work of Delgado Wise is necessary to explain internal and international displacements of labour caused by processes of uneven development within those migrant-sending countries. Finally, and most starkly, there is an acute need for a systematic analysis of *remittance capital* and its macroeconomic implications for economies that have become increasingly dependent upon these flows. These concepts are used to identify cumulatively causal processes at different scales of analysis, from individual agency (*status*) to local institutions (*place*) to local structures (*forced migration*) to global structures (*remittance capital*), and together comprise a multiscalar migration theory, as applied to Sri Lanka. Each concept is considered in more detail below.

Status

In his contributions to dual labour market theory, Piore (1980) draws attention to the socio-economic function of *status* within labour-receiving economies as creating a structural demand for migrant workers. What is overlooked, however, is the accompanying centrality of status tensions as a social mechanism underpinning migration from sending regions. Washington and post-Washington development prescriptions not only produce *forced migration* by eroding the decentralisation of decent work, but also confine available employment to the degraded forms of work demanded by 'competitive' export production. This entails a fictitious commodification of labour, in which human labour is 'disembedded' from its social and cultural meaning and ascribed a purely economic value within the market economy (Polanyi 2001 [1944]). The deprivation of esteem inherent to the fictitious commodification of labour – often manifesting in social stigma directed towards the performance of such work – creates a strong incentive to reclaim *status* through other means. Empirical findings from this research suggest that although temporary labour migration is routinely exploitative and degrading, it often carries a sense of prestige within migrant communities. It is plausible that confining degraded work to socially invisible foreign employment offers migrants an opportunity to avoid stigma and re-author their experiences by constructing narratives of success upon their return.

The conspicuous consumption of remittances augments this notion and suggests that *status* is itself one of the key incentives for engaging in migration. Here, conspicuous consumption is not ascribed a pejorative value – as has been the case in studies that decry such remittance use as wasteful or non-productive (de Haas 2010) – but as an agentic means of reclaiming *status* by signifying the hallmarks of 'migrant success'. By invoking Veblen's concept of pecuniary emulation (Veblen 2009 [1899]), the construction of migrant success is seen to convey a false prosperity that nonetheless encourages further migration amongst those attempting to emulate returnees' apparent wealth. Although Veblen's overall body of work is far removed from Marxian analysis, pecuniary emulation is complementary insofar as offering a social theory of consumption that can be meaningfully linked to patterns of production and capital accumulation. In doing so, it offers greater practical utility than Marx's own, more abstract conceptualisation of consumption as the realisation of value necessary to reproduce the capitalist mode of production (Marx 1981 [1867]). As such, considerations of *status* demand to be understood as a fundamental social dynamic that – interrelated with processes of uneven development – influence and sustain decisions to engage in temporary labour migration.

Forced migration

The term *forced migrati*on is typically applied to the displacement of populations by conflict or natural disasters, but has been used by Delgado Wise to explain processes of economic upheaval arising from the restructuring of capitalist production (Delgado Wise 2009). Here, *forced migration* relates specifically to the 'de-structuring' of labour, wherein decent living and working conditions associated with local employment are structurally undermined by the centralisation of productive activity (Delgado Wise 2009). The hegemony of neoliberal economic governance has effected a qualitative shift in the developmental role of the state, as protectionism and decentralised industrial policies have steadily given way to efforts to promote industry by attracting FDI in geographically concentrated EPZs. With privatisation and economic deregulation erstwhile undermining traditional and agricultural livelihoods, the declining availability of decent work engenders forced economic migration – both internally and internationally – to centres of production and employment. This economic restructuring finds its roots in local class struggles, wherein economic policies promoted under the banner of economic growth have served as a means to extend and strengthen the interests of local capitalists (Harvey 2007). This process has reconfigured people and spaces to connect with global markets, entailing *forced migration* where the intensification of uneven development produces a need to migrate internally or internationally out of economic necessity.

Place

By analysing the geographic intersection of class, ethno-religious background and local institutions, complex and distinctive migration practices can be identified. This recognition pushes back against tendencies to homogenise temporary labour migrants, as inherent to notions of a uniform 'reserve army of labour' as to the neoclassical rendering of migrants as *homo economicus*, and instead emphasises the important locational differences that arise from the contextual specificities of migrant-sending countries. These locational differences can meaningfully affect who migrates and under what circumstances, which may in turn help explain and analytically situate differing migration outcomes within and between particular migrant communities. *Place* furthermore evokes a sense of spatial fixity that constrains labour relative to the mobility of capital, here represented by the employers, recruitment agents, sub-agents and labour brokers that together comprise the 'merchants of labour'. Determining how the merchants of labour exploit the limitations of place and local practices can afford additional explanations for why certain migrant communities appear to fare better than others. Locational differences in the severity of recruitment fees and the extent of migration-related debt suggest that processes of uneven development have, in turn, produced uneven migration experiences that exacerbate underlying disadvantages. In this regard, *place* essentially serves as an analytical intermediary that expounds the institutional ties between individual migrant households and broader structures of the local economy.

Remittance capital

Even among the more critical pockets of the migration literature there is a frequent and persistent assumption that remittances are a beneficial source of developmental capital for countries of origin. However, there has been insufficient scrutiny of the role remittances play at the macroeconomic level. Although representing large sums of money in aggregate, remittances are dispersed amongst individual households where they typically facilitate basic consumption and financing improvements to housing, education, healthcare and small investments (Piper 2010). While sending governments cannot directly capitalise on these financial flows, international remittance transfers amass foreign exchange earnings that can offset trade deficits and prevent currency depreciation. This can improve access to international loans and the ability to repay existing debt. Thus, while temporary labour migration is effectively subsidising the productive and reproductive capacity of foreign economies, the remittances received in exchange play a structural role in financing development projects that might otherwise be unviable. However, the sustained inflow of remittance receipts can cause currency overvaluation that undermines trade competitiveness to the detriment of export production, impeding the diversification of local manufacturing industries and the potentially significant source of trade revenue and employment growth they represent. In this sense, migrant-sending countries run the risk of becoming remittance-dependent and unable to retract from a structural commitment to foreign employment without critically destabilising the local currency and the select forms of capital accumulation it supports. Compounding this problem is the observation that remittance expenditure can be import-stimulating and generate demand for other economies where consumer goods are more likely to be manufactured.

A note on methodology: from theory to fieldwork

A multiscalar theory of migration, by its very nature, demands an accompanying research methodology that can uncover meaningful findings at multiple levels of analysis. If temporary labour migration's relationship with uneven development is to be understood on global and local scales it is important to contextualise the internal dynamics of migration as well as to gather macroeconomic data. This observation directly informed the decision to employ a multi-sited research strategy that could account for key locational and demographic differences produced by processes of uneven development. It similarly determined the use of a mixed-methods approach that allowed quantitative migration data to be recorded without compromising qualitative insights into the intricate social realities of migration across different contexts. This research philosophy involved the incorporation of two distinct phases of research: a primary phase comprised of 100 semi-structured interviews with returned migrants of various backgrounds and a secondary phase involving a smaller series of in-depth interviews with key stakeholders from civil society and government organisations in order to triangulate location-specific findings for countrywide significance.

Within this general approach, three of my theoretical foci – *forced migration*, *place* and *status* – translate into overarching research questions that span the migration process from departure to reintegration. To what extent has uneven development engendered *forced migration* into urban and international employment? How have locational differences and specific migration practices shaped the conditions and outcomes of foreign employment? How do conditions of local employment affect notions of self-esteem and does migration offer an opportunity to reconstruct social status? These three questions form a multiscalar line of enquiry that assesses the structural causes, social institutions and individual pressures of systemic labour migration from Sri Lanka. Returned migrants served as the sole participant demographic for the first phase of fieldwork, their lived experiences during pre-departure, migration and reintegration offering insights into temporary labour migration as an individual, institutional and structural process. The fourth theoretical foci – *remittance capital* – addresses macroeconomic outcomes of temporary labour migration that could not be addressed directly through interviews with migrant returnees. Triangulation in the second phase of research was therefore vital in allowing detailed household-level findings to be extrapolated in relation to Sri Lanka's broader developmental context, which forms the basis of discussion in Chapters 6 and 7.

Conclusion

This chapter has reviewed the migration-development debate in parallel with de Haas's prominent interpretation of its central debates, both to contextualise the emergence of 'post-Washington' migration policy and to expose the subtle realignment of migration theory within these same ideological parameters. It has specifically drawn attention to the way in which historical-structuralist perspectives have been more readily delegitimised than disproven, while the core assumptions of neoclassical economic theory have been repackaged in the NELM and positioned as a supposed 'middle-ground' to the migration-development debate. I then revisited the underlying Marxian root of historical-structural perspectives to address existing limitations of the approach and offer a coherent framework in which to reconcile individual realities with economic structures that appreciably shape them. Marxian analyses of uneven development examine global patterns of capital accumulation, but also the contextually specific spread and evolution of capitalist social relations throughout the Global South (Brenner 1977). Emphasising the multiscalarity inherent to this approach, particularly by drawing attention to the importance of geography and local institutions as intermediaries between overarching structures and individual agency, allows for a historical-structural approach that both accommodates and explains a diversity of migration outcomes. The following chapter extends this historical-structural analysis to the uneven development of Sri Lanka's economy to situate the emergence of temporary labour migration as a livelihood and as a strategy of accumulation.

Notes

1 The conflation of neo-Marxist and dependency approaches as 'historical-structuralism' is here a reflection of tendencies to do so within the migration-development literature, which situates them under the same umbrella. It should be noted that, independent of the migration-development debate, these are distinct and complex literatures that cannot adequately be consolidated as 'historical-structuralism'.

2 The Washington Consensus refers to a set of economic policy prescriptions backed by the 'Washington Institutions' – chiefly the IMF and World Bank – and intended to promote free-market development in underdeveloped regions. More generally, it refers to the enshrining of neoliberal economy theories in development policy and practice.

3 The most recent UN High-Level Dialogue on International Migration and Development in 2013 saw a considerable embrace of managed migration policies by labour-sending countries as well as labour-receiving ones. This stands in contrast to greater scepticism expressed by developing economies at the previous dialogue in 2006.

4 A theory put forward by Arghiri Emmanuel in the 1950s, and subsequently adopted by dependency theorists, in order to substantiate the Singer-Prebisch book. It contends that the exchange of low value-added (peripheral) products with high value-added (core) products constitutes an exploitative transferral of surplus value from the periphery to the core.

References

Abreu, Alexandre. 2012. 'The New Economics of Labor Migration: Beware of Neoclassicals Bearing Gifts'. *Forum for Social Economics* 41 (1): 46–67.

Agunias, Dovelyn. 2006. 'Remittances and Development: Trends, Impacts, and Policy Options – A Review of the Literature'. Washington DC: Migration Policy Institute.

Beijer, G. 1970. 'International and National Migratory Movements'. *International Migration VIII* (3): 93–109.

Binford, Leigh. 2003. 'Migrant Remittances and (Under)Development in Mexico'. *Critique of Anthropology* 23 (3): 305–36.

Brenner, Robert. 1977. 'The Origins of Capitalist Development: A Critique of Neo-Smithian Marxism'. *New Left Review* I (104): 25–92.

Castells, Manuel. 1999. *The Informational City: Information Technology, Economic Restructuring, and the Urban-Regional Process*. Reprinted. Oxford: Blackwell.

Castles, Stephen. 2006. 'Guestworkers in Europe: A Resurrection?' *International Migration Review* 40 (4): 741–66.

Castles, Stephen. 2010. 'Understanding Global Migration: A Social Transformation Perspective'. *Journal of Ethnic and Migration Studies* 36 (10): 1565–86.

Castles, Stephen. 2013. 'The Forces Driving Global Migration'. *Journal of Intercultural Studies* 34 (2): 122–40.

Castles, Stephen and Godula Kosack. 1973. *Immigrant Workers and Class Structure in Western Europe*. London: Oxford University Press.

Chang, Ha-joon. 2003. *Kicking Away the Ladder Development Strategy in Historical Perspective*. London: Anthem Press.

Clemens, Michael A., Çağlar Özden, and Hillel Rapoport. 2014. 'Migration and Development Research Is Moving Far Beyond Remittances'. *World Development* 64: 121–24.

Cohen, Robin. 1987. *The New Helots: Migrants in the International Division of Labour*. Aldershot: Gower.

Cornia, Giovanni Andrea, ed. 2004. *Inequality, Growth, and Poverty in an Era of Liberalization and Globalization*. Oxford: Oxford University Press.

De Silva, S. B. D. 2013. *The Political Economy of Underdevelopment*. Colombo: Routledge.

Delgado Wise, Raúl. 2009. 'Forced Migration and US Imperialism: The Dialectic of Migration and Development'. *Critical Sociology* 35 (6): 767–84.

Delgado Wise, Raúl and Humberto Márquez Covarrubias. 2009. 'Understanding the Relationship between Migration and Development: Toward a New Theoretical Approach'. *Social Analysis* 53 (3): 85–105.

Emmanuel, Arghiri. 1972. *Unequal Exchange: A Study of the Imperialism of Trade*. London: New Left Books.

Friedman, Thomas L. 2000. *The Lexus and the Olive Tree*. London: HarperCollins.

Gibson-Graham, J.K. 2006. *A Postcapitalist Politics*. Minneapolis, MN: University of Minnesota Press.

Giddens, Anthony. 1984. *The Constitution of Society: Outline of the Theory of Structuration*. Berkeley, CA: University of California Press.

Gunder Frank, Andre. 1966. 'The Development of Underdevelopment'. *Monthly Review* 18 (4): 17.

Haan, Arjan de. 1999. 'Livelihoods and Poverty: The Role of Migration – A Critical Review of the Migration Literature'. *The Journal of Development Studies* 36 (2): 1–47.

Haas, Hein de. 2007. 'Remittances, Migration and Social Development: A Conceptual Review of the Literature'. 34. Social Policy and Development Programme Paper. UNRISD.

Haas, Hein de. 2010. 'Migration and Development: A Theoretical Perspective 1'. *International Migration Review* 44 (1): 227–64.

Haas, Hein de. 2012. 'The Migration and Development Pendulum: A Critical View on Research and Policy: The Migration and Development Pendulum'. *International Migration* 50 (3): 8–25.

Harris, J., and M. Todaro. 1970. 'Migration, Unemployment and Development: A Two-Sector Analysis'. *The American Economic Review* 60 (1): 126–42.

Harvey, David. 2007. 'Neoliberalism as Creative Destruction'. *The Annals of the American Academy* 610 (March): 22–44.

Hujo, Katja, and Nicola Piper. 2010. *South–South Migration: Implications for Social Policy and Development*. New York: Palgrave Macmillan.

Kapur, Devish. 2003. 'Remittances: The New Development Mantra?' Prepared for G-24 Technical Group Meeting, 15–16 September. New York: United Nations.

Katz, Eliakim, and Oded Stark. 1986. 'Labor Migration and Risk Aversion in Less Developed Countries'. *Journal of Labour Economics* 4: 131–49.

King, Russell. 2012. 'Theories and Typologies of Migration: An Overview and a Primer'. Willy Brandt Series of Working Papers in International Migration and Ethnic Relations. Malmö: Malmö University.

Lauby, Jennifer, and Oded Stark. 1988. 'Individual Migration as a Family Strategy: Young Women in the Philippines'. *Population Studies* 42: 473–86.

Marx, Karl. 1981. *Capital: A Critique of Political Economy. Vol. 1*. London: Penguin.

Mies, Maria, and Vandana Shiva. 1993. *Ecofeminism*. London: Zed Books.

Morawska, Ewa. 1990. 'The Sociology and Historiography of Immigration'. In *Immigration Reconsidered: History, Sociology and Politics*, edited by Virginia Yans-McLaughlin, 187–240. New York: Oxford University Press.

Morawska, Ewa. 2012. 'Historical-Structural Models of International Migration'. In *An Introduction to International Migration Studies*, edited by Marco Martiniello and Jan Rath, 55–75. Amsterdam: Amsterdam University Press.

Nikolinakos, Marios. 1975. 'Notes Towards a General Theory of Migration in Late Capitalism'. *Race and Class* 17 (1): 5–17.

Onis, Ziya, and Fikret Senses. 2005. 'Rethinking the Emerging Post-Washington Consensus'. *Development and Change* 36 (2): 263–90.

Papademetriou, Demetrios G., and Philip L. Martin, eds. 1991. *The Unsettled Relationship: Labor Migration and Economic Development. Contributions in Labor Studies, no. 33*. New York: Greenwood Press.

Petras, James. 1981. 'Dependency and World System Theory: A Critique and New Directions'. *Latin American Perspectives* 8 (3/4): 148–55.

Phillips, Nicola. 2009. 'Migration as Development Strategy? The New Political Economy of Dispossession and Inequality in the Americas'. *Review of International Political Economy* 16 (2): 231–59.

Piore, Michael J. 1980. *Birds of Passage: Migrant Labor and Industrial Societies*. Cambridge: Cambridge University Press.

Piper, Nicola. 2010. 'All Quiet on the Eastern Front? – Temporary Contract Migration in Asia Revisited from a Development Perspective'. *Policy and Society* 29 (4): 399–411.

Polanyi, Karl. 2001. *The Great Transformation: The Political and Economic Origins of Our Time*. Boston, MA: Beacon Press. First published 1944.

Portes, Alejandro, and John Walton. 1981. *Labor, Class, and the International System*. Burlington, MA: Academic Press.

Rankin, Katharine N. 2001. 'Governing Development: Neoliberalism, Microcredit, and Rational Economic Woman'. *Economy and Society* 30 (1): 18–37.

Sassen, Saskia. 1988. *The Mobility of Labor and Capital: A Study in International Investment and Labor Flow*. Cambridge: Cambridge University Press.

Sassen, Saskia. 1991. *The Global City: New York, London, Tokyo*. Princeton, NJ: Princeton University Press.

Stark, Oded. 1984. 'Migrant Decision Making: A Review Article'. *Journal of Development Economics* 14 (Spring): 80–93.

Stark, Oded, and David Bloom. 1985. 'The New Economics of Labour Migration'. *American Economic Review* 75: 173–8.

Stark, Oded, and J. Edward Taylor. 1989. 'Relative Deprivation and International Migration'. *Demography* 26: 57–70.

Stiglitz, Joseph E. 2003. *Globalization and Its Discontents*. New York: W.W. Norton.

Van Hear, Nicholas. 2010. 'Theories of Migration and Social Change'. *Journal of Ethnic and Migration Studies* 36 (10): 1531–6.

Veblen, Thorstein. 2009. *The Theory of the Leisure Class*. Oxford: Oxford University Press. First published 1899.

Wallerstein, Immanuel Maurice. 2004. *World-Systems Analysis: An Introduction*. Durham, NC: Duke University Press.

Wickramasekara, Piyasiri, International Labour Office, and Bureau for Workers' Activities. 2011. *Circular Migration: A Triple Win or a Dead End?* Geneva: ILO.

Williamson, John, and Institute for International Economics (US), eds. 1990. *Latin American Adjustment: How Much Has Happened?* Washington, DC: Institute for International Economics.

World Bank. 2006. *Global Economic Prospects: Economic Implications of Remittances and Migration*. Washington, DC: World Bank.

World Bank. 2011. *Migration and Remittances Factbook 2011*. Washington, DC: World Bank.

2 The political economy of uneven development in Sri Lanka

It is necessary to contextualise the present centrality of temporary labour migration in Sri Lanka – as a livelihood strategy, a recruitment business and a pillar of macroeconomic stability – as the outcome of historically formed political-economic structures of uneven development. Sri Lanka's economic landscape has been transformed by structures of imperialism, within which local class formations and a logic of accumulation by subordination have taken shape. The economic subsumption of caste, ethnic and gender relations under postcolonial articulations of nationalism have overseen the preservation of uneven development processes from one epoch to another, exacerbated by neoliberal reforms enacted in 1977. The 'open economy' period channelled existing ethnic and gendered discrimination into specific avenues of capital accumulation, entrenching an uneven and exclusionary vision of development that has since become status quo. It is against the backdrop of this neoliberal restructuring that temporary labour migration has taken root as one of a limited number of livelihood strategies for populations geographically and demographically excluded from development.

This chapter outlines recent macroeconomic shifts that have propelled Sri Lanka to its current political-economic juncture and situates the role of labour migration within it. The first section briefly outlines class relations and capital accumulation strategies formed under colonialism. The second section focuses on economic reconfigurations following the 1977 neoliberal turn, examining how Sri Lankan neoliberalism was assembled from its own social milieu and appropriated the logic of accumulation by subordination first exercised under colonialism. The final section addresses labour migration more specifically, by examining the changing demographics and policy responses to migration since its widespread occurrence in the late 1970s.

Accumulation by subordination in colonial and post-colonial Sri Lanka

The modern political economy of Sri Lanka cannot be understood independently of its history with colonialism. Overlapping waves of colonial invasion by the Portuguese, Dutch and British have altered the structure of Sri Lanka's social and economic institutions: the traditional monarchy was progressively undermined by military incursions and the entrenchment of foreign administration; extraction economies arose around the regional trade of cinnamon, gems and agricultural produce; and, under the British, tea plantations were established as a central feature of the economy (Jayawardena 2000). The last and most enduring of these shifts, from exploitation by extraction to exploitation by production, is a defining feature of British imperialism as a more explicitly capitalist form of colonialism (McNally 2006). The logic of imperial capitalism demands a reconfiguration of the social relations of production in order to facilitate the capital accumulation for which it exists. In Sri Lanka this did not entail a comprehensive adoption of capitalist social relations, but rather the strategic assimilation of the existing mode of production – including its ethnic, gender and caste divisions – into a quasi-capitalist mode of production. What emerges in Sri Lanka, as elsewhere in the colonised world, is the emergence of an incomplete capitalist transformation characterising what Paul Baran has dubbed 'a twilight world, neither wholly feudal nor capitalist' (in Jayawardena 2000, xxiii).

Much has been written about the class relations and structures of production underpinning Sri Lanka's colonial economy, most notably Kumari Jayawardena's seminal exploration of the rise of the colonial bourgeoisie *Nobodies to Somebodies* (2000) and S. B. D. De Silva's expansive *The Political Economy of Underdevelopment* (2013 [1982]). I will avoid going over ground that has been so expertly covered, save to make one observation about the enduring salience of the plantation economy: that it set an influential precedent for capital accumulation by way of ethnic and gendered subordination. In leveraging the cultural subjugation of Indian Tamils (and particularly Indian Tamil women) to maintain a semi-feudal workforce whose mistreatment garnered little political traction, the British effectively mapped out a blueprint for wealth creation that has since been reproduced in varying contexts and become the defining dynamic of Sri Lanka's uneven development. This logic, which I term *accumulation by subordination*, differs importantly from its kindred concept of accumulation by dispossession (Harvey 2003). Whereas Harvey's concept refers to the manner in which transfers of land and wealth facilitate capital accumulation by centralising the ownership of assets, accumulation by subordination refers to the mobilisation of ethnic and gendered discrimination to legitimise and maintain the expropriation of these resources – and of labour itself – from vulnerable populations. In this manner, the predatory practices of dispossession described by Harvey are not only enacted, but are reproduced and preserved as a continuing basis for accumulation under a semi-feudal arrangement of capital and labour relations. In the case of the plantation economy, the Indian Tamils were already dispossessed of land and labour by economic upheavals in India that resulted in their forcible displacement to Sri Lanka. Their subsequent subordination as a socially and culturally removed ethnic minority has maintained an overtly ethnicised system of indentured plantation labour that continues to the present day (Jayawardena and Kurian 2015).

The forging of Sri Lanka's post-colonial identity largely occurred under an ethos of patriarchal ethno-nationalism, through which accumulation by subordination was rearticulated to construct economic and social advantages over women and ethnic minorities (Withers and Biyanwila 2014). Both the leftist Sri Lanka Freedom Party (SLFP) and right-wing United National Party (UNP) voiced claims to nationhood steeped in Sinhala-Buddhist exceptionalism and attendant patriarchal norms. The SLFP, in power from 1956 through to 1977, pursued a protectionist economic agenda committed to the expansion of public services, welfare and import-substitution industrialisation. Within this 'closed economy' model, gendered and ethnic discrimination was more a matter of restrictions to public-sector employment, which was seen as the rightful preserve of Sinhalese men, than direct exploitation in nascent industries. Sri Lankan Tamils were all but excluded from bureaucratic positions with the passing of the 'Sinhala Only Act' in 1956, enshrining Sinhalese as the only official language of Sri Lanka (Nissan and Stirrat 1990). At the same time, women of all ethnicities had limited access to public-sector jobs and were largely confined to forms of work seen as a natural extension of reproductive labour: textile production, tea picking and domestic work (Jayaweera 2002).

The closed economy model was thrown into disarray when, in 1973, the global oil crisis provoked a sharp increase in the price of Sri Lanka's main imports – petroleum and petroleum-related products – relative to its small stream of predominantly agricultural exports (Kelegama 2006). The continued imposition of strict trade restrictions in a context of underwhelming domestic production soon manifested in a scarcity of many basic foodstuffs and consumer goods that, in turn, proved conducive to corruption and public discontent. Sri Lanka's political and economic crises intensified by the mid-1970s and left Sirimavo Bandaranaike's SLFP government on a precarious footing, rapidly losing public credibility through the imposition of strict rationing quotas amidst burgeoning unemployment (Kottegoda 2004). Accumulation by subordination had established a labour market segmented by ethnicity and gender, but Sri Lanka's political and economic institutions were left on the brink of collapse and the closed economy model was no longer a viable vehicle for its deployment as a developmental project.

Sri Lankan neoliberalism

In 1977, following delayed elections and dwindling popularity, the SLFP government of Sirimavo Bandaranaika was ousted in a landslide victory to the UNP, headed by J. R. Jayawardene. The UNP advocated a policy platform that might be considered only the second example of neoliberalism worldwide,[1] promising sweeping economic liberalisation as a panacea for the macroeconomic quagmire of the closed economy period (Richardson Jr. 2004). The structural impact of these reforms has since seen 1977 interned in popular consciousness as a pivotal turning point in Sri Lanka's social and economic history.

The 'open economy' story spans the foundation of modern Sri Lanka's economic pillars, the interrelated beginnings of an epoch-defining civil war and continues to define the current 'post-war' developmental context. This section analyses the specific character of Sri Lanka neoliberalism and its revitalisation of 'accumulation by subordination'. It details the dramatic political-economic restructuring that took place following the 1977 elections and situates within these shifts the intensification of uneven development processes that exploit and exclude along and across class, ethnic and gendered divisions. These processes are explored in relation to the economic expressions of ethnic violence bookending the civil war, the reorientation of capital accumulation within export processing zones and the garment industry, and the burgeoning growth of temporary labour migration. It is no coincidence that the employment of Sri Lanka's working-class is almost entirely accounted for by the armed services, garment manufacturing and temporary labour migration (Shastri 2004). All three trends reproduce the same mechanics of accumulation by subordination and uneven development enshrined in the colonial plantation economy: the systematic exploitation of disempowered populations to underpin capital accumulation for an insular bourgeois minority.

Jayawardene's election as prime minster was swiftly followed by the passing of a new constitution that transferred his leadership to the executive post of president. Utilising additional legislative powers conferred to the presidency, Jayawardene oversaw the implementation of a package of free-market policies that rapidly deregulated and privatised the Sri Lankan economy. A floating exchange rate was adopted, import and migration controls were dismantled, the banking system and credit supply were substantially deregulated and blueprints were laid down for a large export processing zone just north of Colombo, in Katunayake (Richardson Jr. 2004). This geographic reconfiguration of export production was accompanied by the simultaneous abandonment of decentralised state-run industries, curtailing the provision of local employment opportunities for rural populations and particularly for women hitherto working within village workshops established by the national handloom industry (Kottegoda 2004). The rural poor were further disadvantaged by the abolition of rice subsidies, on which the country had relied since independence and the undermining of public healthcare and education by the rise of privatised alternatives (Gunasinghe 2011).

Yet these free-market reforms were not paired with a typically neoliberal fiscal stance. In a bid to galvanise the economy for export production the new government channelled massive capital expenditure into agriculture, industry, housing and infrastructure projects (Richardson Jr. 2004). Though successful in stimulating short-term growth and a marked increase in low value-added industrial exports, government expenditures were largely financed by developmental aid, international loans and foreign exchange receipts earned from remittances. Together, these sources of capital represented a new web of macroeconomic dependencies and constraints. Thus, the early boom accompanying Jayawardene's liberalisation program was short-lived. By 1982 government debt had tripled, inflation was high and trade deficits – no longer safeguarded by import restrictions – were increasing rapidly (Kelegama 2006). Debt servicing took up a growing portion of government revenue and precipitated heavy cutbacks to already strained developmental and welfare projects, while spiralling inflation caused ongoing reductions in real wages and the post-independence trend towards distributional equality began reversing under intensified capital accumulation (Indraratna 1990; Richardson Jr. 2004).

The new macroeconomic tensions of Sri Lankan neoliberalism produced and sustained three broad and interrelated trends: increasing ethnic violence and the wartime economy; internal migration to find work in the urban export economy; and countrywide recourse to international migration as a livelihood strategy. All three structural shifts were fundamentally catalysed by the rationale of centralising economic activity in select urban settings of the Sinhalese-majority Western Province. As Kelegama notes:

> The development of industrialisation that emerged after a decade of liberalisation was very much lopsided with less diversification and was highly urban-based. Out of the industrial exports nearly 60 percent originated from the textile and garment sector and 70–80 percent of the industry in output terms was concentrated in the Western Province.
>
> (2006, 202)

Neoliberal development continued to exclude the Sri Lankan Tamil population clustered in the north and east, but also fostered incendiary ethnic tensions amongst economically disaffected Sinhalese poor, many of whom in turn found military employment as the armed services swelled during the civil war (Shastri 2004). For the rural Sinhalese population, diminishing local employment opportunities betwixt the feminisation of urban export manufacturing dramatically reconfigured the working lives of young women, large numbers of whom began migrating internally to support themselves and their families by labouring in the growing garment industry. Similarly, the pervasive decline of rural livelihoods alongside the relaxation of migration policies engendered growing temporary labour migration to West Asia. Women, in particular, were departing in large numbers, both deterred by the deepening stigma surrounding garment work and incentivised by high demand for migrant domestic workers following India, Pakistan and Bangladesh's recent prohibition of female migration (Eelens, Mook, and Schampers 1992). In path-dependant fashion these broad structural trends have matured since the 1977 turn to become increasingly embedded features of the Sri Lankan economy: ethnic violence has eventually resolved as a post-war strategy of accumulation by dispossession; feminised (and more recently ethnicised) manufacturing has become entrenched as a key export industry; and the remittances received from labour migration have comprised an ever-greater slice of the foreign exchange earnings financing trade deficits and loan repayments.

Ethnic violence and the open economy

The causality between economic restructuring in 1977 and the outbreak of civil war in 1983 is contested in Sri Lanka, complicated by the existence of competing and highly politicised interpretations of accountability for the conflict. Sri Lanka's macroeconomic problems during the neoliberal period are often attributed to the war, an assessment made particularly compelling when considered in light of post-war investment and the tourism boom along Sri Lanka's south-west coastline. But while the emigration of Tamil refugees has unambiguously been linked to the war, data from the Sri Lankan Bureau of Foreign Employment (SLBFE) clearly demonstrates that large-scale temporary labour migration of Sinhalese and Muslim populations began almost immediately after migration restrictions were lifted in 1977 (SLBFE 2012). In a similar vein, arguments that the war impeded economic development tend to lose credibility when confronted with more substantiated evidence that the 1977 economic reforms aggravated existing ethnic tensions (Richardson Jr. 2004). While the Tamil population continued to experience discrimination within the open economy, so too did the Sinhalese poor endure material hardships. Living amidst polarising class relations, but without the ethnically entitled patronage of the state-regulated economy, many working-class Sinhalese developed an acute sense of relative deprivation (Gunasinghe 2011). Popular discontent was not directed at the state, partially because the state's economic accountability was concealed behind the supposed impartiality of the free market and partially due to violent repression of the labour movement (Biyanwila 2011). Discontent was instead readily lent to ethnic antagonisms being stirred by unscrupulous politicians (Manor 1984; Tambiah 1986) and Sinhalese capitalists struggling against Tamil and Muslim businesses benefiting from transnational trade connections after the removal of import restrictions (Gunasinghe 2011). Thus, despite only two notable ethnic clashes in the 60 years prior, the 1977 elections preceded six years of incessant ethnic rioting and culminated in the 1983 Black July riots that left up to 3,000 Colombo Tamils dead, left thousands more internally and internationally displaced, and catalysed the commencement of civil war (Gunasinghe 2011).

The war itself was undeniably harmful for Sri Lanka's economy insofar as it deterred FDI, disrupted the tourist economy and prompted huge swathes of GDP to be earmarked for military expenditure over public investment. However, the rapid growth of the armed forces also acted as an economic 'safety valve' providing mass employment for the same economically marginalised Sinhalese men left politicised by their relative deprivation in the wake of economic reforms. Indeed, alongside export manufacturing and migration, the armed services formed (and remain) one of three major avenues of employment in the post-1977 economy (Shastri 2004). The wartime economy was thus sustained through the contradiction of its own inception; class antagonisms and unemployment produced under neoliberalism were vented through the conflict they helped create and so obfuscated deep-seated macroeconomic frailties. Acute class inequalities were therefore maintained throughout the conflict, even if the war itself curtailed the extent to which investment and accumulation could be undertaken by local capitalists. In 2009, a harrowing end to the war eased these constraints and paved the way for 'post-war reconstruction' in the manner of accumulation by dispossession. Unwilling to demilitarise its 200,000-strong army – both for reasons of structural unemployment and the forceful preservation of Tamil subordination – the Sri Lankan government has since overseen investment in retail franchises, tourist developments and the planned opening of new industrial parks and export processing zones (JDI 2011). Given that capital investment in the north and east is typically sourced from outside these regions, the state appears complicit in preserving ethnic fractures by transitioning military conquest into economic subjugation.

The gendered economy of export production

The 1977 reforms entailed significant reconfigurations of the nature and extent of women's participation in paid employment (IPS 2013), with female labour force participation rates jumping markedly despite 40,000 job losses associated with the decline of the local handloom industry (Kottegoda 2004). This increase is given meaning by the creation of several EPZs that centralised garment manufacturing in urban areas, most prominently the Katunayake and Biyagama EPZs located just outside of Colombo (Sivananthan 2008), as part of the government's concerted attempt to further integrate the labour of young Sinhalese women into global production networks. The geographical reconfiguration of the economy around urban export production reinforced existing patterns of uneven development by undermining rural employment opportunities and necessitating internal migration to EPZs in order to find work.

Yet the defining feature of this new avenue of accumulation was its specific subordination of a gendered (and more recently ethnicised) workforce. A sexist rhetoric of 'nimble fingers' (Elson and Pearson 1981) was mobilised alongside existing patriarchal parameters to construe garment work as an extension of household care work, and thus the domain of women's work in form and in function. Patriarchal notions of what constitutes 'appropriate' work marginalise a majority of Sri Lankan women from better-paid work in high-growth and professional industries, irrespective of qualifications and educational attainment (Gunatilaka 2013; Kotikula and Solotaroff 2006). At the same time, this rhetoric ensures that women remain over-represented in the most labour-intensive, poorly remunerated occupations that together comprise the backbone of Sri Lanka's export economy (Kotikula and Solotaroff 2006). In the post-war period this has been compounded by ethnic discrimination, as Tamil women fleeing poverty in the underdeveloped north – many of whom are internally displaced persons – have been integrated into the garments industry on unequal terms (Fernando 2013). Tamil women working in the Katunayake EPZ have been seen to experience discrimination in terms of employment and working conditions, while their segregation from Sinhalese women is reportedly being used by employers to shore up ethnic tensions and undermine attempts at collective bargaining (Fernando 2013).

A contradiction thus emerges, wherein social constructions of women as bastions of reproductive labour are fractured by the reality of a sexual division of labour that situates women as breadwinners working within the most exploitative tiers of production. Women constitute approximately 85 per cent of all employees within Sri Lanka's EPZs (DOLUS 2010), while also comprising the majority of estate workers within tea and rubber plantations (Kotikula and Solotaroff 2006) and, until very recently, the majority of temporary labour migrants (SLBFE 2016). Tea and garments alone account for over half of all Sri Lanka's goods exports, while migration brings in remittances equivalent to 63 per cent of exports (CBSL 2018). A patriarchal mode of production, formalised under colonialism and restructured through neoliberalism, has curtailed women's economic life to the performance of menial labour in circumscribed spheres of work: indentured to plantations, exploited in factories or without rights within the private homes of foreign employers (Withers and Biyanwila 2014).

While the extent of women's participation in these avenues of employment is substantially tempered by religious background, with notably less participation in the domestic workforce from Muslim and Christian women (Gunatilaka 2013), what is fairly universal are the long hours, low-wages and lack of labour rights typically associated with the feminisation of export production as a cheaper, more 'competitive' alternative to unionised male labour (Standing 1989, 1999). Despite the adverse conditions of women's employment and its significance for the export economy, women's increased participation in productive employment has politicised tensions between socially ascribed work and care roles. Young women working in garment factories are pejoratively branded *Juki girls* or *Juki pieces* (in reference to a common brand of sewing machine), connoting disposability and sexual promiscuity, with the inference that work and urban life has compromised the chastity and respectability that women are expected to embody as symbols of the nation (Lynch 2007). Women are thus subordinated, materially and culturally, as an exploitable mainstay of productive and reproductive labour.

Temporary labour migration: foundations of the remittance economy

A third reconfiguration of economic life in the 'open economy' is found in the beginnings of temporary labour migration to West Asia. In addition to liberalising labour migration itself, the Jayawardene government privatised the role of the Foreign Employment Unit (established by Bandaranaike just a year earlier), allowing recruitment agencies to proliferate within a loosely regulated system of migration practices (Gamburd 2000). Local and regional contexts conspired to make recruitment a lucrative business. Oil-driven accumulation in the Persian Gulf had created huge surpluses and attendant demand for migrant labour to perform the manual work necessitated by infrastructural expansion and the domestic labour sought by increasingly wealthy West Asian households. At the same time, declining rural livelihoods and the lack of decent work generated under neoliberal patterns of accumulation left much of the Sri Lankan population predisposed to meet such demand – particularly women, whose opportunities were greater due to the excess demand created by the prohibition of female migration amongst other labour-sending countries.

While foreign incomes could outstrip local wages for male and female migrants, the increasing costs of recruitment fees meant that agencies, sub-agents and brokers – the so-called merchants of labour – were accumulating significant wealth while migrants themselves faced difficulty financing their placements abroad (Eelens and Speckmann 1992). These escalating financial obstacles, paired with the well-documented physical and psychological hardships of indentured employment in West Asia (ILO 2010), speaks to temporary labour migration's emergence as a survival strategy pursued less by choice than by necessity. At the same time, the state itself benefitted greatly from increasing departures. Temporary labour migration circumvented pressure to generate employment locally, stymieing potentially destabilising political and economic tensions, while remittances brought in foreign exchange 'urgently needed to sustain the economic policies of the UNP government' (Eelens, Mook, and Schampers 1992, 4). By effectively deferring the contradictions of uneven development, the structural dynamics of temporary labour migration have safeguarded the continuation of accumulation by subordination elsewhere in the economy, while creating new opportunities for the merchants of labour to amass wealth.

Managing migration: demographic change and policy responses

The demographics of migration

Migration, both of labour and of political refugees, has been an increasingly prominent feature of post-independence Sri Lanka. In particular, the late 1970s and early 1980s can be identified as a period of pronounced out-migration in both respects, with Sri Lankans migrating temporarily to the Persian Gulf to meet burgeoning demand for cheap labour or resettling in the West in order to escape growing sectarian violence. These parallel streams of migration also have distinct ethnic characteristics, with the vast majority of refugees having come from the island's Tamil minority, while labour migrants have historically been of Sinhalese or – especially in relation to population size – Muslim background (Eelens and Schampers 1992). Surveying the demographic shifts within both these categories of migration, including the more recent influx of Tamils into processes of temporary labour migration, offers an important reflection of the changing social and economic dynamics of Sri Lankan migration.

In short, the 1977 neoliberal turn and commencement of full-blown civil war in 1983 served as catalysts for labour and political migration respectively (Sriskandarajah 2002). Since that time, capital transfers originating from both channels of migration have endured as economic mainstays in regional and national contexts. With imports invariably outstripping exports, remittance income has become a key source of foreign reserves and a widely acknowledged macroeconomic remedy to Sri Lanka's unfavourable Balance of Payments scenario (IPS 2012). Despite the ubiquity of remittances themselves, the demographics of migration have altered substantially over time. One of the most striking changes has undoubtedly been the proliferation of the Tamil diaspora and the capital transfer associated with it, though these migrations fall beyond the purview of my research and have been discussed in detail elsewhere (Sriskandarajah 2002; Spencer 1990). Temporary labour migrants, on the other hand, have historically originated from Sinhala-Buddhist and (relative to population size) Muslim and Sinhala-Catholic communities outside the regions affected by civil war. Previous studies have indicated that Muslims are four times more likely to emigrate than other Sri Lankans living in Colombo, owing to West Asian employers' demand for workers with a compatible religious orientation (Mook 1992), while there appears to be a similar bias to Sinhala-Catholics on account of their monotheistic beliefs (Spaan 1992; Gamburd 2000). More recently, Tamils have also begun migrating for foreign employment in growing numbers, having previously been excluded from regular temporary labour migration due to the effects of the civil war. In the years immediately following the end of the war, major urban centres in the Northern and Eastern Provinces had shown the greatest year-on-year increases in migrant departures, despite a relative lack of government training and administrative outreach to these communities (SLBFE 2012).

However, the most striking feature of Sri Lanka's labour migration is the historically large number of women involved in the migratory process. Though early statistics are somewhat unreliable and reported estimates at times conflicting, there is a consensus that women accounted for roughly 70 per cent of all labour migrants by the mid to late 1980s (Gamburd 2000). The commencement of mass labour migration from Sri Lanka coincided with other South Asian labour-sending nations implementing morally or religiously driven policies to retract domestic workers from foreign employment, at a time when the demand for domestic workers in the West Asia was growing steadily (Eelens, Mook, and Schampers 1992). Consequently, the demand for domestic workers increased dramatically and Sri Lankan women – many frustrated by the lack of domestic employment opportunities within a rapidly liberalising economy or stigma in the garments industry – were quick to take up these positions (Gamburd 2000). Male labour migrants from the same period were principally low-waged workers temporarily employed as construction labourers on projects in the Gulf region. Though male workers were in a clear minority during the 1980s, there has been a trend towards the de-feminisation of migrant labour flows since the mid-1990s (IPS 2012). This is likely the result of sustained demand for construction workers in West Asia, as reflected by increasing numbers of low-waged male migrants, but also a consequence of social backlash against young mothers' involvement in domestic worker migration and subsequent implementation of the FBR (IPS 2012; ILO 2018). Irrespective of fluctuating gender patterns, the prevalence of low-waged workers endures. Despite government programs to bolster skilled migration, 'low-skilled' workers (including domestic workers) still account for 89 per cent of all labour migrants (CBSL 2018).

Current government policies to promote labour migration

Over the past decade the economic salience of temporary labour migration has increased substantially, reflected by a dramatic increase in both migrant outflows (SLBFE 2012) and remittance income as a percentage of net export earnings (IPS 2012). During this same period, the prevailing philosophy of actively promoting foreign employment intensified, culminating in the creation of the Ministry for Foreign Employment Promotion and Welfare (MFEPW) in 2007. The ministry overlooks the function of both the SLBFE and the Sri Lanka Foreign Employment Agency (SLFEA), whose role involves exploring and catering to skilled job markets abroad, and operates in alignment with the government's policy commitment to 'make every effort to be a provider of globally employable, competitive human capital' (MFP 2006, 176). Under the MFEPW's guidance, policy emphasis has shifted away from the formalisation of the migration process – an objective largely attained, with the exception of rampant sub-agent malpractice (ILO 2013) – and towards efforts to reshape the composition of Sri Lanka's foreign labour force. There is a pervasive sentiment, both within the MFEPW and SLBFE itself (MFEPW 2012; SLBFE 2012) and amongst broader governmental and independent economic assessments (MFP 2006; IPS 2012), that Sri Lanka must transition from supplying 'low-skilled' to 'skilled'[2] workers in order to achieve greater developmental outcomes from temporary labour migration. Though the desire to curtail 'low-skilled' labour is frequently discussed in reference to the growing catalogue of social ills associated with mass migration of female domestic workers, the underlying assumption behind refocusing on skilled labour migrants is unanimously predicated on the expectation of increased wages and – by extension – a net increase in remittances (IPS 2014).

The importance of skilled migration in contemporary policy discourse has also borne serious implications for the protection of migrant workers. While the MFEPW has worked closely with the ILO in compiling the National Labour Migration Policy and states a commitment to 'promote opportunities for all men and women to engage in migration for decent and productive employment in conditions of freedom, equity, security and human dignity' (MFEPW 2008, 7), there is limited discussion of how such an outcome can be achieved for 'low-skilled' workers. Indeed, the protection of 'low-skilled' workers is framed in much the same light as it was in earlier decades, that is, hinging on the presence of Sri Lankan diplomatic missions in labour-receiving nations, the pursuit of bilateral agreements and memoranda of understandings, and the need to further monitor the recruitment process at home (MFEPW 2008). The enduring nature of migrant abuse in spite of the prolonged implementation of these strategies does, however, cast doubt over the efficacy of such measures. The MFEPW concludes that in light of continuing human rights abuses endured by 'low-skilled' workers, 'the ultimate protection to all migrant workers is the possession of skills' (MFEPW 2008, 10). Similar rhetoric about the 'limited bargaining power' of 'low-skilled' vis-à-vis skilled labour is found from the SLBFE (2012) and together with MFEPW policy initiatives aimed at 'securing employment opportunities for skilled workers in safe and regulated work environments' (MFEPW 2008, 10) represents a tacit conflation of migrant training and migrant protection. Indeed, the mission statement of the ministry highlights 'the development of skills as a main and effective means of protection for migrant workers and their families' (MFEPW 2008, iv). In doing so, however, it also represents a weakening policy resolve towards defending the rights and working conditions of the vast majority of migrants who remain firmly within the 'low-skilled' category. In practice, recent SLBFE activity reports indicate a prioritisation of compensatory measures over worker protection, while – contrary to stated policy intentions – pre-departure training programmes remain predominantly tailored to 'low-skilled' vocations (MFEPW 2012).

The economic imperative of obtaining greater remittances appears to outweigh the government's commitment to both skilling and protecting migrant workers. At a migration policy symposium held in 2014, the secretary of the MFEPW spelt out the government's explicit intention of increasing annual remittances from the US$6.4 billion received in 2014 to US$10 billion by 2016 (IPS 2014). In order to achieve this target, several policy tools were highlighted, including the recent mandate by the SLBFE that all migrant domestic workers must attain a National Vocational Qualification (NVQ) Level Three certificate prior to migration. The outcome of the three-week course – which covers housekeeping, food preparation, personal hygiene and care for children, the infirm and the elderly (SLBFE 2015) – was deemed a necessary step in 're-branding' Sri Lankan domestic workers as 'domestic housekeeping assistance', a move in turn designed to attract higher wages and therefore increased remittances (IPS 2014). This 'upskilling' is effectively symbolic, as the NVQ course content differs in no discernible way from existing two-week pre-departure training conducted by the SLBFE (GIC 2015), and belies the government's intention of profiting further from 'exporting' Sri Lankan labour for the West Asian 'market'. The explicit rhetoric of labour commodification expressed during the symposium is congruent with the SLBFE's recent adoption of the nationalistic term *rativiru* (lit: migrant hero), both echoing the language of migrant heroism employed in the Philippines (Guevarra 2010) and an allusion to the local term *ranaviru* (lit: war hero). This labelling homogenises a diverse migrant population as an economic army doing duty for Sri Lanka and offers symbolic dignity to placate the dehumanisation inherent within the fictitious commodification of migrants as human exports. A lack of genuine resolve in addressing the training and reintegration of migrant workers – particularly in the majority Tamil Eastern Province, where there is an insufficient distribution of migrant support and training services (SLBFE 2012) – further exposes the remittance-centric underpinnings of existing migration policy despite rhetorical commitments to skilled labour migration.

The prevailing paucity of skilled migrant workers is, beyond government policy, indicative of a structural shortage of skilled labour in Sri Lanka's domestic workforce (SLBFE 2012). The Rajapaksa government's development manifesto specified an acute need to address Sri Lanka's 'low-skill' and largely informal workforce and foster skilled labour in order to facilitate envisioned industrial diversification, service sector growth and overall international competitiveness (MFP 2006). The incumbent Sirisena government maintains this concern. Supporting this emphasis on producing skilled labour, the Institute of Policy Studies (IPS) observes a discrepancy between emerging industrial and service opportunities and a lack of skilled labour to fill these potential jobs (IPS 2012). However, the IPS also notes an inherent strain in developing a skilled labour force at home and abroad; with the rate of foreign employment outstripping domestic employment growth, there is an appreciable challenge in retaining an adequate number of skilled workers within Sri Lanka itself (IPS 2012).

This is problematic, not only for internal economic development, but for the macroeconomic impact of remittances. Even optimistic understandings of the migration–development nexus contend that the retention of skilled workers is a decisive factor in a nation's ability to translate remittances into output growth (Abella and Ducanes 2007), thus exposing a fundamental tension within Sri Lanka's policy objective of simultaneously encouraging skilled labour formation in national and international contexts. Despite the IPS's acknowledgement that policies promoting skilled labour migration 'will need to be re-evaluated' (IPS 2012, 87), the current lack of policy discussion rings true to Abella and Ducanes's warning that 'expectations of large remittances make it easier for the policymakers to avoid or postpone making hard and painful decisions' (2007, 75). With remittance earnings playing an increasingly vital role in financing Sri Lanka's substantial trade deficit, the reframing of migration policy in terms of attaining dramatically increased annual remittances by increasing labour migration to West Asia – skilled or otherwise – appears to confirm the presence of a deepening remittance-dependency.

Conclusion

This chapter has reviewed Sri Lanka's history of uneven development in order to contextualise the emergence of temporary labour migration and background the macroeconomic conditions against which its developmental implications play out. Sri Lanka's increasing reliance on foreign employment has been identified as a logically consistent outgrowth of historical structures of uneven development and an interrelated rationale of accumulation by subordination. Examining the asymmetrical spread of capitalist social relations over time, it has argued that an important precedent was set during British imperialism, wherein ethnic and gendered discrimination was leveraged as a basis for establishing and legitimising the exploitation of marginalised populations. Accumulation by subordination was first exercised under a semi-feudal mode of production in the estate sector (and prevails there today), was resuscitated under market conditions following Sri Lanka's embrace of neoliberalism and endures as developmentally excluded populations continue migrating to West Asia for work. The role of economic policy in catalysing and entrenching these movements of labour is examined, covering successive efforts to regularise and promote temporary labour migration, including current efforts to encourage skilled migration to the detriment of the vast majority of migrants that fall outside this category. Complementing the theoretical framework introduced in Chapter 1 with a careful examination of the research context, this chapter prefaces the discussion of fieldwork findings that follows in Chapters 3, 4 and 5.

Notes

1 Following Pinochet's 1973 US-backed coup in Chile, Sri Lanka was the next country to implement far-reaching neoliberal reforms before the popularisation of those economic policies in the UK and US. It represents an oft-overlooked case study in the development of neoliberalism in practice.

2 It should be noted that the social construction of 'skills' and their subsequent codification as 'unskilled', 'low-skilled' or 'highly-skilled' is deeply flawed and reproduces power imbalances along gender, race and class lines (Warhurst, Tilly, and Gatta 2017). The skill categories discussed here reflect those in use by the Sri Lankan government and are made necessary by the context of discussion.

References

Abella, Manolo, and Jeffrey Ducanes. 2007. 'Is Transnationalism a New Paradigm for Development?' In *Migration and Development: Perspectives from the South*, 65–75. Geneva: IOM International Organization for Migration.

Biyanwila, Janaka. 2011. *The Labour Movement in the Global South: Trade Unions in Sri Lanka*. London: Routledge.

Central Bank of Sri Lanka (CBSL). 2018. 'Economic and Social Statistics of Sri Lanka 2018'. Colombo: Central Bank of Sri Lanka.

De Silva, S. B. D. 2013. *The Political Economy of Underdevelopment*. Colombo: Routledge.

Department of Labour (DOLUS). 2010. 'Promoting Fundamental Principles and Rights at Work in Sri Lanka (2009–2011)'. Colombo: Department of Labour.

Eelens, Frank, and Toon Schampers. 1992. 'Survival Migration: The Sri Lankan Case'. In *Labour Migration to the Middle East: From Sri Lanka to the Gulf*, 27–40. London: Kegan Paul International.

Eelens, Frank, and Johann Dirk Speckmann. 1992. 'Recruitment of Labour Migrants for the Middle East'. In *Labour Migration to the Middle East: From Sri Lanka to the Gulf*, 41–62. London: Kegan Paul International.

Eelens, Frank, T. Mook, and Toon Schampers. 1992. 'Introduction'. In *Labour Migration to the Middle East: From Sri Lanka to the Gulf*, 1–27. London: Kegan Paul International.

Elson, Diane, and Ruth Pearson. 1981. '"Nimble Fingers Make Cheap Workers": An Analysis of Women's Employment in Third World Export Manufacturing'. *Feminist Review* 7 (Spring): 87–107.

Fernando, Mangala. 2013. *Ethnic Discrimination: The Post Armed Conflict Economic Challenges of Tamil Women*. Colombo: Women's Centre Sri Lanka.

Gamburd, Michele Ruth. 2000. *The Kitchen Spoon's Handle: Transnationalism and Sri Lanka's Migrant Housemaids*. Ithaca, NY: Cornell University Press.

Government Information Centre (GIC). 2015. 'Training for Migrant Workers'. Colombo: Government Information Centre.

Guevarra, Anna Romina. 2010. *Marketing Dreams, Manufacturing Heroes: The Transnational Labor Brokering of Filipino Workers*. New Brunswick: Rutgers University Press.

Gunasinghe, Newton. 2011. *Newton Gunasinghe: Selected Essays*. Edited by Sasanka Perera. Colombo: Social Scientists' Association.

Gunatilaka, Ramani. 2013. *Women's Participation in Sri Lanka's Labour Force: Trends, Drivers and Constraints*. Colombo: International Labour Organisation.

Harvey, David. 2003. *The New Imperialism*. Oxford: Oxford University Press.

Indraratna, A. D. V. de S. 1990. *The Agonies of a Small Open Economy (Sri Lanka) and Remedial Options Open to It*. Armidale, N.S.W.: Faculty of Economic Studies, University of New England.

Institute of Policy Studies (IPS). 2012. *Sri Lanka: State of the Economy 2012*. Colombo, Sri Lanka: Institute of Policy Studies of Sri Lanka.

Institute of Policy Studies (IPS). 2013. *Sri Lanka: State of the Economy 2013*. Colombo, Sri Lanka: Institute of Policy Studies of Sri Lanka.

Institute of Policy Studies (IPS). 2014. 'Summary Report: International Conference on Policies for Mainstreaming Migration into Development in Sri Lanka, 14 August 2014. Colombo: Institute of Policy Studies of Sri Lanka.

International Labour Office (ILO). 2010. *International Labour Migration: A Rights-Based Approach*. Geneva: International Labour Office.

International Labour Organisation (ILO). 2013. *Recruitment Practices of Employment Agencies Recruiting Migrant Workers: A Review Aimed at Improving Recruitment Regulations and Drafting Recruitment Guidelines*. Colombo: ILO.

International Labour Organisation (ILO). 2018. 'Sri Lankan Female Migrant Workers and the Family Background Report'. Colombo, Sri Lanka: International Labour Organisation (ILO).

Japan Development Institute (JDI). 2011. 'The Study on the FDI Promotion Policy Review and SEZ Development Strategy for Sri Lanka'. Japan: Engineering and Consulting Firms Association, Japan Development Institute.

Jayawardena, Kumari. 2000. *Nobodies to Somebodies: The Rise of the Colonial Bourgeoisie in Sri Lanka*. Colombo: Social Scientists' Association and Sanjiva Books.

Jayawardena, Kumari, and Rachel Kurian. 2015. *Class, Patriarchy and Ethnicity on Sri Lankan Plantations: Two Centuries of Power and Protest*. Telangana: Orient Blackswan.

Jayaweera, Swarna, ed. 2002. *Women in Post-Independence Sri Lanka*. New Delhi: Sage Publications.

Kelegama, Saman. 2006. *Development Under Stress: Sri Lankan Economy in Transition*. London: Sage Publications.

Kotikula, Aphichoke, and Jennifer Solotaroff. 2006. 'Gender Analysis of Labor in Sri Lanka's Estate Sector'. Washington, DC: World Bank.

Kottegoda, Sepali. 2004. *Negotiating Household Politics: Women's Strategies in Urban Sri Lanka*. Colombo: Social Scientists' Association.

Lynch, Caitrin. 2007. *Juki Girls, Good Girls: Gender and Cultural Politics in Sri Lanka's Global Garment Industry*. Ithaca, NY: Cornell University Press.

Manor, James, ed. 1984. *Sri Lanka in Change and Crisis*. New York: St. Martin's Press.

McNally, David. 2006. *Another World Is Possible: Globalization and Anti-Capitalism*. Winnipeg: Arbeiter Ring Publishing.

Ministry of Finance and Planning Sri Lanka (MFP). 2006. 'Mahinda Chintana: Vision for a New Sri Lanka'. Colombo: State Printing Corporation.

Ministry of Foreign Employment Promotion and Welfare (MFEPW). 2008. 'National Labour Migration Policy for Sri Lanka'. Colombo: Ministry of Foreign Employment Promotion and Welfare.

Ministry of Foreign Employment Promotion and Welfare (MFEPW). 2012. 'Performance 2011'. Colombo: Ministry of Foreign Employment Promotion and Welfare.

Mook, T. 1992. 'Middle East Migration at the Micro Level'. In *Labour Migration to the Middle East: From Sri Lanka to the Gulf*, edited by Frank Eelens, Toon Schampers, and Johann Dirk Speckermann, 107–36. London: Kegan Paul International.

Nissan, Elizabeth, and R. L. Stirrat. 1990. 'The Generation of Communal Identities'. In *Sri Lanka: History and the Roots of Conflict*, 19–44. London: Routledge.

Richardson Jr., John M. 2004. 'Violent Conflict and the First Half Decade of Open Economy Policies in Sri Lanka: A Revisionist View'. In *Economy, Culture and Civil War in Sri Lanka*, edited by Deborah Winslow and Michael D. Woost, 41–72. Bloomington, IN: Indiana University Press.

Shastri, Amita. 2004. 'An Open Economy in a Time of Intense Civil War: Sri Lanka, 1994–2000'. In *Economy, Culture and Civil War in Sri Lanka*, edited by Deborah Winslow and Michael D. Woost, 73–92. Bloomington, IN: Indiana University Press.

Sivananthan, A. 2008. 'Promoting Decent Work in Export Processing Zones (EPZs) in Sri Lanka'. Colombo: International Labour Organisation.

Spaan, E. J. A. M. 1992. 'Socio-Economic Conditions in the Gulf States'. In *Labour Migration to the Middle East: From Sri Lanka to the Gulf*, edited by Frank Eelens, Toon Schampers, and Johann Dirk Speckmann, 87–106. London: Kegan Paul International.

Spencer, Jonathan, ed. 1990. *Sri Lanka: History and the Roots of Conflict*. London: Routledge.

Sri Lanka Bureau of Foreign Employment (SLBFE). 2012. *Annual Statistical Report of Foreign Employment 2011*. Colombo: Sri Lanka Bureau of Foreign Employment.

Sri Lanka Bureau of Foreign Employment (SLBFE). 2015. 'Housekeeping Assistant Training'. Colombo: Sri Lanka Bureau of Foreign Employment.

Sri Lanka Bureau of Foreign Employment (SLBFE). 2016. 'Different Perspectives of Departure Details'. Colombo: Sri Lanka Bureau of Foreign Employment

Sriskandarajah, Dhananjayan. 2002. 'The Migration-Development Nexus: Sri Lanka Case Study'. *International Migration* 40 (5): 283–307.

Standing, Guy. 1989. 'Global Feminization Through Flexible Labour'. *World Development* 17: 1077–95.

Standing, Guy. 1999. 'Global Feminization Through Flexible Labour: A Theme Revisited'. *World Development* 27: 583–602.

Tambiah, Stanley Jeyaraja. 1986. *Sri Lanka: Ethnic Fratricide and the Dismantling of Democracy*. Chicago, IL: University of Chicago Press.

Warhurst, Chris, Chris Tilly, and Mary Gatta. 2017. *A New Social Construction of Skill*. Edited by John Buchanan, David Finegold, Ken Mayhew, and Chris Warhurst. Vol. 1. Oxford University Press.

Withers, Matt, and Janaka Biyanwila. 2014. 'Patriarchy, Labour Markets and Development: Contesting the Sexual Division of Labour in Sri Lanka'. *IIM Kozhikode Society & Management Review* 3 (1): 33–43.

3 In search of the 'good life'

Uneven development and forced migration

This chapter explores how temporary labour migration has, with varying degrees of locational difference, constituted *forced migration* in a manner logically consistent with Sri Lanka's continuing economic reliance on strategies of accumulation by subordination described in the previous chapter. Uneven development, intensified during the 1977 neoliberal restructuring, has selectively exploited vulnerable demographics while marginalising others entirely. The concurrent deregulation of foreign employment has, in turn, provided an open door for those unwilling or unable to find work within the degraded conditions of local employment. Operating as a macroeconomic 'safety valve', labour migration has simultaneously alleviated the governing onus of job creation, shaped a lucrative new recruitment industry for capital and become a survival strategy for working populations marginalised by their class, ethnicity and gender. However, the impact of these processes cannot be generalised; the very notion of uneven development implicitly addresses the asymmetrical manner in which structural shifts play out across local contexts. By analysing the importance of locational differences, complex and distinctive migration practices can be identified. In each fieldwork location the relative degradation of local employment was seen to force workers to migrate, internally or internationally, as a survival strategy. However, the circumstances under which migration occurred – the relative costs of, benefits from and dependency on migration – varied appreciably from one community to another, reflective of prevailing developmental disparities and location-specific migration strategies. What emerged was a broad spectrum of migration outcomes shaped by social topography and tempered by individual circumstance, but nonetheless gravitating towards one-off, transient or insufficient returns.

The chapter draws on a range of qualitative and quantitative fieldwork data in order to contextualise the relationship between lived experiences of *forced migration* and the structures of uneven development that define Sri Lanka's economic landscape. The first section examines the various reasons for migration throughout the four communities researched in the study, drawing analytical connections between the widely cited need to travel abroad in order to earn a liveable income and the conditions of local employment. The prevalence and nature of *forced migration* is further substantiated by consideration of the perceived benefits of migration: what was hoped for and what was gained in lieu of local employment opportunities. Establishing that the 'good life' sought by migrants is largely analogous to conditions of decent employment that have been undermined by uneven development, it then explores the disconnect between entrepreneurial investment and other developmental 'wins' anticipated by the mainstream migration literature and the dominant empirical reality of remittance-led subsistence. Characterising the stubborn challenges of reintegration as symptomatic of the structural conditions producing *forced migration* itself, it then examines the path dependency emerging from this contradiction: that initial migration tends to produce repeat or 'flow-on' migration in order to preserve remittance streams for economic survival.

Forced migration: the decline of traditional livelihoods

Reasons for migration

Given the extent of temporary labour migration from Sri Lanka, one of the most immediate questions to be addressed is *why* so many people are opting to migrate, particularly given general awareness of the dire working conditions to be found in West Asia.

The NELM and other neoclassical-informed theories of migration answer this question by postulating migrants' rational calculation of local and foreign income differentials, whether individually conceived or as part of a greater household strategy to diversify income streams and hedge against risk. Yet the mere identification of income differentials as economic push/pull factors does little to explain underlying developmental conditions or the specific patterns of migration they produce. Sri Lankan incomes were worse than those available to migrant workers in the Persian Gulf long before migration began taking shape as a livelihood strategy in 1977. So too are migrant incomes in West Asia significantly lower than those available to migrant workers in other parts of the world, yet migration to West Asia remains accountable for 89 per cent of Sri Lanka's foreign employment (SLBFE 2016). Of course, both of these facts point to an obvious conclusion: income differentials are analytically unhelpful without recognition of the way movements of human labour are regulated by, and contingent upon, developmental strategies and migration policies in both labour-sending and labour-receiving economies. The structural and institutional characteristics that shape demand for migrant labour in receiving economies have been meaningfully explored in Piore's (1980) work on dual labour market theory. Delgado Wise's (2009) conceptualisation of *forced migration* offers theoretical complementarity for sending economies by drawing connections between the structures and institutions of uneven development and the emergence of labour migration as a survival strategy. For Sri Lanka, the conspicuous burgeoning of foreign employment departures alongside neoliberal economic restructuring suggests an intimate connection between economic development and 'decisions' to migrate. During 1977, which represents a watershed year, an unsuccessful commitment to decent and decentralised local employment gave way to centralised and intensified strategies of accumulation that forced marginalised populations into specific pathways of foreign employment for economic survival.

A sense of *forced migration*, most often attributed to those internally displaced by war and natural disaster rather than economic migration (Castles and Miller 2007), was clearly discerned from interviews conducted with migrant returnees. In aggregate, a telling 96 per cent of respondents indicated that they would not have migrated if they were able to earn a liveable wage from local work. The economic necessity of migration was further probed to distinguish between unemployment and underemployment[1] as the principal source of pressure, with 22 per cent identifying a lack of work as their reason for migration compared to 66 per cent who expressed a need for better wages. These findings resonate with the notion of uneven development in a highly informal agricultural economy,[2] where rank unemployment is rarely as encumbering as the degraded terms of local employment arising from the decline of traditional livelihoods in favour of concentrated urban production. Unemployment and underemployment are here intimately linked, with the insufficient creation of local jobs fostering a reserve army of labour whose acute need for work exerts downwards pressure on existing wages and ensures a prevalence of precarious and unsustainable livelihoods (Arunatilake 2012).

Across each fieldwork location traditional agricultural livelihoods were seen to produce insufficient income to support basic economic subsistence for most households, with women's employment in the garment industry, itself a driver of internal migration, the only prominent source of stable breadwinner employment outside of foreign employment.

As one male returnee from Negombo explained:

> I couldn't save in Sri Lanka, I had to migrate to afford a house and land. Sri Lanka is a good country, but we can't live off our earnings.

Another returnee, a woman working in a small plantation in Akmeemana, told of her own struggles as a breadwinner:

> I got only Rs150[3] per day for plucking tea leaves. Even my husband was looking for a job for so long, but could not find any. That is why I left the three children with my husband and went abroad.

The situation was seen to be worse in Thavapuram, where the aftermath of civil war intersected with underdevelopment, as illustrated by a young mother's reflections:

> Here, I could not get a job. Nobody, no organisations, helped me at the time of my husband's death … I had no income to raise my kids. I have no parents, only a sister and her husband. Her husband's legs are not functional, he cannot walk. Because of that, I could not depend on them and had to migrate in search of a living.

This sentiment of reluctance to leave Sri Lanka (and invariably one's family) in the face of financial necessity was common to all communities surveyed, with a few notable exceptions arising from those who wanted to leave their home communities for personal reasons, ranging from social stigma to domestic abuse, fleeing war and a sheer curiosity to experience life abroad. It is important to note that the personal and distressing nature of some of these reasons for migration may have precluded respondents from openly discussing these experiences, potentially downplaying their significance. Qualitative studies into the experiences of migrant domestic workers in Sri Lanka have, for example, stressed that some women pursue migration chiefly to escape domestic abuse and repressive gender roles in their local community (Smith 2010; Kottegoda *et al.* 2013).

Locational difference

While *forced migration* was seen to occur across all fieldwork locations (see Figure 3.1), migration practices differed in each context. In large part a reflection of the geographical spread of local employment prospects, this was also seen to be informed by cultural distinctions arising from ethno-religious difference and the character of local institutions. Some key considerations here include the community's proximity to EPZs and urban centres; the relative strength of traditional livelihood activities as a component of identity; the nature of local gender roles – that is, varying by ethno-religious norms; the relative degree of cooperation within a given community; the extent of destruction caused by armed conflict and the 2004 tsunami; and the extent of local knowledge about migration practices. Within specific communities, pertinent threads can be drawn together to depict the emergence of specific migration practices that, although unified by *forced migration*, produce varying effects regarding the circumstances and outcomes of foreign employment. Locational differences are further explored through the concept of *place* discussed in Chapter 4, but the contextualisation of each migrant community involved in the study is necessary to provide a background to all research findings. A brief overview of the key variations detected between fieldwork locations is offered to illustrate these differences and provide a community context in which to anchor ongoing exploration of individual experiences.

Akmeemana

The Sinhala-Buddhist community in Akmeemana shares many similarities with that of Negombo, in that traditional livelihoods, both paddy cultivation and fishing, have been progressively eroded while tourism and garments production have provided alternative work nearby in Galle. Despite these growing industries, the community has a long-standing involvement with temporary labour migration and it endures as a commonplace livelihood strategy. This is largely because the handful of local garment factories provide limited and stigmatised

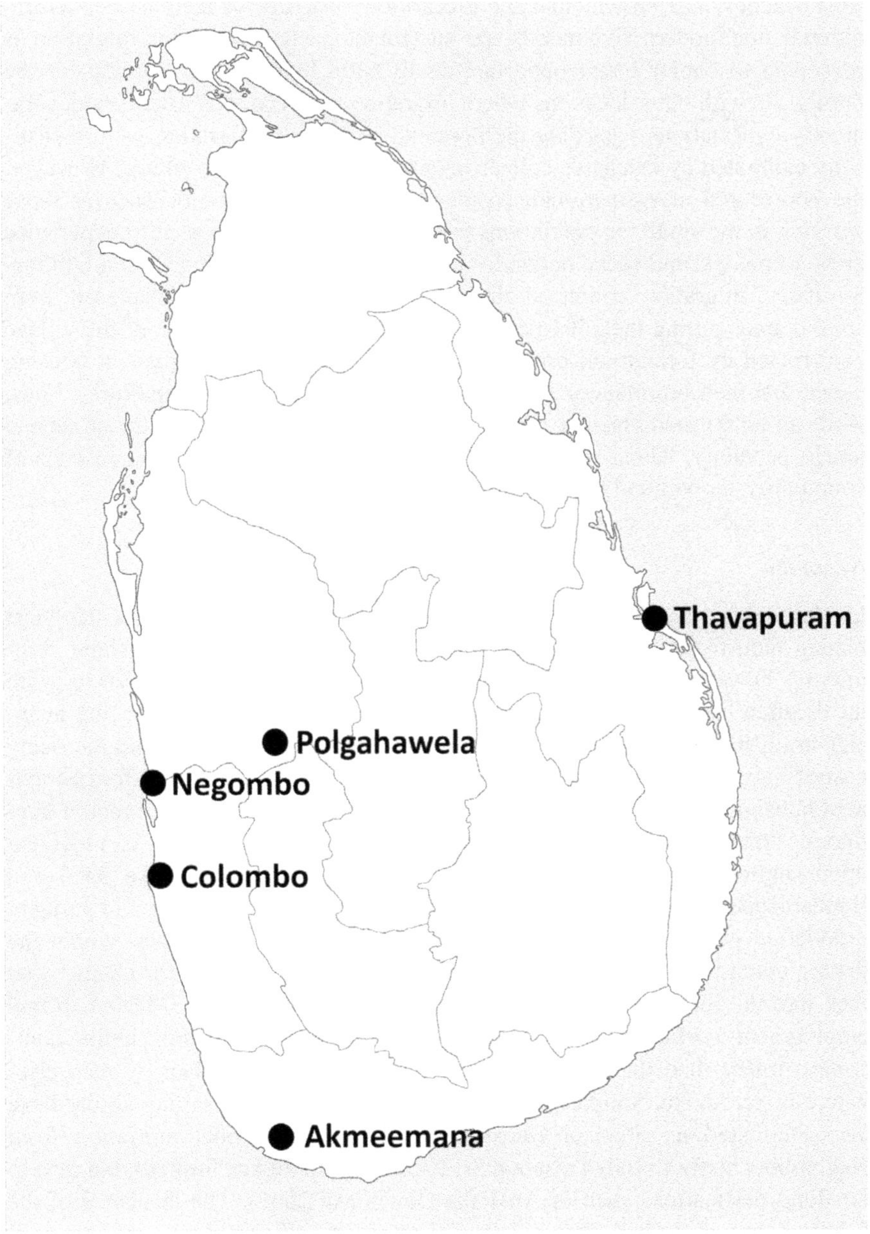

Figure 3.1 Map of fieldwork locations.

jobs for young women, while the expansive tourist operations along the south-west beaches offer only menial and precarious work. Locals feel that neither traditional nor modern livelihoods are sustainable, whereas labour migration is perceived to confer better opportunities to build housing and provide for the family. As with other locations where migration has been long established, community expectations regarding the potential benefits of migration were realistically calibrated by extensive collective experiences within the village. However, the poorer and more marginalised members of the community, such as those working in the small tea plantations in the nearby hills, were seen to experience greater financial and social hardships in arranging and benefiting from migration. Similarly, migration conferred different outcomes for those displaced from coastal areas during the 2004 tsunami and now living in a portion of the village constructed by foreign-aid projects, as the pre-existence of permanent housing meant that their remittances could be directed towards other expenditures. Thus, while an established practice alongside the limited opportunities of the urban and tourist economy, labour migration was seen to occur in the relative absence of community support and tempered by socio-economic circumstances.

Negombo

In Negombo, traditional livelihoods are explicitly intertwined with the local fishing industry, one of the oldest and largest in Sri Lanka. The fishing community, however, remains one of the poorest in the Western Province, with locals often living in thatched housing along Negombo lagoon and facing financial strain from increasing competition with commercial trawlers and the rising cost of living. Conditions of poverty, and particularly the desire to afford permanent housing, has encouraged a sustained history of migration as a modern livelihood strategy, although this has occurred alongside other employment opportunities afforded by physical proximity to the Katunayake EPZ and Bandaranaike International Airport: Negombo is the primary location of garment production in Sri Lanka and a prominent tourist hub. Membership within the fishing community has strong (and often divisive) implications for identity that feed into the formation of location specific migration practices. Men often find employment working as ship-hands and captains for West Asian shipping companies, rather than the more typical labouring work undertaken by men elsewhere in Sri Lanka. Similarly, knowledge of sea routes and sailing ability have also facilitated an atypical concentration of irregular boat migration from Negombo, chiefly to Italy (where a Sri Lankan diaspora has formed), but also to far-flung destinations such as Australia (Jayatilaka 2005). The insularity of the fishing community, including cultures of drinking and gambling, was also seen to prompt some to migrate to West Asia as a means of escaping the trajectory of life in a context of tightknit social relations and diminutive prospects of upwards mobility. Finally, as a port of early settlement by Dutch and Portuguese colonialists, Negombo has one of the most concentrated Catholic populations in Sri Lanka. Numerous Catholic community and philanthropic organisations exist as a consequence, often extending support to migrant returnees who have experienced trauma during foreign employment, sometimes in conjunction with the Women's Centre of Sri Lanka, a nascent cross-occupational women's union based nearby in Ja-Ela.

Polgahawela

Polgahawela, like elsewhere in rural Sri Lanka, has experienced declining traditional livelihoods without even the mild offsets afforded by geographical proximity to centralised production and tourism. A flagging rubber plantation to the north of the village provides some work for the community, however the local economy is seen to revolve around merchant activity facilitated by the logistical advantage of being situated at a major intersection of road and rail routes connecting Colombo with Kurunegala and other regional cities. In the Muslim community surveyed, the effects of developmental marginalisation were exacerbated by religiously proscribed gender norms that make women's internal migration to live and work away from home (i.e. in the garments industry) socially unacceptable. However, as part of a recurrently discriminated ethnic group living in fragmented pockets throughout Sri Lanka, the Polgahawela Muslims were seen to possess particularly strong community bonds and support networks. In the context of foreign employment this communal interdependence, along with specific ethno-religious characteristics, has produced distinctive and favourable migration practices. Principles of Islamic banking prohibit making interest on loans which, along with the intra-communal practice of *zakat* (the religious obligation to make charitable giving), has resulted in an informal system of group funding for potential migrant's recruitment fees that sidesteps the deleterious reliance on moneylenders seen in other fieldwork locations. Moreover, with West Asian employers exhibiting a preference for Muslim workers, and Sri Lankan Muslims generally more amenable to working in West Asia on account of the same religious affinity, there exists a mutual reciprocity of non-economic incentives that has historically generated greater demand for Polgahawela's Muslim migrants. Not only has this tended to amount to lower recruitment fees and higher wages, it has also resulted in current migrants 'brokering' the direct employment of friends and relatives to prospective employers in West Asia, thereby circumventing the costs and complications of recruitment agents.

Thavapuram

The Tamil-Hindu community in Thavapuram, a small village north of Batticaloa on Sri Lanka's east coast, is distinguished from the other fieldwork locations on account of its embroilment in civil war and relatively recent exposure to temporary labour migration as a livelihood strategy. With much of the Eastern Province contested by the LTTE (Liberation Tigers of Tamil Eelam) until 2007, migration had until that time occurred outside the purview of government regulation and mainstream recruitment practices and was largely characterised by informal and refugee flows. The commencing of widespread temporary labour migration clearly coincided with the Sri Lankan government regaining control of the Eastern Province, when recruitment agencies began operating in this hitherto unexposed community and offered relatively attractive alternatives to existing employment in an impoverished region characterised by severe underdevelopment, human and infrastructural war losses, coastal tsunami damage and precarious seasonal agriculture worsened by recent droughts. A combination of poverty and limited community knowledge of migration practices have resulted in Thavapuram experiencing particularly dire outcomes from foreign employment. On the one hand, having minimal existing assets to leverage has left prospective migrants dependent on taking usurious loans from moneylenders in order to finance recruitment fees, resulting in crippling debt repayments. On the other, a lack of experience with temporary labour migration has left the community vulnerable to exploitation from recruitment agencies in Colombo who, via a network of subagents and local brokers, have been seen to deceive potential migrants with inflated recruitment costs and promised salaries far beyond those actually received. Insufficient government regulation of migration practices in this region, evidenced by a lack of SLBFE offices and involvement with local government, combines with a palpable air of desperation to engineer a situation where those with the greatest disadvantage are burdened with the most adverse pathway to foreign employment.

These four fieldwork locations are united by shared structural economic pressures that have culminated in experiences of *forced migration*; community-specific tensions are facets of a singular process of uneven development that coordinates accumulation by subordination along geographical and cultural axes while forcing the ostracised remainder into foreign employment. The dwindling viability of traditional livelihoods and insufficient generation of decent employment alternatives is a common experience of Sri Lanka's working poor. However, as demonstrated above, the nuances of uneven development – its geographic parameters, cultural antagonisms and intersection with ethnic and gendered subordination – have produced markedly different migration practices between places and peoples. These differences are an important reminder of the multiscalarity of migration dynamics. Structures of global capital have clearly hewn an overarching passage of temporary labour migration from Sri Lanka to West Asia, but the scope of experiences within this broad corridor of movement is moulded by countrywide patterns of uneven development and the nature of local institutions that have arisen in response to these asymmetries. It is therefore meaningless to speak of Sri Lanka's labour migrants as a homogenised whole, just as much as it is pointless to emphasise individual agency without contextualising the structural limitations to its exercise. Place, then, serves as something of an intermediary between uneven development and the multitude of lived experiences nestled within those structures. This is discussed further in Chapter 4. Having been outlined in general terms, the diverse conditions under which Sri Lankans migrate are repeatedly drawn on when interpreting the implications of *forced migration* arising from research findings. The first theme to be explored as such is the notion of 'the good life', a frequently cited aspiration of migrant returnees across all four fieldwork locations.

'The good life' – migrant aspirations and the benefits of foreign employment

Pre-migration hopes and expectations

One recurrent theme I encountered when interviewing returnees about their reasons for migrating was the desire to successfully lead a 'good life', something unanimously felt to be unachievable by working locally in Sri Lanka. Unpacking the personal meaning ascribed to notions of a 'good life' – the idealised social and economic circumstances to be attained through migration – thus provides a nuanced means of understanding of what is left wanting, personally and materially, as a consequence of uneven development. The four dominant themes emerging from migrants' remittance priorities (housing, education, business investment and day-to-day consumption) are all reflected in returnees' discussions of 'the good life'. Locational differences in migrants' hopes proved very limited, with business investment consistently emerging as the leading aspiration after housing. Given that migrants' ambitions and general conceptions of good living were far more consistent across different communities than the actual outcomes of migration experiences, the following discussion of recurrent themes does not delve into location-specific variations.

Housing

When asked what her main expectations were before travelling abroad, a female returnee from Akmeemana replied frankly:

> Our only idea was to build a house. To be happy in life. To provide for the children's education, to eat and buy clothes.

These sentiments encapsulated the simple aspirations expressed by a majority of the returnees I interviewed. That the construction of a house stands apart as a preliminary objective is meaningful in illuminating migrants' interpretation of 'the good life'. Ownership of a permanent dwelling can be seen both as a precondition for other improvements to household well-being and as a 'big ticket' asset that is relatively more difficult to finance under conditions of local employment than the smaller recurring payments demanded by education fees and household consumption. In the first instance, a brick-and-mortar housing confers numerous safety, health and livelihood advantages over thatched housing and other temporary dwellings: namely the physical security of the home, access to running water and proper sanitation systems, and the ability to run electricity through the house.

As a senior director at the IPS explained:

> [housing] is normally a priority because most of them [migrant workers] stay in poor houses, and maybe when they come back they might be thinking of a larger family or having an additional room and renting that room out. Housing receives priority. And you see if they are going from a mud hut or a house without electricity, afterwards they bring these electrical items and they must have proper electricity connections to use them. They bring washing machines, proper water lines, etcetera – all those fall into place when you have a proper house.

Permanent housing thus offers a stable platform from which reproductive labour can be reduced and child-rearing eased, allowing for home conditions that are potentially more conducive to children's education and alternative income strategies, such as rent and self-employment. Indeed, hopes to acquire land and housing are often intimately tied to considerations of family and intergenerational well-being. This is additionally important in situations where migrants have unmarried daughters, for whom a permanent house can later serve as an important form of dowry payment for a 'good marriage' and upwards social mobility such weddings can allow for.

This interrelationship between housing and intergenerational well-being is reflected in one Thavapuram woman's unequivocal response to why she chose to migrate for work:

> I have neither land nor house for my three girl children. So, I went there to build a house for them.

Speaking more directly to the importance of housing as a dowry payment, a project coordinator at the Colombo ILO office observed:

> You can give your daughter in marriage, if you have a house, especially if it's permanent. All of them have dwellings, but it doesn't necessarily mean that they are permanent dwellings. So they go overseas in order to earn to build a permanent house, brick-and-mortar walls and roofs and windows.

That housing is a primary ambition of migrant workers is, however, also an overt testament to prevailing conditions of underdevelopment amongst Sri Lanka's working poor, and the unfeasibility of making land purchases and household construction within the confines of local avenues of employment.

A woman from Negombo explained that her alternative to migration, garment work, would not provide the income needed to build a house:

> We had many financial problems. We didn't have a house to stay in. It was difficult to stay in my mother's house. I hoped to build a house of our own. That's why I went.... There were no such opportunities here. The only

> opportunity was in a garment factory. But the salary was not enough at that time.

A middle-aged mother, also from Negombo, discussed additional limitations to working in the garment industry:

> I am a mother of three children. Even my husband is sick. There was no job. We lived in a rented house. There were so many problems. I could not even go to a garment factory, because they did not take any workers if we did not know sewing. I did not know sewing, so I also could not go. Garment factories take those who are young and those who know sewing using machine. But, anyone can go abroad as a housemaid. That is why I went.

For many, remitted income from foreign employment is the only means of amassing sufficient savings for land and housing. Women's remittances are particularly important in this regard, as female migrants often exclusively performed care work prior to foreign employment, their newfound wages thus complementing, rather than substituting for, existing household income.

Education

Migrants' ability to provide for their children's education was another key ambition prior to migration, particularly amongst female migrants, and an important intergenerational element of living 'the good life'. When asked about conditions of local employment in Sri Lanka, many migrants noted that there are no good jobs available unless you have skills and a good education – at once an expression of resignation for their own working futures and an insight into the importance attributed to providing reputable education for their children.

Of all migrant returnees interviewed, including those whose migration was ultimately fruitless in terms of remitted income, 58 per cent committed remittances towards their children's education, with outlays ranging from basic book and uniform purchases to after-school tuition costs and private schooling fees. Despite Sri Lanka's long-standing commitment to universal free education, the popular conception of 'good education' as a private expense rather than a public assurance was clear.

For some it stood apart as a top priority, as was the case with a young Negombo woman:

> I wanted my sisters and brothers to be educated and for my parents to live happy without being in debt.

Another, a mother from Thavapuram, made clear the centrality of education in her hopes to better her children's lives:

> I wanted to educate my kids and provide them with a fine life, which I did not experience. I wanted to make their lives better.

A common sentiment that transpired from the interviews was that a good education would lead to good employment (i.e. a stable, respected and decently remunerative job) that would then serve as the bedrock for their children's ability to live a good life in Sri Lanka. The importance of this connection was made evident by returnees who reported the chief benefit of their migration as being able to help their children or siblings find decent employment. Tacitly, migrants also implied that, having found decent employment, their children would then be positioned to support the family beyond what they themselves could.

A director of the Centre for Migration Research and Development (CMRD) further contextualised the recurrent research finding that migrants saw education as a significant investment:

> I mean there is a whole discussion going on that the Sri Lankan government is not investing enough money in education. So currently the quality of our higher education is very low, it's down, so we have to supplement, which is why the whole tuition industry has come up. Investments in basic human capital, I don't think it's happening, that's why people have to find their own ways, private education and private healthcare have boomed – it's now a huge industry.

Business investments

The desire to invest remittances in a business, typically informal self-employment, was a strong priority amongst male migrants and frequently tied to the notion of living 'independently' or 'freely'. Ninety-six per cent of migrants desired to work within their home communities and expressed disinclination to migrate for reasons other than sheer necessity. Reflecting this sentiment, business investments and informal self-employment can be interpreted as a means of achieving sustainable income locally while achieving independence from the debt and economic subsistence otherwise characteristic of life on the wrong side of uneven development.

A young father in Negombo told of his struggles supporting his family as a waged worker:

> If I could manage here I won't go. There are opportunities here. You can manage with the daily wage, but it's not enough as I have two children.

When asked what he hoped to achieve by migrating, he echoed a commonly held hope that business ownership would allow for a sustainable life in Sri Lanka:

> I wanted to go and do the same job that I was doing here [welding] and then come back and develop my own welding business here. And then educate my children.

In a few instances, business ambitions transcended the desire to cleave out a sustainable form of self-employment for the returnee and their family, instead being conceived as a gateway to deriving rentier income. A woman in Thavapuram described this connection between her business hopes and property investment, explaining that her dreams were to:

> save some money and buy an auto, engage in business, at least long enough to buy some plots to lease.

A man from Polgahawela had similarly entrepreneurial desires. When asked how he had hoped to spend his income, he explained his business plan:

> First, I want to buy vehicles, for business purposes, like having vans for hire.

On the whole, though, migrants' notions of business did not coalesce with intent for capital accumulation or rent seeking so much as they reflected a need for stable self-employment outside of the vicissitudes of traditional livelihoods and waged work. This is reflected in the particularly high number of participants who articulated their business plans in the purchasing of a trishaw taxi: a relatively affordable, low-return investment that nonetheless allows returnees to work at their own discretion and with a sense of independence.

Day-to-day consumption

Being able to finance daily household expenses – the ability to pay bills, provide sufficient food and other incidentals such as basic clothing – was another key priority for returnees. However, being able to pay for day-to-day consumption was not typically discussed as an ambition in its own right, as even the most destitute of potential migrants tended to hope for greater returns from their foreign employment. Often this basic provision was mentioned as an attendant goal to building a house, investing in education or starting a business. Nonetheless, that providing for household consumption costs featured as a fairly common pre-migration goal speaks to the difficulty of simply 'getting by' on local wages, a situation that is further illustrated when discussing the prevalence of household indebtedness in the following chapter.

Understanding migrant aspirations

The Sri Lankan migrants interviewed were seen to conceptualise 'the good life' as an assemblage of basic needs, within which status consumption played an important but subservient function to the consolidation, sustainable reproduction and intergenerational improvement of household well-being. The complex dynamics of status consumption is returned to in detail in Chapter 5. For now, migrants' reflections on 'the good life' is contextualised to situate those hopes in relief of deepening developmental shortcomings and declining welfare provisioning accompanying Sri Lanka's neoliberal governance.

A quantitative insight into pre-departure aspirations is gained by tallying migrants' self-identified remittance priorities, disaggregated by gender to account for social norms and important practical differences between men and women's foreign employment. When migrants' top remittance priorities are considered, a clear emphasis on the construction of housing is seen across both sexes, followed by children's education for women (see Table 3.1) and business investments for men (see Table 3.2). When migrants' secondary priorities are considered the picture becomes slightly more balanced, with women preferencing expenditure evenly on education and housing and men focusing on business slightly ahead of housing and consumption. From this simple snapshot arises a gendered matrix of remittance priorities, wherein the ambitions of female migrants are chiefly centred upon the provision of housing and education, while male migrants are typically concerned with housing, business and day-to-day household consumption.

Assessing the need for housing as a general indication of insufficient incomes cutting across local working conditions of both men and women, subsequent gendered distinctions can plausibly be located in the feminisation of breadwinner employment despite the stubborn persistence of a sexual division of care work (Kottegoda 2004; Jayaweera and Dias 2009; Withers 2016). The decline of traditional livelihoods alongside the feminisation of export production has meant that women have frequently supplanted men as the primary income earner; yet resultant crises of masculinity have tended to reinforce, rather than compensate

Table 3.1 Top remittance priority for women

Category	*Frequency*	*Percentage*
Business	2	3.4
Consumption	1	1.7
Debt repayment	4	6.8
Education	9	15.3
Healthcare	1	1.7
Housing	39	66.1
Jewellery and clothing	1	1.7
Other	2	3.4
Total	59	100.0

Table 3.2 Top remittance priority for men

Category	*Frequency*	*Percentage*
Business	13	31.7
Debt repayment	3	7.3
Housing	22	53.7
Other	3	7.3
Total	41	100.0

for, the gendered allocation of reproductive labour (Gamburd 2000). Female migrants' emphasis on their children's education might thus be construed as an extension of socially ascribed care duties, whereas male migrants' greater concern with starting a business is perhaps reflective of the need to find new avenues of income in lieu of decent employment within traditional occupations. That male and female migration are, within a single household, typically mutually exclusive supports this interpretation. Although diminished, men's local incomes can contribute to day-to-day consumption costs, thus freeing up women's remittances for large investments in housing and education. Conversely, if men's migration necessitates women residing at home (i.e. isolated from centralised labour markets) their remittances will likely have to cover day-to-day consumption in addition to competing business or housing objectives.

That migrants feel compelled to travel abroad in order to sufficiently educate their children and safeguard their future employment opportunities speaks to two structural features of Sri Lanka's uneven development, both with common origins in neoliberal restructuring: polarising income inequality across skill categories and the increasing de facto privatisation of the national education system.

The first of these issues has, by and large, already been discussed: declining working conditions for Sri Lanka's poor, and particularly those dependent on rural livelihoods, are linked to the 1977 economic reforms and the government's implicit abandonment of prior commitments to providing decent, decentralised employment. Intensified capital accumulation following the deregulation of the economy has overseen the concentration of local capital and limited FDI into select 'growth industries', predominantly garment manufacturing and the plantation economy, but more recently including a range of service industries: finance, logistics, telecommunications, information technology (IT), business process outsourcing (BPO), tourism and retail (IPS 2017). Incomes within these service industries are substantially higher than the national average and dwarf the incomes of those, like many migrants, straddling the national poverty line (DCS 2017). Historically, access to these jobs, along with desirable public service positions, has been governed by a mixture of discriminatory factors (Little and Hettige 2014). Colombo's elite schooling institutions, whether public or private, have long been the domain of the urban elite and function as veritable incubators for those working in the best-paid professional and administrative vocations. Exclusion from the most reputable schools – whether by class, gender or ethnicity – highlights the degree to which education overlaps with patriarchal ethno-nationalism in producing differentiated working entitlements (Little and Hettige 2014).

Sri Lanka's increasing polarisation of incomes across skill categories has occurred hand-in-hand with declining standards of public education and healthcare resulting from dwindling government investment in the universal welfare framework erected following independence (IPS 2013). Instead, the steady privatisation of the education system – evidenced by the growth of private schools and tutoring (IPS 2013; Little and Hettige 2014) – has shaped the pathway towards acquiring 'decent education' and vocational prospects. Within this privatised system, burgeoning expenditure by relatively wealthy Sri Lankans on private tertiary and vocational training ensures a continuity between class background and access to decent employment, to the obvious detriment of the poor who remain dependent on under-funded public schooling, which in itself is often abandoned out of the necessity to work (Little and Hettige 2014). Similarly, a proliferation of private healthcare expenditure amongst Sri Lanka's 'middle class', amidst the government's declining commitment to public health infrastructure (Abeykoon 2002), reflects a shift in who is able to access quality care. Thus, somewhat paradoxically, the working poor within a country that has historically prided itself on a universally free education and healthcare system (and resultantly healthy human development indicators) feel compelled to migrate in order to afford private services that may improve their children's prospects.

However, as the senior director at IPS explained, these priorities may also become more important throughout the course of migration:

> Although there is free education and free healthcare the whole system has become so very complicated and cumbersome. The quality of services has deteriorated in both health and education. For migrants, the type of education they are looking for you may not get from the present education system. And even in the health care system they maybe not be satisfied with the quality of state hospitals because, after all, these migrants experience better quality facilities abroad and they would have heard about better education systems in those countries. So since the aspirations are high, they would like to go for private health insurance, pay for a better education, all this comes with the broadening of the mind.

Migrants' desires to start a business are the product of the same climate of underdevelopment, but typically address returnees' own ability to earn a sustainable income upon reintegration, distinct from educational investment as an intergenerational strategy to secure a 'good life' for the family. Ambitions to invest in some form of business were consistent across rural and urban contexts, reflecting the prevailing inadequacy of local employment for the working poor in both milieus. It also speaks to the growth of what has, perhaps too leniently, been branded Sri Lanka's 'middle class', within which small business owners are a key constituent (IPS 2013). Short of possessing the educational qualifications necessary to find work in formal-sector employment, informal self-employment is construed as migrant returnees' most promising avenue for improved local earnings and upwards social mobility. However, the experiences of returnees interviewed suggested that achieving business or self-employment outcomes from migration were fraught with complications.

The challenge of reintegration: investment, subsistence and dependency

Remittance expenditure

When interviewed, migrant returnees were asked to identify the main categories of remittance expenditure that occurred during and after their migration in order to juxtapose previously established remittance priorities against their actual expenses. Again, disaggregated by gender, the results reflect a clear disparity between anticipated and actual remittances uses. For women (see Table 3.3), housing emerged as the predominant category of remittance expenditure, consistent with pre-migration priorities, albeit with diminished frequency on account of unanticipated categories of expenditure. Debt repayments, jewellery and clothing purchases, day-to-day consumption and healthcare all featured more significantly than was expected prior to migration, redirecting anticipated remittance use from housing and education alike. For men (see Table 3.4), the effects were more pronounced, with housing and business expenses featuring far less than anticipated, while debt repayments and day-to-day consumption commanded dramatically increased proportions of remittance expenditure. In both cases a number of 'other' expenses arose, most often related to marriage arrangements and dowries, while 'NA' cases represent situations where no expenditures

Table 3.3 Top remittance expenditure for women

Category	*Frequency*	*Percentage*
Business	2	3.4
Consumption	4	6.8
Debt repayment	10	17.0
Education	7	11.9
Healthcare	2	3.4
Housing	24	40.7
Jewellery and clothing	4	6.8
Other	2	3.4
NA	4	6.8
Total	59	100.0

Table 3.4 Top remittance expenditure for men

Category	*Frequency*	*Percentage*
Business	2	4.9
Consumption	8	19.5
Debt repayment	15	36.6
Housing	11	26.8
Other	4	9.8
NA	1	2.4
Total	41	100.0

were able to be made due to foreign employment being cut short by illness or income being withheld by employers.

Narrowing the focus of analysis to patterns of investment relative to subsistence consumption, it becomes apparent that business outlays were a much slimmer percentage of primary remittance expenses than anticipated, while the opposite was true of day-to-day consumption. This inversion of expectations takes on further significance when considering the frequency with which *any* form of business expenditure was made in each fieldwork location (see Table 3.5). With debt repayment accounting for 32 per cent of primary remittance expenditures in Negombo and 44 per cent in Thavapuram – as opposed to 12 per cent in both Akmeemana and Polgahawela – it is unsurprising that business investments were least common in the two most impoverished communities. Moreover, with Polgahawela already a merchant community with a favourable migration culture and Akmeemana experiencing informal self-employment opportunities tied to local tourism, there are differences of place and practice that may go some way in accounting for higher business expenditure in those communities. Nonetheless, the implications are intuitive: those who are most disadvantaged are least likely to engage in business.

Business investments

Business investments, like education expenses, can encompass a broad array of outlays. These were seen to range from merchant trading to shopkeeping and sole-traders to a diverse spectrum of informal self-employments such as operating a trishaw, home textile work, food preparation and handicraft production. Gendered differences occur here too, as men tended to start business ventures with the aim of providing the primary income stream for the household, whereas women were often involved in less lucrative home production, perhaps reflecting the greater social pressures associated with the decline of traditionally male livelihoods. In general, however, the majority of remittances spent on business tended to amount in small expenditures on home production (such as selling beedis,[4] making tea cloths or trading livestock) or 'one-off' asset purchases (such as a trishaw, van or fishing boat) enabling informal self-employment capable of generating subsistence income. In only very few instances were larger investments made, and such businesses failed as often as they succeeded.

Table 3.5 Business expenditures by location

Location	*Frequency*	*Percentage*
Akmeemana	10	40.0
Negombo	5	20.0
Polgahawela	9	36.0
Thavapuram	3	12.0
Total	27	27.0

One woman from Akmeemana – the most successful interviewed in that community – used remittances from her time abroad to start a home textile business, which has since become the main livelihood for the family. The impact of her migration was profound, both for her immediate family and her siblings, but she was quick to acknowledge the good fortune of obtaining a company-arranged visa to work abroad, first in garments and then in nursing:

> I supported my siblings by paying for their education, which allowed them to get good jobs as a teacher and a police officer. Migration also allowed me to open my business, which we have since lived off. I was successful because I was able to get a company visa and work in decent conditions. A company visa is very good.

Conversely, an elderly man from the same street lamented his decision to migrate, as he gave up a stable job driving a bus for the Ceylon Transport Board in the hope of using remittances to start a business in tourism:

> I did manage to save for a van to do guided tours, but it was an outdated model and I had not enough English, so the business failed. Everything changed for the worse. I had no benefit, I only lost my CTB job by taking a gamble on migration.

In most cases, however, spending money on business ventures was clearly not possible. When asked whether any remittances were put towards business investments, a young woman from Polgahawela replied:

> No. I could not save money for that. My earnings were just enough to look after my kids. I spent it to bring up the children and for household expenses. Therefore, I could not save anything during my two years of stay.

Another man, from Akmeemana, simply laughed:

> What nonsense, we could do nothing at all with the money.

Migrants' general struggle to realise business aspirations, and, even then, doing so almost exclusively by way of menial self-employment, speaks to the general challenge of reintegration facing returnees. Even in Akmeemana and Polgahawela, where remittances were more often spent on business, daily expenses were as often a primary remittance expense as in Negombo and Thavapuram, and were therefore seen as a ubiquitous component of remittance expenditure regardless of location. This reflects both the limitations of foreign earnings – particularly once recruitment costs, underpayment, foreign expenses, remittance fees and unplanned purchases are accounted for (discussed further in Chapter 4) – as well as the steep cost of living in Sri Lanka. When speaking to migrant returnees it was not uncommon to hear that migration had brought little or no benefits to the family, despite a lengthy time spent working abroad.[5] Instead, the main outcome of migration had been to oversee household subsistence with remittance income, sometimes to no greater effect than by working within Sri Lanka.

A Polgahawela man explained his experience after two years abroad:

> I returned home the same as the way I left. Had I been here during that time, I could have earned Rs1,000 per day and had a good time with my family. Instead, I left the children and went there for a low salary job. Thinking about this situation, I was worried a lot there.

When asked whether his family had benefited from his migration, a middle-aged man from Akmeemana lamented simply:

> No. Because everything I earned went into paying the loan I took to leave.

His neighbour, a young mother, was similarly regretful, having spent a year and a half in Saudi Arabia:

> My only happiness is that the children could eat something at home. Other than that, there was nothing to be happy or satisfied about the money I earned and sent back to Sri Lanka.

While subsistence could generally be achieved during migration, migrants faced difficulty channelling remittances into sustainable income-generating activity – by investment or employment – upon their return to Sri Lanka. Only 31 per cent of all returnees reported that their family had received any employment or income-earning benefits from their migration, with those responding affirmatively including those who subsequently helped another family member find work abroad. This was particularly true of the more disadvantaged communities in Negombo and Thavapuram, whose relative lack of reported employment benefits are highlighted in Table 3.6. Indeed, even those who had been successful in fulfilling more straightforward ambitions, such as building a house, were seen to have made multiple trips abroad in order to do so. The more stints of foreign employment that had been made, the more likely returnees were to report

Table 3.6 Employment benefits by location

Location	*Frequency*	*Percentage*
Akmeemana	11	44.0
Negombo	7	28.0
Polgahawela	11	44.0
Thavapuram	2	8.0
Total	31	31.0

beneficial outcomes from foreign employment. Only after three separate trips had been made was migration seen to be clearly beneficial for the household (see Table 3.7), notwithstanding a potential self-selection bias in that migrants are unlikely to continue working abroad if the first experience did not prove beneficial.

This finding is corroborated by a broader migrant reintegration study by the ILO in Colombo, which demonstrates that the number of separate trips undertaken is a key determinant of positive migration outcomes (ILO 2013). Instead of resulting in development-catalysing entrepreneurship, it is clear that for a majority of the returnees interviewed foreign employment was largely a means of subsistence, requiring multiple trips to attain tangible benefits and offering little by way of sustainable income prospects upon return.

As the CMRD director pointed out, the struggle to make business investments tenable is often a trigger for repeat migration:

> They would come back and say, you know, we tried to open a business but we couldn't make any money from it. They are basically losing their money back in Sri Lanka, but they need to keep finding ways to keep maintaining the income, so they decide to migrate again.

Remittance dependency: repeat and flow-on migration

For the returnees interviewed, *forced migration* took on an iterative and intergenerational aspect. The same conditions of uneven development causing Sri Lanka's working poor to pursue temporary labour migration, in conspiracy with the generally adverse conditions of employment in the Gulf, prevented returnees' remittances from financing sustainable benefits upon their return. Struggling to reintegrate, often socially as much as financially (ILO 2013), migrants frequently engage in repeat migration in order to sustain the remittance transfers that the household may now be reliant upon (Brochmann 1993).

As an officer within the Department of Labour put it:

> Rural areas have high unemployment – only one class is doing this thing [migration]. Repeat migration happens because returnees expect debt and financial difficulty in Sri Lanka and so they go again.

Table 3.7 Overall benefit by number of trips

Number of trips	*Frequency*	*Beneficial migration %*
One	42	47.6
Two	34	58.8
Three	8	100.0
More than three	16	87.5
Total	100	–

Women tended to repeat migrate more often than men (see Table 3.8), perhaps reflective of domestic worker migration being a comparatively cheaper and more reliable source of income than men's foreign employment. Alternatively, some households practice 'flow-on' migration, in which another family member travels abroad to preserve this stream of remittances. This often entails a returnee's spouse making a stint abroad to do their part in earning for the family, but also extends to situations where migrants' hopes for their siblings' or children's employment prospects are eventually played out by securing foreign employment, perhaps under slightly more favourable circumstances by paying higher recruitment fees for skilled placements. In all cases, difficulty finding commensurate local employment upon reintegration – particularly if changing consumption habits or incomplete investments have placed additional demand on household finances – makes the resumption of foreign employment hard to avoid.

Housing projects and iterative lifestyle changes can be particularly path dependent in this manner.

Discussing migrants' ambition to build housing from remittances, a program officer on the Swiss Development Corporation's (SDC) migration project observed:

> Maybe a few of them take initiative to build houses or they start building houses, but it's a process in which you need more money, so two years of contract is inadequate. You would start, but you are unable to continue.... Of course, there is no plan for the house at first and they also do not really know how to build such a big house. How much money will they need? Will they be able to earn that money within the two years of contract? So they don't plan according to what they would be able to gain. It's all that they want ... they want to build a big house, but a two-year contract and the money that goes into that is not adequate to build the house, look after children, look after the day-to-day expenses and so on.

Speaking in a similar vein, the ILO project officer remarked on the cumulative causation of lifestyle adjustments enabled by an initial migration:

> Your children say 'Mum, we need something bigger. Why don't you go overseas again and earn it and come back?' So then the family tends to

Table 3.8 Repeat migration

Number of trips	*Women %*	*Men %*
One	37.3	48.8
Two	33.9	34.2
Three	10.2	4.9
More than three	18.6	12.2
Total	100.0	100.0

> depend on the money the mum sends and then they don't want her back; they want her to constantly be overseas and have a regular flow of income. Sometimes when she comes back, they continue to lead the lifestyle of when money was coming regularly. And then they get into even more debt because their lifestyles don't change with the change in income. And then that causes people to keep going again.

A contradiction thus takes shape at the intersection of *forced migration* and migrants' aspirations for a 'good life' defined by and large by access to basic goods, decent employment and intergenerational well-being. The inability to realise these goals within Sri Lanka's prevailing climate of underdevelopment forces migrants abroad into foreign employment under a range of unfavourable circumstances, with structures of uneven development, location-specific migration practices and individual circumstances all contributing to the extent to which remittances can be put towards intended use. However, short of sustainable business investment or otherwise achieving sustainable incomes upon reintegration, the partial realisation of other goals – housing, education, greater disposable incomes and comfortable lifestyles – establishes a path dependency on repeat migration that can span decades of an individual's life or flow-on migration that entails multiple generations working abroad for survival.

Conclusion

This chapter has examined the way in which structures of uneven development have shaped the causes for and outcomes of temporary labour migration throughout Sri Lanka. Neoliberal economic restructuring has disrupted traditional livelihoods while channelling particular categories of labour into narrow and degraded job openings in export industries, resulting in unemployment and underemployment that, particularly in the rural economy, has amounted to conditions of *forced migration*. Migrants' aspirations affirm this analysis, as the 'good life' sought across each of the migrant communities studied was seen to reflect little more than the basic outcomes of a sustainable livelihood. The outcomes of migration were, however, seen to intersect with prevailing underdevelopment in a manner that stifled key ambitions while fostering economic subsistence and a prevalent dependency on repeat or flow-on migration to sustain remittance flows. These findings challenged expectations of migrant entrepreneurship commonly voiced in mainstream migration-development literature. Yet, while uneven development represents an encompassing structural impetus for *forced migration*, variations in migration outcomes across different migrant communities emphasise that experiences of migration-development are not uniform and cannot be adequately analysed from a structural-level analysis alone. This recognition paves the way for a more attentive analysis of the geographical and institutional nuances of *place* in the following chapter.

Notes

1 Underemployment is here framed simply as wages or hours deemed insufficient by the worker.
2 Calculations vary, but tend to peg informal employment at around 70 per cent of all employment (Arunatilake 2012).
3 Discussions of income and expenses are discussed with reference to Sri Lankan rupees (Rs) throughout the empirical section of the book. For reference, 100 rupees is equivalent to US$0.55 as of January 2019, while one 'lakh' – i.e. Rs100,000 – amounts to US$550.
4 Hand-rolled cigarettes.
5 On occasion this reflected a mismanagement of remittances by family left behind, but 84 per cent of respondents said they were happy with the way remittances had been spent by their families left behind, the remaining 16 per cent of discontented respondents also including those who had income withheld and could not remit.

References

Abeykoon, Palitha. 2002. 'Case Study: Sri Lanka'. In *Long-Term Care in Developing Countries: Ten Case Studies*, 332–58. Geneva: World Health Organisation.

Arunatilake, Nisha. 2012. 'Precarious Work in Sri Lanka'. *American Behavioral Scientist* 57 (4): 488–506.

Brochmann, Grete. 1993. *Middle East Avenue: Female Migration from Sri Lanka to the Gulf.* Boulder, CO: Westview Press.

Castles, Stephen, and Mark J. Miller. 2007. *The Age of Migration: International Population Movements in the Modern World.* 3rd edition. Houndmills: Palgrave Macmillan.

Delgado Wise, Raúl. 2009. 'Forced Migration and US Imperialism: The Dialectic of Migration and Development'. *Critical Sociology* 35 (6): 767–84.

Department of Census and Statistics (DCS). 2017. *Sri Lanka Labour Force Survey: Annual Report – 2017.* Colombo: Department of Census and Statistics.

Gamburd, Michele Ruth. 2000. *The Kitchen Spoon's Handle: Transnationalism and Sri Lanka's Migrant Housemaids.* Ithaca, NY: Cornell University Press.

Institute of Policy Studies (IPS). 2013. *Sri Lanka: State of the Economy 2013.* Colombo: Institute of Policy Studies of Sri Lanka.

Institute of Policy Studies (IPS). 2017. *Sri Lanka: State of the Economy 2017.* Colombo: Institute of Policy Studies of Sri Lanka.

International Labour Organisation (ILO). 2013. *Reintegration with Home Community: Perspectives of Returnee Migrant Workers in Sri Lanka.* Geneva: International Labour Organisation.

Jayatilaka, Danesh. 2005. 'Research Study on Human Smuggling in Sri Lanka: Windows for Intervention by the International Organization for Migration'. Colombo, Sri Lanka: International Organization for Migration.

Jayaweera, Swarna, and Malsiri Dias. 2009. 'Gender Roles and Support Networks of Spouses of Migrant Workers'. In *Gender and Labour Migration in Asia*, 43–115. Geneva: IOM International Organization for Migration.

Kottegoda, Sepali. 2004. *Negotiating Household Politics: Women's Strategies in Urban Sri Lanka.* Colombo: Social Scientists' Association.

Kottegoda, Sepali, Ramani Jayasundere, Sumikā Perērā, and Padma Atapattu. 2013. *Transforming Lives: Listening to Sri Lankan Returnee Women Migrant Workers.* Colombo: Women and Media Collective.

Little, Angela, and S. T. Hettige. 2014. *Globalisation, Employment and Education in Sri Lanka: Opportunity and Division.* Florence: Taylor and Francis.

Piore, Michael J. 1980. *Birds of Passage: Migrant Labor and Industrial Societies*. Cambridge: Cambridge University Press.

Smith, Monica. 2010. 'Erasure of Sexuality and Desire: State Morality and Sri Lankan Migrants in Beirut, Lebanon'. *The Asia Pacific Journal of Anthropology* 11 (3–4): 378–93.

Sri Lanka Bureau of Foreign Employment (SLBFE). 2016. 'Different Perspectives of Departure Details'. Colombo: SLBFE.

Withers, Matt. 2016. 'Sri Lanka: Working Realities and Gendered Fictions'. In *Women, Work and Care in the Asia-Pacific*, edited by Marian Baird, Michele Ford, and Elizabeth Hill, 148–64. London: Routledge.

4 The cost of being exploited

Fees, debts and the merchants of labour

The previous chapter explored how the causes and outcomes of Sri Lankan temporary labour migration are intimately tied to processes of uneven development, varying across fieldwork location but nevertheless converging upon a collective experience of forced migration. This chapter further analyses the manifestation of structural inequalities through the medium of *place* by unpacking the localised practices of the 'merchants of labour' and the disparate costs and conditions of migration they produce. Locational differences in the extent of recruitment fees and migration-related debt further suggest that processes of uneven development have, in turn, produced uneven migration experiences that exacerbate underlying developmental contradictions. *Place* – representative not only of the geographical manifestation of class, gender and ethno-religious structures, but also the networks and institutions that bind their interactions with one another and the broader economy – is fundamental in mediating the interplay between individual experiences and overarching constraints. Building on the previous chapter's introduction to distinctive migration cultures emerging across each fieldwork location, this chapter explores the employment hurdles faced by each migrant community to demonstrate how the 'merchants of labour' employ strategies to exploit communal practices encumbered by their spatial fixity.

As in Chapter 3, qualitative and quantitative fieldwork data is used extensively in order to discuss the costs and conditions of temporary labour migration with direct relation to the lived experiences of migrants themselves. The first part of the chapter addresses the cost of migrating and prevalence of debt across each of the four fieldwork locations, exploring research findings that suggest the most socio-economically disadvantaged migrate under the most difficult circumstances. In the following section, these uneven costs and conditions of migration are analysed in relation to pertinent local institutions, emphasising the relationship between geography, communal knowledge and the strategies employed by agents and intermediaries, demonstrating how recruitment practices map onto, and strategically exploit, patterns of uneven development. Finally, the chapter reflects on popular responses to migrant exploitation, navigating the tense coexistence of a patriarchal media backlash to women's migration alongside a muted policy impetus to promote further migration.

The demographics of debt

Recruitment methods and associated expenses

Temporary labour migration has been accompanied by the proliferation of private recruitment agencies that coordinate the supply of Sri Lankan labour to foreign employers (ILO 2013). Despite modest policy reforms designed to tighten recruitment practices and cap fees, most notably the SLBFE Act 21 of 1985, private agencies continue to thrive within a loosely regulated environment and constitute a major local industry. Of the three major pathways for arranging foreign employment – through private recruitment agencies, the SLBFE or personal contacts – private recruiters have historically dominated and continue to account for 60 per cent of current placements (ILO 2013). Recruiters make commission on foreign job orders, but also derive profits from charging recruitment fees to prospective migrants in Sri Lanka, making most job placements via a private agency a substantial expense.

Domestic worker migration has been a partial exception to this practice, as legal reforms to fee structures for low-salary positions in 1994 (ILO 2013) combined with high demand for domestic workers from foreign employers have meant that recruiters will often offer more favourable terms to fill job orders. For other categories of migrant workers, the charging of exorbitant recruitment fees, well above the maximum amount stipulated by the SLBFE, remains rife (ILO 2013). Yet with migration through private contacts either dependent on pre-established networks or equally as costly, and state-provisioned recruitment narrowly focussed on limited bilaterally agreed contracts, private recruiters retain a stranglehold on arranging foreign employment contracts (ILO 2013). A slew of associated expenses – including medical costs to secure a clean bill of health, visa and passport fees, air tickets, mandatory insurance fees and mandatory training fees for domestic workers – are typically reflected in agency recruitment fees. Those migrating through a personal contact typically bear these costs on an ad hoc basis. Migrants' relative reliance on these two principal strategies for arranging employment, and the extent of the costs involved in either, were seen to vary across fieldwork locations and individual circumstances.

Quantitative data gathered from interviews with returned migrants suggested that the predominant means of arranging foreign employment was by way of recruitment agents, accounting for 70 per cent of all departures. This is broadly consistent with SLBFE estimates, which identify that agency recruitment accounted for approximately 67 per cent of foreign employment placements in 1999, the median year of emigration in the study (SLBFE 2012). Private employment arrangements via family and friends comprised the next most common means of placement, followed by a single SLBFE placement and two anomalous instances of company-arranged job placements. This trend was broadly consistent across all fieldwork locations, with the exceptions of the Polgahawela Muslims, who experienced a notably more balanced proportion of agency-arranged employment relative to private placements, and the Thavapuram Tamils, who were disproportionately reliant on recruitment agents (see Table 4.1).

Table 4.1 Method of arranging employment

Method	*Akmeemana %*	*Negombo %*	*Polgahawela %*	*Thavapuram %*
Family or friends	20.0	28.0	40.0	20.0
Private agent	72.0	68.0	60.0	80.0
SLBFE	4.0	0	0	0
Other	4.0	4.0	0	0
Total	100.0	100.0	100.0	100.0

Variations in the method of arranging employment were, however, eclipsed by a more pronounced locational disparity in the actual expenses associated with arranging migration. Achieving a meaningful cross-locational comparison of these costs necessitated a limited examination of recruitment between 2000 and 2013, as the Thavapuram Tamils only began participating in temporary labour migration at the turn of the millennium and inflation-adjustment of earlier migrations from other locations were unfeasible due to the historical volatility of the Sri Lankan rupee. Disaggregating by gender and skill level, the data revealed that the average recruitment costs for the most typical categories of temporary labour migration (female domestic workers and male low-waged workers) were substantially higher in Thavapuram relative to all other locations (see Figure 4.1). In the case of Thavapuram's domestic workers, the average expenses to arrange migration were more than triple that of the other fieldwork locations over the same time period. Using the same criteria of comparison to assess the average income gained from these placements reveals that higher recruitment costs were not reflective of better job positions abroad (see Figure 4.2). Indeed, male low-waged workers from Thavapuram were seen to receive substantially

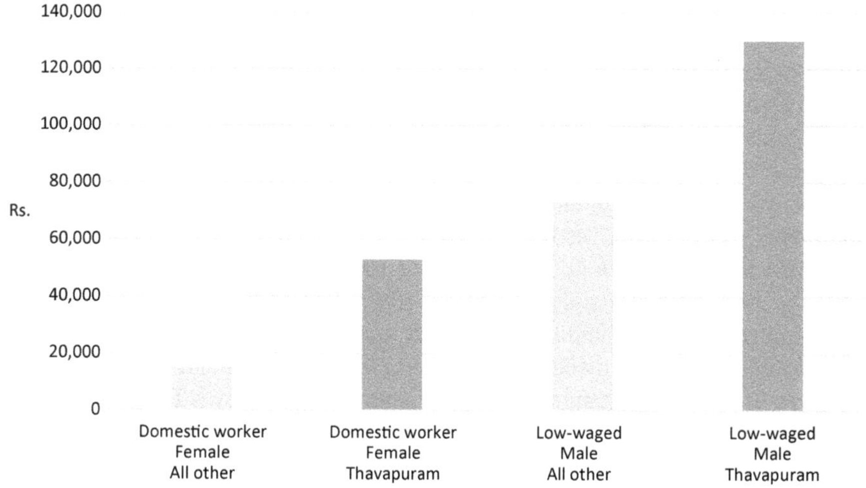

Figure 4.1 Recruitment costs in Thavapuram, 2000–2013.

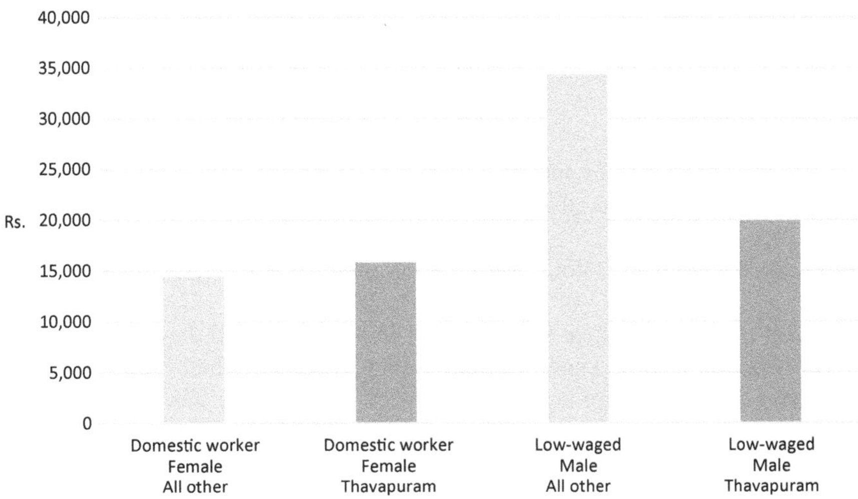

Figure 4.2 Migrant incomes in Thavapuram, 2000–2013.

less income than similarly skilled workers from other locations, despite paying notably higher fees to arrange their employment. These findings suggest that migrants from the most socially and materially disadvantaged community participated in foreign employment under the costliest circumstances.

Qualitative findings substantiated this apparent disparity, uncovering varying personal narratives of recruitment experiences across the four fieldwork locations. In communities with a long history of temporary labour migration, participants often discussed recruitment as a relatively simple process – either casually facilitated by friends and family, or arranged straightforwardly through a local agency. These lived experiences shed light on the relationship between place, the method of arranging employment and the costliness of those practices.

Akmeemana and Negombo

In Akmeemana, one woman explained how the recruitment agents facilitated her placement and covered the upfront costs, offering an interest-free monthly repayment plan as a means of financing the process:

> The agency does everything. I didn't pay anything, the agency took repayments from my salary. I got Rs18,000 per month, the agency took Rs3,000 per month.

Another, living just a few doors down, also arranged her employment via a private agency, but hinted at the advantage of being able to utilise local knowledge to choose which recruiter to use:

> Yes, it was through an agency, but a person that we knew recommended the agency to me.

In Negombo, similar themes emerged. A young mother recently returned from Saudi Arabia told that:

> We did not spend any money.... They did not even charge me. They gave me the insurance and all and then they sent me.

When asked why she was not charged for her placement, she responded:

> I don't know. The agent said that they do not charge and they send for free. Previously I did not know that they even give money when we go. The first time I did not receive any money. But the second time they said that they will give me Rs15,000 – but they gave only Rs10,000.

An earlier migrant domestic worker from Negombo was not subject to the same lack of fees, but could partially leverage her pre-existing employment in the nearby Katunayake EPZ to finance her placement:

> I went through an agency. At that time, it was Rs25,000. I borrowed and I also had some money saved from my job at Katunayake. I pawned some jewellery to a bank as well. I can't remember how much the interest was, but I earned there and paid it off.

Other Negombo migrants were able to draw on established networks to arrange their employment through friends and family.

One woman, an older migrant, told of how easily this arrangement took shape for her:

> No. I didn't find out about any jobs. I had no brains to do that, so one of my friends sent a ticket and I decided to go ... I asked this uncle to ask from his daughter to send me a ticket from a good place and in one week's time I received a ticket from her. It was my decision and I gave Rs2,000 to my friend as an appreciation.

Another, a more recent migrant worker, retold how she was actively recruited by a family friend:

> Yes, I got the job through an aunt who had lived in Bahrain for 12 years. She said there is a need for someone to look after a baby and asked me if I would like to take the job. We had financial problems so I asked my mother if she could look after my child and I left for Bahrain to work as a nanny ... I went to work for the sister of the madam my aunt was working for. She got me the ticket and then deducted the amount from my salary.

In both Akmeemana and Negombo, there was a palpable sense that arranging migration was an established practice. A concentration of private agencies within these urban, Sinhalese communities – both with a long history of migration – makes it likely that competitively favourable recruitment practices have become a necessity of doing business. With potential migrants able to choose between a number of agencies in facilitating their employment, or perhaps draw on personal connections abroad, it would appear difficult for agencies to charge recruitment fees beyond what communal knowledge of migration practices stipulate as an acceptable price. Moreover, for some female domestic workers, prior access to stable employment opportunities in nearby EPZs mean that existing income can assist in financing whatever recruitment fees do arise.

As one woman from Akmeemana explained, her employment in a garments factory directly catalysed her trip abroad:

> I only left the factory because I decided to go abroad. I wanted to go abroad with my friends from work … we paid about Rs5,000 each and went altogether.

Polgahawela

In Polgahawela, where Muslims had been involved in temporary labour migration since its very beginnings, even more favourable terms of recruitment were observed. For a number of Polgahawela migrants, including men seeking low-waged work, visas were arranged primarily through friends or family already abroad and without charge.

One particularly successful migrant explained how he started working as a private driver in the UAE:

> I got my visa and tickets sent from Dubai. I didn't pay anything, I got it freely.

Another man received his visa freely from friends, only using recruitment agencies to find an employer:

> Both the times, my friends sent me the visas and then I took the help of agents. I did not spend much on my journey.

An older migrant woman, who left for Kuwait as a domestic worker in the 1990s, explained that she was paid a considerable amount by the agency through which she arranged her employment:

> I went through an agency, they organised the visa and other matters … I didn't pay, the agency had given money to me to go abroad, around Rs30,000. No deductions, the agency had done everything for me, my medical and visa matters were also looked after by the agency before I was sent for foreign employment.

Here migration was not only well established, but a practice favourably shaped by heightened foreign demand for Muslim workers and a communal interdependency strengthened by religious ethics. West Asian employer preferences for Muslim workers are well-documented (Gamburd 2000), translating into higher commission for recruiters able to supply such workers, likely undercutting the importance of profiting from recruitment fees. Contrarily, it makes sense that recruitment agents would offer cash incentives to Muslim workers in order to fulfil these more lucrative job orders. Moreover, adherence to the Islamic pillar of *zakat*, within which *riba* (any excess over and above the principal loan, such as interest) is considered *haram*, was seen to eventuate in altruistic practices of 'paying forwards' the cost of migration. This involved existing migrants arranging visas and employment free of charge for friends and family at home, with the expectation that the recipient would subsequently extend the favour to other prospective migrants within the community. The costs associated with arranging employment in Polgahawela were, in this sense, greatly reduced. This affirms other research findings that suggest migrants using informal networks are more likely to express satisfaction and report 'success' than those using recruitment agents (Shah 2000).

Thavapuram

In contrast, insights into the experiences of Thavapuram migrants revealed less surety in arranging migration, including the costs to be paid and the trustworthiness of private agents and brokers.

One woman, having recently returned from Jordan, spoke of paying recruitment fees far greater than agencies would be able to charge in other parts of the country:

> I went through an agency. I paid Rs100,000. This amount included training, medical and other charges.

Having emigrated as a domestic worker in 2008, long after limits to domestic worker recruitment charges had been established and amidst high demand from foreign employers, there should have been no fee levied at all.

The severity, and arbitrariness, of these charges are highlighted by the more lenient arrangement experienced by a neighbour, migrating as a domestic worker just two years later:

> I went through an agency – we didn't spend. They gave Rs20,000 and even paid for my passport.

However, the agency was complicit in glossing over the potential hardships of the job:

> The first month was so difficult – they beat me and then I went to another house because they didn't pay my salary. The agency said the work is good and easy, so I didn't think about it much.

Elsewhere in the community, a young man seeking low-waged work expressed uncertainty regarding the substantial placement costs he paid to an agency:

> The first time I went via an agency to Saudi Arabia and my second time my brother sent a visa and I went to Qatar.... My first time I didn't know about this matter of what amount I should pay to go there and I spent Rs25,000 for a medical matter because they said I was sick. In total I paid Rs145,000.

Another man, who had recently returned from working as a mason in Qatar, explained that even arranging foreign employment by way of private contacts was very costly:

> Someone, a friend of my friend, sent me a visa and I spent nearly 110,000 on the process. I gave 60,000 to the person who sent the visa.

As suggested by the quantitative snapshot provided earlier in the chapter, migrants from Thavapuram were seen to experience greater costs in arranging migration, most likely arising from a limited community understanding of migration practices and recruitment standards found elsewhere in Sri Lanka. With labour migration having only taken place in any substantial way since the turn of the millennium, there was not the same measure of experiences and existing migrant networks to draw upon. Moreover, being geographically isolated from urban centres – where recruitment agencies and SLBFE offices are concentrated – it would appear that those agents who are active in remoter communities like Thavapuram exercise a monopolistic presence. Given that arranging migration commands such an expense, it would appear that private contacts who are capable of facilitating placement might likewise be inclined to gain from these lucrative fees by charging similar amounts in return for visa and work arrangements. This practice of extorting informal 'recruitment fees' has been documented as part of the ILO's research into strategies of arranging foreign employment (ILO 2013).

Migrant indebtedness

The previous section established that participation in temporary labour migration was disproportionately expensive for the most underdeveloped community studied. However, the need to pay higher placement costs with relatively less financial and material assets poses a secondary dilemma regarding the availability of financing options and the prevalence of debt amongst returnees. Findings suggested that locational differences in the expenses associated with the arrangement of foreign employment were compounded by significant disparities in the levels of migration-related indebtedness that returnees experienced within each community. Quantitatively, this relationship – that is, between varying recruitment costs, structural disadvantage and migration-related indebtedness – is explored across each community through three data points: the methods of financing recruitment costs, the prevalence of migration-related loan repayments as a remittance expense, and the severity of debt expressed as the length of loan repayments.

Methods of financing costs

Migrants were seen to rely on a variety of means to finance the costs associated with migration, be they all-inclusive recruitment fees or private expenses for visas and tickets. Three general strategies can be identified: reliance on personal assets (including savings, pawned jewellery and mortgaged housing); non-interest loans from friends, family and agents (which may or may not entail repayment); and high-interest loans from local moneylenders. The ability to pursue one strategy over another is reflective of the degree to which individual agency has, through the intermediary of place, been restricted by structural inequalities. Generally speaking, those with material assets can afford to self-finance migration; those who have fewer resources but are anchored within a strong community can instead borrow from friends and family; while those with neither assets nor a developed community are limited to private loans which, in the absence of collateral, are invariably subject to high interest.

Table 4.2 demonstrates the extent to which each fieldwork location used particular financing strategies, corroborating this analysis. In Negombo a combination of private assets (albeit very little in the form of savings) comprised the main method of financing, followed closely by borrowing from friends and family and a 20 per cent reliance on moneylenders. In Akmeemana the composition is similar, with moneylending again accounting for 20 per cent, but with community lending taking precedence over private assets (the majority of which were savings). Polgahawela stands apart, as no migrants were reliant upon moneylenders. Loans from friends and family accounted for almost half of all financing methods, the remainder of which came largely from savings and assets. Yet most telling is the pattern of financing in Thavapuram, where 68 per cent of migrants were reliant on moneylenders, while the rest pawned jewellery and mortgaged their houses in lieu of savings or communal lending.

Table 4.2 Method of financing foreign employment

Method	*Akmeemana %*	*Negombo %*	*Polgahawela %*	*Thavapuram %*
Agent loan	0.0	0.0	8.0	0.0
Family or friends	36.0	24.0	44.0	0.0
Moneylender	20.0	20.0	0.0	68.0
Mortgaged house	4.0	16.0	0.0	12.0
Pawned jewellery	0.0	8.0	8.0	4.0
Savings	20.0	4.0	20.0	0.0
Other	8.0	20.0	8.0	0.0
NA	12.0	8.0	12.0	16.0
Total	100.0	100.0	100.0	100.0

The prevalence and severity of debt

The composition of financing strategies within each fieldwork location appeared to have direct implications for the prevalence and severity of migration-related indebtedness.

The prevalence of migrant debt amongst each community was examined by simply measuring how many migrants spent a portion of their remitted income repaying migration-related loans. In Negombo this amounted to 56 per cent of migrants. In Akmeemana and Polgahawela, where communal loaning and private savings were highest, 44 per cent of migrants spent remittances on loan repayments. In Thavapuram, where reliance on moneylenders was rife, 80 per cent of migrants used remittances to finance debt.

However, gauging the prevalence of loan repayments offers only a partial characterisation of indebtedness. More telling is the amount of time that was taken to repay the loan, as this holistically portrays the interrelationship between the size of the loan, the interest charged and the amount of foreign income earned to facilitate repayment. Table 4.3 shows how these repayment periods varied by location. Most migrants from Negombo and Akmeemana were able to pay off their migration-related debts within one year of commencing foreign employment (although long-term debt remained more common in Negombo). In Polgahawela, most migrants repaid loans within six months, with very few individuals continuing to live in debt beyond this timeframe. In Thavapuram, however, not only was debt the most prevalent, but also the most severe: very few migrants had paid off their debt within the first year, with most migrants either indebted for multiple years or still encumbered by repayments.

The greater proportionality of recent emigrations from Thavapuram only partially accounts for the high number of migrants still repaying debt; departures taking place after 2010 only account for 40 per cent of migrants within this category, suggesting that at the time of research (in 2014) the majority of those still repaying loans had been encumbered by debt for anywhere between 4 and 11 years. This severity of structural indebtedness was not observed in any other fieldwork location.

The personal reflections of participants in Thavapuram give greater insight into how the spatial and institutional context of *place* has produced such significant debt amongst migrant returnees.

Table 4.3 Length of debt repayments

Length	*Akmeemana %*	*Negombo %*	*Polgahawela %*	*Thavapuram %*
Less than six months	24.0	24.0	40.0	16.0
Less than one year	20.0	12.0	4.0	0.0
One to two years	8.0	12.0	8.0	12.0
More than two years	4.0	12.0	0.0	12.0
Still repaying	0.0	0.0	0.0	40.0
NA	44.0	40.0	48.0	20.0
Total	100.0	100.0	100.0	100.0

One man, when asked about the conditions of his loan, explained:

> I took a loan but didn't know the interest rate. It took almost two years to pay off. I didn't get enough income to pay it off soon.

When asked how his remitted income was spent, he provided a telling glimpse into how high recruitment costs, a lack of financial resources and poor working conditions could easily conspire to produce acute indebtedness:

> I paid off debts and did nothing else – it had almost doubled after interest.

Another male migrant in the community told of a similar outcome:

> I thought migration would mean earning a bit more money to improve my fishing business. I paid off the interest and debt, but only brought Rs4,000 when I returned.

Further, it became clear that migration and debt bore another kind of relationship in Thavapuram, wherein paying off pre-existing debt – accrued in lieu of stable local employment – was sometimes the primary reason for pursuing foreign employment in the first place.

When asked what her pre-migration goals were, a recently returned domestic worker explained:

> I thought of paying off my debts, which were over two lakh.[1] I paid one lakh, but after coming back I applied for another loan to settle the rest. I had many plans – to build a house, spend for the kids, etc. – but nothing materialised.

The common shortfall of this strategy was encapsulated by the experiences of another returnee who sought foreign employment for the same reason. When asked how his remittances were spent, he said:

> The money was used purposively, but only repaid our debt. Beyond that, I had to repay debt from the ticket fees and had to pay interest money on top of that – too much of a financial problem. I didn't have a good life from foreign employment and I only finished repaying one debt, but now have to settle more, so I'm not happy.

These experiences all hint at the formation of a contextually specific condition of uneven migration in Thavapuram where civil war, economic marginalisation and a dearth of migration knowledge have together culminated in an environment where migrants are subjected to prohibitive recruitment fees prior to migration and severe debt upon return. The previous chapter revealed that temporary labour migration had, across the board, brought little of its presumed economic benefits to the returnees interviewed. Yet while inordinate fees, extortionate loans and migrant indebtedness were experienced by some returnees in other fieldwork locations, in no other community was it observed with the same prevalence and severity as it was in Thavapuram.

In order to understand why the most disadvantaged community would migrate under the most costly and unrewarding terms, it is necessary to understand how the 'merchants of labour' navigate and exploit the geography of Sri Lanka's uneven development.

Mapping the merchants of labour

The term 'merchants of labour' has been used to describe the network of businesses facilitating temporary labour migration: foreign and local recruitment agencies, sub-agents, labour brokers, money transfer agencies, financiers and informal migrant networks that can negotiate foreign employment (ILO 2006). In Sri Lanka's case, the government, too, joins the ranks of these merchants of labour, as the promotion of foreign employment has become a key developmental strategy (discussed further in Chapter 6). No matter whether these institutions are operating in unison (as with foreign and local agencies) or in competition (as with informal migrant recruiters), their interrelationship at any given time defines the pathways and contours of the employment system characterising the 'supply' of migrant labour.

Focussing more narrowly on recruitment processes, the Sri Lankan ILO country office has partially mapped these interactions as they stand within the prevailing regulatory environment. Attention is given primarily to the interactions between local recruitment agencies, foreign agencies and employers, and the Sri Lankan government's foreign and domestic regulatory bodies: diplomatic missions and the SLBFE respectively. In short, foreign employers and agencies are required to register with, and submit all job orders to, the Sri Lankan diplomatic mission in their country, after which Sri Lankan agencies respond to these approved job orders by liaising with the SLBFE to acquire official grants for procurement and recruitment fees to be charged (ILO 2013).

Despite the importance of the regulatory shifts that have over time led to the current institutional framework, recognition that temporary labour migration unfolds in a context of uneven development places equal importance on the spatial dimensions of the recruitment system. This is most apparent in regard to the relationship between local recruitment agencies and prospective migrants. A relatively uncomplicated recruitment process, wherein local agencies fulfil job orders by recruiting migrant workers from a dormant 'job bank' of pre-registered migrants, may well exist in some urban settings where there is a sufficient mass of aspiring migrants. However, the preponderance of sub-agents and local labour brokers acting as private intermediaries between agencies and migrants suggest an altogether more convoluted chain of recruitment practices that take on explicit geographical characteristics.

Chapter 2 described how an ingrained logic of accumulation by subordination has positioned urban capital to exploit and marginalise vulnerable – and mostly rural – populations. Examining the geographical concentration of recruitment agencies relative to the district-level distribution of departures seems to reaffirm this pattern of uneven development. Recruitment agencies are overwhelmingly concentrated in Sri Lanka's largest urban centres, Colombo and Gampaha, while migrants themselves originate from a wide range of localities, and increasingly from the marginalised Northern and Eastern Provinces (SLBFE 2012; IPS 2013). With only a handful of local recruitment agencies operating in Sri Lanka's more remote districts,[2] unlicensed sub-agents play a fundamental role in recruiting migrants on behalf of registered recruitment agencies in Colombo and other urban centres. For example, in Batticaloa district – where Thavapuram is located – 2011 saw 16,163 departures despite there being just eight registered agencies in the area, only one of which sent more than 100 workers (SLBFE 2012). Arranging foreign employment in these locations is therefore not a simple and mutually enacted coordination between prospective migrants and local agencies. Rather, it entails a more complex chain of top-down recruitment that spans physical distance and encompasses the vested interest of multiple private actors, the most prominent of which are sub-agents, whose involvement as an intermediary in rural recruitment is modelled in Figure 4.3.

Sub-agents operate by extending the recruitment operations of registered agencies beyond their immediate area of business, travelling across Sri Lanka to fulfil existing job orders by enlisting prospective migrant workers, typically from rural communities or marginalised regions. Sub-agents will often employ labour brokers, generally well-respected points of contact within the local community, to help drum up interest and identify prospective migrants. In other instances, sub-agents are themselves embedded as trusted members of these communities.

As the project coordinator at the Colombo ILO office explained:

> They [recruitment agents] have personnel asked to go to particular areas. Not that they originate from Colombo, Kurunegala or Galle, these are people who are well known in the community, who people trust and call 'big-brother', or 'uncle' or 'aunty' or whoever. So the sub-agents work on

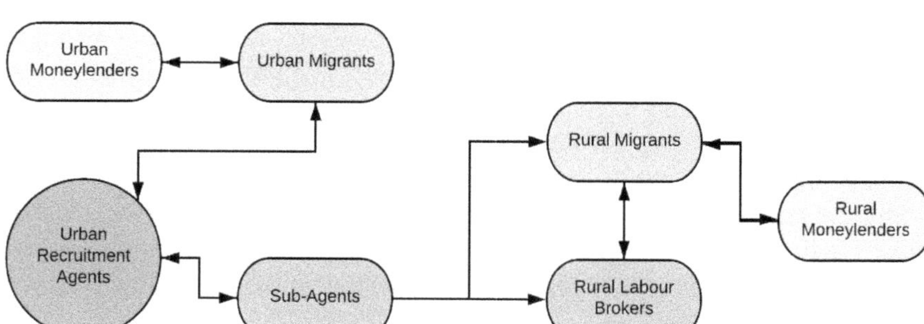

Figure 4.3 Temporary labour migration recruitment networks in Sri Lanka.

> that trust. So sub-agents, either they are people who have gone overseas and come back themselves – previous migrant workers – or they are approached by someone from an agency saying 'Look, I'll pay you this much, if you can get me ten people'. Because each licensed recruitment agency gets a quota, say 150 workers to Qatar for domestic work. So within a 60-day period, they have to get the passport, get the pre-departure training done, get the visa sorted out and send them. So they pay people quick money to find the 150 people.

However, these additional links in the chain of recruitment means that there are a greater number of private actors seeking to make a return on the job order. Sub-agents and labour brokers tend to engage in malpractice and inflate recruitment fees in order to maximise their stake in arranging the supply of labour, yet as individual actors are difficult to regulate (ILO 2013). Moreover, recruitment agencies themselves are not held accountable for these practices, as sub-agents and brokers have no formal ties to the licensed agent handling the job order. For recruitment agencies, this practice offers a cheaper and less labour-intensive option of recruiting migrants from distant regions and disparate communities than establishing official subsidiary agencies in new locations. Meanwhile, the healthy earning potential of the unofficial merchants of labour embedded within this recruitment network – the sub-agents, labour brokers and moneylenders – provides cumulatively causative institutional reinforcement to underscore the path dependence of this recruitment strategy.

The strategy itself, however, is facilitated by a central feature of accumulation by subordination: the mobility of capital over the fixity of labour embedded in *place*. For the most marginalised, *place* denotes disadvantage expressed geographically as isolated communities with degraded local employment, weak institutions and an incomplete knowledge of migration practices.

When interviewed, the SDC program officer spoke to the importance of *place* in Thavapuram:

> I would say that in Thavapuram migration, for most families, is a new phenomenon. Because Batticaloa is one of the districts that has experienced 30 years of conflict on top of the tsunami, so it's double heat. But if you look at a community in the south, this has not been the experience. So these are also, I'm not generalising it, but most of the communities in the south are well established. In the sense that the community is stable, right? But if you look at the communities in the north and east, they are more unstable. Because of the war they lost everything, faced repeated displacement and there were no jobs, and then more operations and crises have repeated throughout their lives. In this case, migration was not a priority or possibility.

However, the intensity of the war also bore important implications for recruitment networks, as the program officer continued to explain:

> There were years in which people would not move out of the districts so they never had a chance of coming to Colombo and migrating, right? And the agents were so scared to go and work in these districts, because their personal security was their main concern.

In Thavapuram, pre-existing marginalisation has been compounded by decades of civil war and the 2004 tsunami, accounting for the community's postponed participation in temporary labour migration. This delay, exacerbated by an uneven distribution of official migrant services in the Eastern Province (SLBFE 2012), has resulted in a nexus between unestablished local expectations of the migration process and the savvy of merchants of labour with three decades of accumulated experience from running businesses elsewhere in the country. As might be expected, prospective migrants' deficient understanding of the standards and procedures of recruitment forms a basis for their exploitation by sub-agents and brokers.

The ILO project coordinator explained how a lack of information and poorly distributed government services had affected migration in Batticaloa and its surrounding communities:

> Post-conflict migration has increased, but with little information. For example, Batticaloa itself doesn't have a foreign employment bureau district resource centre. There are 25 resource centres in the country, but Batticaloa itself doesn't have one. There's one in Ampara, there's one in Kalmunai, and there is one in Vavuniya, but not in Batticaloa. So this is probably a reason, because everybody is told, 'Go to the foreign employment bureau office, or the district centre in your district.' Even to go to the district office, they would probably only go if there was a problem. They would first be approached by a sub-agent, and after that they would only go to the district office for their registration or signing of a contract. Before that, they probably wouldn't go at all. So the chances of getting migration information is very limited, because they are already approached by sub-agents at the village level, while it takes about two hours to get to the district centre. The only incentive is to sign your contract at home, but by that time you've already paid whatever to the sub-agent and this and that.

A representative of the Ministry of Labour and Labour Relations reaffirmed these concerns, noting that:

> Most migrants from rural areas don't even know about the SLBFE – only the man or woman in their village who is a broker for an agent.

The ability of sub-agents and labour brokers to mobilise and navigate gaps in government coverage and established communal knowledge allows them, in essence, to calibrate expectations as to the cost and procedure of recruitment.

The SDC program officer spoke on this topic, based on his organisation's own fieldwork in Batticaloa:

> But this Batticaloa, being a new community … is also hugely lacking in information. Ideas have been given to rural communities that the migration for domestic workers is subject to the payment of money … we realise when we start working with these communities, these communities do not understand that there is a SLBFE in that district which is solely responsible for this issue, to whom they can go and check information they do not know. So everything is – starting from the first till the end – everything is channelled through the recruitment agents and they merely depend on all what is said by the recruitment agents. They are the first meeting point, because people do not know where to go and ask, people do not know the entire reality, they do not know about the documents, about also the language issues. These are also communities that have never been to the cities to understand how the whole process works. So all that is spilled out by the agent is taken for granted, is fully trusted, and people find themselves signing on white papers. When our partners started telling women during the awareness program that they don't have to pay, just we could see from their 'Ah, should we pay? Can we go free of charge?' and then there is 'Oh, I paid 50,000. I paid 60,000'. It's the lack of information.

Such instances of malpractice – not limited to inflating recruitment fees, but also including the deliberate issuing of misinformation regarding wages and conditions in order to entice potential migrants – are well documented throughout Sri Lanka (ILO 2013). However, it is capital's ability to traverse the terrain of uneven development and exploit disadvantaged populations constrained by *place* that is fundamental in explaining how and why these strategies are employed in some locations more than others. For Thavapuram, the consequences of these networked recruitment practices are striking. Reeling from the overlapping adversities of underdevelopment, war and natural disaster, migrants from Thavapuram were already ill-positioned to finance the costs of migration and reap beneficial outcomes after their return. But, further disadvantaged by incomplete information and exposure to institutionalised malpractice, the likelihood of positive experiences proved particularly slim – the real beneficiaries being the moneylenders, brokers and sub-agents orchestrating the supply of labour to recruitment agents. While migration still bore mixed (and generally negative) outcomes throughout other fieldwork locations, recruitment methods were altogether more direct and transparent, so that migrants within those communities were not handicapped with the same degree of pre-migration indebtedness that a majority of those in Thavapuram were encumbered by.

The dire consequences of sub-agent activity in Sri Lanka are widely acknowledged by the ILO (2013), state regulators (Martin 2012) and, judging from day-to-day conversations held in Colombo, the general public. In light of popular awareness, the following and final section of this chapter considers how adverse migration outcomes have been reflected in policymaking and the media.

Regulation and representation

Policy responses

The actions of unauthorised sub-agents have been widely condemned, both by international organisations such as the ILO (2013) and Human Rights Watch (2007), and by vested government and industry bodies such as the SLBFE and the Association of Licensed Foreign Employment Agents (ALFEA). The call for greater regulation has been unanimous; even ALFEA, which represents the interests of licensed recruitment agencies, has been outspoken in its concern for the impact of sub-agent malpractice on the wider industry.

Interviewed in an English-language weekend newspaper, *The Sunday Times*, ALFEA president Faizar Mackeen spoke out against sub-agents and the absence of an effective regulatory response:

> This is not good for business, it is also dangerous since there is no accountability should something go wrong at either end because these people are not registered and would be hard to trace in an eventuality. Not only that, many of those involved in such rackets are rogue sub-agents operating in various parts of the country and the authorities have done very little to rope them in.... If this is allowed to continue foreign principals would look elsewhere for future recruitment and we may lose out in the market.
>
> (Berenger 2012)

Despite expressing concerns that are chiefly a reflection of self-interest, specifically that foreign demand for Sri Lankan workers could decline on account of malpractice, there appears to be a consensus between business and civil society that the government needs to tightly regulate sub-agent activity. Yet there has been little by way of official policy response, despite pressure from the Colombo Process[3] to tighten regulations (Agunias, Aghazarm, and Battistella 2011) and Sri Lanka's official migration policy acknowledging the severity of the issue and the responsibility of the government in resolving it:

> Malpractices by private recruitment agencies and the gaps in the regulatory framework for local agents of recruiting agencies (known as sub-agents) lead to exploitative and abusive situations for migrant workers.... The State has the final responsibility in all recruitment processes, derived from its commitment to protecting workers within a secure and equitable labour migration process.
>
> (MFEPW 2008, 10–11)

When interviewed, a general manager for the SLBFE explained that a new regulatory framework redressing gaps within the existing legislation was soon to be put before parliament:

> [The existing legislation] was enacted in 1985. We did certain amendments from time to time, but still it had a lot of loopholes. It clearly mentioned the

> role of the recruitment agents and the bureau, but the sub-agent is in-between – he is not recognised and he is not legalised.... Ultimately what we decided was to introduce a new system, we proposed a new act that is called Sri Lanka Migration Employment Authority Act that is now put to the parliament and the parliamentary commission is looking after that and I think most probably before the end of this year come it will come into practice. It will definitely identify the role of the sub-agent. What are their limits? How they can do it? Everything is covered. Whatever the problems we had for the last 20 years is covered by that particular act. So once this act is enacted definitely this problem will be solved because we'll be going get the support in a legalistic manner.

The Act intends to establish a Migration Employment Authority to replace the SLBFE while creating new guidelines for sub-agents that will provide a legal basis for prosecuting misconduct. However, legislating against sub-agent malpractice and actually enforcing those standards are two separate challenges. While moves to create a legal rationale for regulation is welcomed, it remains unclear as to how the SLBFE will ensure that unauthorised sub-agents – reportedly numbering more than 10,000 (*The Sunday Times* 2014) – will be registered and made compliant with new rules when they are presently able to operate inconspicuously. Recruitment agencies can be held accountable, as their business is conducted from fixed offices, whereas sub-agents ply their trade without such constraints. Furthermore, the implementation of the Sri Lanka Migration Employment Authority Act itself appears to have been delayed indefinitely, with no mention of the policy going into effect more than four years after it was widely anticipated to be passed into law.

Media coverage

In contrast, the Sri Lankan government has been quick to offer policy responses to other issues concerning migrant welfare that receive considerably greater media attention, namely the abuse of domestic workers and the social consequences of 'absent' mothers and 'left-behind' children. The 2013 execution of Rizana Nafeek sparked a revitalisation of media coverage around the physical abuse of Sri Lankan women working abroad and concomitant concerns over the domestic fallout of women's migration.

Ceylon Today, a popular English-language daily, published an editorial entitled 'Enough is Enough', in which the author captures the national political investment in private female bodies when decrying:

> Why do we continue to expose our girls to such ignominious situations? Do we not have any other avenues for foreign exchange other than selling our women? Sri Lanka, the country we are proud to be born into, is now known as the country of housemaids.
>
> (Yahampath 2013)

The Sri Lankan government responded shortly after Nafeek's beheading by introducing the FBR, which increased the minimum age of prospective migrant domestic workers to Saudi Arabia to 25 and – in response to further public concern over the 'heavy social cost on the children they leave behind' (Weeraratne 2014) – placed restrictions on prospective migrant women with young children (ILO 2018). The centrality of gendered subordination within these debates is clear. An editorial from another English-language tabloid, the *Daily Mirror*, asked: 'What is more important – a mother's right to choose her job or a child's need to be raised by her mother?' (Weeraratne 2014). The government, too, suggests that family problems arising from migration are the onus of women migrants. The chairman of the SLBFE was quoted as saying, 'We have witnessed several broken homes since mothers have been working abroad' (*Daily Mirror* 2013), while the Sri Lankan ambassador to Kuwait stated, 'We are paying the price – the social impact is huge, families are breaking up' (Daily Mirror 2014).

These sentiments, consistently mobilised by government representatives and the Sri Lankan tabloid press, reflect a tradition of patriarchal ethno-nationalist rhetoric, first articulated by middle-class Sinhalese Buddhist men seeking to define and subordinate women's lives within the domestic sphere in the wake of receding colonialism (de Alwis 1996). In practical terms, it is rhetoric used to bolster the ideological construction of a sexual division of labour that locates Sri Lankan masculinity in the performance of productive labour and femininity in the performance of care and domestic work (Gamburd 2000). The very construction of this division, however, is made increasingly fragile by the stark social and economic reality of women's productive labour as temporary labour migrants. These combined tensions have amounted to a weak policy approach to migrant welfare. On one hand the government seeks to ingratiate patriarchal notions of protection though conditional restrictions to domestic worker employment, while on the other it fails to generate meaningful policy responses to the abuse and exploitation perpetuated by recruitment practices for fear of disrupting the economic contribution of migration.

The government appears to have been superficially restricting female migration in the name of protecting workers and their families, while surreptitiously taking steps to encourage continued and more profitable migration by female domestic workers. By planning to 'rebrand' Sri Lankan domestic workers as 'domestic housekeeping assistance' without meaningfully increasing pre-departure training or skills assessment, policymakers have demonstrated a commitment to 'exporting' Sri Lankan labour for the West Asian 'market'. The government's stated intention to substantially increase annual remittances through traditional channels (IPS 2014) – that is, predominantly by way of domestic worker migration to West Asia – provides little incentive to regulate the network of sub-agents and brokers upon which much of that pathway is built.

A general consequence of this policy and media antagonism is that the government has become chiefly concerned with regulating the popular representation of migrant issues, that is, the social edifice of a patriarchal backlash to women's employment. Migrant welfare has become increasingly framed as an issue of individual accountability, typically falling at the feet of female domestic workers for having supposedly shirked maternal duties. Meanwhile, restrictions imposed on the merchants of labour, which carry less ideological saliency and greater economic risk, have been conspicuously toothless. That the higher costs and greater indebtedness resulting from sub-agent recruiting falls mainly on the socially and economically marginalised is likely an added determinant of the government's muted response, mirroring a lack of genuine resolve in providing a sufficient distribution of migrant support and training services in the Eastern and Northern provinces (SLBFE 2012).

Conclusion

This chapter has extended the analysis of *forced migration* introduced in Chapter 3 by drawing attention to the significant institutional differences bound up in the geographic, demographic and cultural fixity of *place*. It has demonstrated how prominent recruitment strategies intersect with locationally specific migration practices in a manner that influences both the cost of migrating and the prevalence of migration-related indebtedness. The practices of the 'merchants of labour' cut asymmetrically across an existing landscape of uneven development, making use of the relative mobility of capital over labour to produce conditions of 'uneven migration' throughout Sri Lanka's rural economy. The institutional characteristics and material limitations of particular migration cultures were seen to either mitigate or exacerbate the extent to which marginalised communities were disadvantaged by uneven migration. Whereas one marginalised community, the Polgahawela Muslims, were able to use ethnic insularity and religious affinities with West Asia to improve the circumstances of their migration, the severity of underdevelopment for the war-affected Tamil-Hindu community in Thavapuram left the group acutely vulnerable to exploitation by recruiters and moneylenders. Ineffective regulatory intervention from the Sri Lankan government, which appears more invested in managing popular opinion, has done little to address this imbalance of recruitment practices. Subjection to forced migration therefore remains tempered by the particular limitations of place and the contrasting mobility of capital, and thus largely reinforces existing developmental disparities. The following chapter explores the complexities of *status* as an expression of migrant agency within and alongside these constraints.

Notes

1 A lakh is a denomination of currency, used throughout South Asia, that represents 100,000 rupees and exchanges at US$560.19 as of 16 March 2019.

2 Those few recruitment agencies that do exist are likely owned and operated as subsidiaries of established recruitment agencies elsewhere in the country – such as 'Trans Gulf East', a branch of 'Trans Gulf' in Colombo and Batticaloa's largest recruitment agency (SLBFE 2012).

3 The Colombo Process, established in 2003, is a forum mediated by the International Organization for Migration (IOM) in order for Asian labour-sending countries to consult with one another regarding regulation, welfare and developmental issues associated with temporary labour migration.

References

Agunias, Dovelyn, Christine Aghazarm, and Graziano Battistella. 2011. 'Labour Migration from Colombo Process Countries: Good Practices, Challenges and Way Forward'. Bangkok: International Organization for Migration (IOM).

Alwis, Malathi de. 1996. 'Gender, Politics and the "Respectable Lady"'. In *Unmaking the Nation: The Politics of Identity and History in Modern Sri Lanka*, edited by P. Jeganathan and Q. Ismail, 137–57. Colombo: Social Scientists' Association.

Berenger, Leon. 2012. 'Three-Wheeler Drivers as Part-Time Sub-Agents a Threat: ALFEA'. *The Sunday Times*, 2012.

Daily Mirror. 2013. 'SL to Cut Down on Maid Exports'. *Daily Mirror*, 2013.

Daily Mirror. 2014. 'SL Mulls Ban on Sending Maids Abroad'. *Daily Mirror*, 2014.

Gamburd, Michele Ruth. 2000. *The Kitchen Spoon's Handle: Transnationalism and Sri Lanka's Migrant Housemaids*. Ithaca, NY: Cornell University Press.

Human Rights Watch (HRW). 2007. 'Exported and Exposed: Abuses against Sri Lankan Domestic Workers in Saudi Arabia, Kuwait, Lebanon, and the United Arab Emirates'. 19 No. 16(C). New York: Human Rights Watch.

Institute of Policy Studies (IPS). 2013. *Migration Profile: Sri Lanka*. Colombo: Institute of Policy Studies of Sri Lanka.

Institute of Policy Studies (IPS). 2014. 'Summary Report: International Conference on Policies for Mainstreaming Migration into Development in Sri Lanka, 14 August 2014'. Colombo: Institute of Policy Studies of Sri Lanka.

International Labour Organisation (ILO). 2006. *Merchants of Labour*. Edited by Christiane Kuptsch. Geneva: Internat. Institute for Labour Studies.

International Labour Organisation (ILO). 2013. *Recruitment Practices of Employment Agencies Recruiting Migrant Workers: A Review Aimed at Improving Recruitment Regulations and Drafting Recruitment Guidelines*. Colombo: ILO.

International Labour Organisation (ILO). 2018. 'Sri Lankan Female Migrant Workers and the Family Background Report'. Colombo: International Labour Organisation (ILO).

Martin, Philip. 2012. 'Reducing Migration Costs and Maximizing Human Development'. In *Global Perspectives on Migration and Development: GFMD Puerto Vallarta and Beyond*, edited by Irena Omelaniuk, 27–52. Global Migration Issues 1. Dordrecht: Springer.

Ministry of Foreign Employment Promotion and Welfare (MFEPW). 2008. 'National Labour Migration Policy for Sri Lanka'. Colombo: Ministry of Foreign Employment Promotion and Welfare.

Shah, Nasra. 2000. 'Relative Success of Male Workers in the Host Country, Kuwait: Does the Channel of Migration Matter?' *International Migration Review* 34 (1): 59–78.

Sri Lanka Bureau of Foreign Employment (SLBFE). 2012. *Annual Statistical Report of Foreign Employment 2011*. Colombo: Sri Lanka Bureau of Foreign Employment.

The Sunday Times. 2014. 'Employment Authority to Regulate Foreign Jobs'. *The Sunday Times*, 2014.

Weeraratne, Bilesha. 2014. 'Restrictions on Female Migrant Workers Discriminatory or Improving Family Wellbeing?' *Daily Mirror*, 2014.

Yahampath, Sita. 2013. 'Enough Is Enough'. *Ceylon Today*, 2013.

5 Manufacturing success

Status and the re-socialisation of migrant labour

This final chapter of fieldwork findings utilises the concept of *status* to situate migrant agency within a framework of temporary labour migration hitherto delineated through the structural and institutional contours of uneven development. *Forced migration*, tempered by the particular limitations of *place*, has given rise to a web of pressures and constraints that expose the conceptual frailty of migrant agency as it is typically conceived, that is, through the lens of free and rational utility-maximisation. For the developmentally marginalised, migration is scarcely voluntary, nor does it often confer sustained (or even immediate) economic benefits. Rather, migration is best understood as a survival strategy intimately tied to Sri Lanka's long history of uneven development. Recast in relation to the gendered socialisation of labour, agency remains a pivotal feature of this strategy. Drawing on Polanyi (2001 [1944]), this chapter examines how the fictitious commodification of Sri Lanka's working classes – within degraded forms of local employment and as 'labour exports' to the Gulf – devalues labour by denying workers' self-esteem in distinctly gendered ways. Synthesising this analysis with Veblen's reflections on consumption (2009 [1899]), it then explores how migrant agency is often expressed through a complex revaluation of migrants' labour, wherein foreign employment offers returnees gender-differentiated opportunities to reconstruct *status* by curating personal narratives of migration and engaging in the conspicuous consumption of remittances. This entails a fundamental paradox, wherein temporary labour migration is frequently abusive and largely unbeneficial in practice, yet by enabling returnees to project material and cultural hallmarks of 'success' is signified as a positive experience. This false pretence of success colours the ambitions and expectations of prospective migrants, inducing a cumulatively causative effect that complements and reinforces the structural and institutional path dependency of temporary labour migration in Sri Lanka.

The first section of this chapter details the exploitation of Sri Lanka's working poor, examining gendered working realities within degraded conditions of local employment and the apparent paradox of locating agency in the typically more exploitative working conditions encountered in foreign employment. The chapter then considers how migrants exercise agency, within the confines of gender norms, as a means of re-socialising their labour by taking ownership of their personal narratives and remitted income to construct or consume *status*. The final section analyses the influence of constructed projections of success that belie the realities of migration as a 'weighted gamble', drawing attention to how the exercise of agency as a superficial re-socialisation of labour creates false expectations for prospective migrants. In this manner, the pursuit of *status* cultivates a social consensus that frequently equates migration with 'success' and harmonises with the structural and institutional pressures of temporary labour migration.

Gendered working realities at home and abroad

Gendered realities of local employment

Examining male and female participants' local occupational categories prior to their migration reveals a clear sexual division of productive and reproductive labour (see Table 5.1). Before leaving for foreign employment, 44 per cent of the women interviewed were performing unpaid care work, while 24 per cent were engaged in informal self-employment and another 24 per cent were 'low-skilled' workers, predominantly within the garments industry. Of the men interviewed, 66 per cent were employed in 'low-skilled' occupations, while engaging in informal self-employment to the same extent as women at 24 per cent. Men were also more often found to be employed in 'high-skilled' occupations or running a business, while absent from the household work performed by women, reflecting Sri Lanka's well-documented gendered asymmetries in skilled and reproductive labour (Gunatilaka 2013).

Interviewees identified a lack of decent local employment as the principal motivation for pursuing foreign employment, reflective of the degraded working conditions underscoring *forced migration* as detailed in Chapter 3. What the interview questions could not capture, however, is the extent to which limited avenues of employment in post-1977 Sri Lanka have intersected with deeply ingrained gendered norms to produce experiences of stigma and exclusion that de-socialises labour by depriving the working poor of *status*. The scope and methodology of the research conducted was not conducive to directly probing these (often sensitive) experiences of stigma found at the intersection of gender

Table 5.1 Occupation before migration

Occupation	*Women %*	*Men %*
Business owner	1.7	4.9
High-skilled	0.0	2.4
Informal self-employment	23.7	24.4
Low-skilled	23.7	65.9
Unpaid care work	44.1	0.0
Unemployed	6.8	2.4
Total	100.0	100.0

and work, but subsequent interviews with key stakeholders corroborated the findings of a number of comprehensive anthropological studies that have explored these tensions in recent years (Gamburd 2000; Kottegoda 2004; Lynch 2007).

Despite their differing foci, these studies all describe the emergence of profound status tension amongst Sri Lanka's poor following the reorganisation of gendered working roles since 1977. In short, the feminisation of breadwinner employment has occurred alongside deepening male underemployment, particularly in the rural economy, prompting a crisis of masculinity that has shaped the social and cultural framing of men's and women's claims to personal integrity. Kottegoda (2004) describes how men have, in the wake of receding employment, turned to ostentatious displays of masculinity by other means, such as gambling, excessive drinking and the conspicuous abstention from care work. Lynch (2007), on the other hand, details how the internal migration of young rural women seeking work in Sri Lanka's EPZs has been accompanied by moral panic over their supposed loss of chastity in the urban milieu, prompting stigmatisation (and devaluation) as *Juki* pieces.[1] Evolving gender norms, strained by a shifting sexual division of labour within a rigid patriarchal framework, have thus produced differentiated challenges to the *status* of male and female workers. Broadly speaking, men are pressured to construct masculinity outside of traditional work roles, while women are expected to navigate stigma and conform to patriarchal expectations while participating in paid work.

These gendered tensions were discussed in the context of feminised labour migration by the SDC program officer, who explained:

> It's a society in which women are primarily responsible for being at home cooking, looking after children, not going for a job, that is mostly the trend in this country for women. Except in the rural areas of course now women are taking higher responsibility. So in those rural areas, in which women do all these household things, the responsibility of earning money lies with the man. When the man does not perform and bring adequate money, it becomes an additional burden of these women, because she has to find the money to feed the children. That is why more and more women are looking for jobs. When a woman looks for a job the man does not take the responsibility of looking after the children.

Gendered realities of foreign employment

Occupation

Even more distinctly than local employment, temporary labour migration is characterised by an unequivocal demarcation of men's and women's work (see Table 5.2). Examining participants' occupational categories during their time working abroad reveals that 93 per cent of women were employed as domestic workers, with only a slim number employed as 'low-skilled' (i.e. non-domestic)

Table 5.2 Occupation during migration

Occupation	*Women %*	*Men %*
Domestic worker	93.2	0.0
High-skilled	1.7	9.8
Low-skilled	5.1	90.2
Total	100.0	100.0

or 'highly-skilled' workers. Conversely, 90 per cent of men were employed as 'low-skilled' workers – a category I used to consolidate a range of jobs that the SLBFE (2012) determines[2] as 'unskilled' (such as labouring, construction and driving) and 'semi-skilled' or 'skilled' (such as carpentry, welding and electrical work) – while the remainder were employed in 'highly-skilled' positions.

Intimately related to occupational categories, gendered differences were also apparent in migrant workers' monthly income and the rate at which remittances were sent home: women averaged a monthly income of Rs14,873 and remitted 85.8 per cent of this income on average, whereas men earned Rs26,402 and remitted 70.7 per cent. As in Sri Lanka, where a stubborn gendered pay gap exists, women's work is devalued in foreign employment and domestic workers command significantly less monthly income than low-waged male workers. However, while live-in positions for domestic workers are ubiquitous and inclusive of basic needs, male workers' higher wages were often offset by expenses in the form of (often hidden) food and accommodation costs, alongside a greater freedom to spend money while socialising. Owing to these differences, women were seen to remit at a higher rate than men, most sending home the entirety of their incomes, save for minor personal expenses or the purchasing of foreign goods to bring back to Sri Lanka.

Working conditions

Working conditions, for both men and women, are seen to be qualitatively worse in West Asia than within Sri Lanka. This is largely due to the presence of the *kafala* system of employment (and a general absence of formal labour laws for foreign workers) throughout the major labour-receiving countries of West Asia: all the Gulf Cooperation Council (GCC) states, along with Jordan and Lebanon (Khan and Harroff-Tavel 2011). The *kafala* system is a sponsorship program that ties the visa and legal status of low-waged migrants and domestic workers to their employment contracts with *kafeels* (employers); they are, as such, unable to leave employment or change employers without compromising the legality of their presence in the host country (Khan and Harroff-Tavel 2011). This visa conditionality affords employers carte blanche over the terms of employment, contravening basic human and working rights and resulting in rampant malpractice:

> As immigration status depends on a contractual relationship, migrant workers can be made to accept terms and conditions of employment at variance with those they were promised before departure from their home countries.
>
> (Khan and Harroff-Tavel 2011, 297)

While my interviews did not specifically probe incidents of abuse or mistreatment given the potentially traumatic nature of these experiences, participants were offered an opportunity to discuss any hardships they encountered while working abroad at their own discretion. These experiences, too, took on starkly gendered differences, deriving from the contrasting forms of vulnerability experienced by migrant domestic workers employed within private households vis-à-vis low-waged migrants labouring under more formal employment arrangements.

Table 5.3 details the main hardships discussed by men and women alike. Only 23 per cent of respondents reported that they had not experienced any hardships during foreign employment, including 27 per cent of women and 17 per cent of men. Some of the most common complaints were experienced by male and female migrants alike, such as being overworked and struggling with foreign foods, languages and climates. Other hardships were more closely aligned with women's working realities. Physical abuse, for example, was almost exclusively experienced by migrant domestic workers, whose confinement to the private sphere of the home[3] renders their working conditions and personal treatment entirely at the discretion of the employer. The vulnerability inherent in this working arrangement is underscored by a recurring observation that instances of physical abuse share little correlation with job experience, but rather arise from the probability and chance of being assigned to a 'good' or 'bad' employer. Particular countries of destination, religious ties and methods of recruitment – that is, random agency placements opposed to direct recruitment via private networks – are pertinent factors contributing to the characterisation of domestic work as a

Table 5.3 Main hardship endured during migration

Occupation	*Women %*	*Men %*
Arrested	1.7	9.8
Deception	1.7	12.2
Food, language or climate	11.9	19.5
Injury or medical issues	11.9	9.8
Overworked	17.0	14.6
Pay withheld	5.1	4.9
Physically abused	13.6	2.4
Underpaid	0.0	4.9
Other	10.2	4.9
None reported	27.1	17.1
Total	100.0	100.0

'weighted gamble' where working conditions and personal safety are highly dependent upon the employer and their family.

Speaking to the arbitrariness of domestic worker abuse, a woman from Thavapuram – an experienced migrant on her third trip abroad – recalled:

> During my third visit to Saudi, in Dammam, I was mistreated. After working for a month, when I asked for my salary, they didn't give it. I told that I have to send it to my kids, then they gave the money. We have to give it to them for the money to be deposited, but they kept delaying. When I asked about it, they twisted my arm and my mistress told her husband and he kicked me and beat me.

Another migrant, a woman from Galle who mortgaged her land to finance her employment as a domestic worker in Lebanon, spoke of similar abuse:

> My time there was very painful. I once got beaten by the master for misplacing one of the children's glasses. I had to wash five bathrooms. While I had my meals, if someone came to that house, I had to go down three stories to open the door. It was so sad. I used to cry all the time. Whenever they went out, they locked me inside.

An older migrant from Negombo, who had made repeated visits to Kuwait beginning in the early 1980s, spoke of helping other domestic workers who were facing abuse:

> I saw how maids were treated in other houses. I saw how maids jumped over the walls. I have helped them as well. I tell my madam, about these maids. I have given food to women who didn't get food to eat.... My madam worked in the Indonesian Embassy. I informed my madam, she would inform our embassy.... There are so many problems. Humiliations, by masters and even children. The children can be very abusive at times, they hit maids, they burn them sometimes.

Meanwhile, those who found work with decent employers avoided instances of abuse and were more likely to express overall satisfaction. Recruitment via private networks is an important factor in this regard, as migrants discussed the benefit of arranging work with an employer who can be vouched for by friends or family members. A woman from Negombo explained:

> The madam and the boss have to be good. Some people say they have had bad experiences, but my Aunt said they [the employers] are good so I was sure.

Elsewhere, the experiences of a Muslim woman from Polgahawela suggest how, in her case, common religious ties may have shaped positive experiences with her employer:

> These three necklaces brother Zareen bought. He was a very good employer and used to give me gifts during charity period, *Sadaqah*.... The employer was good. After I came back to Sri Lanka and went for check-up, I failed my medical, so I informed my employer and they sent money for my operation. After one year they requested me to come back again. But my husband refused.

While overall grievances were slightly lower amongst women interviewed in Polgahawela – where all identified as Muslim and most arranged employment through private contacts – incidents of physical abuse were nonetheless present, suggesting that religious bonds and direct placements only go so far in mitigating the sheer misfortune of working for an abusive employer.

Male workers, on the other hand, were also more likely to experience distinct forms of hardship during their employment, particularly deception regarding wages and – relatedly – being arrested for contravening visa conditionality. Agents or employers were seen to deceive male migrants by offering greater wages during recruitment than were actually paid under employment, with income shortfalls arising either from sheer underpayment (often achieved by way of duplicate contracts) or by exacting hidden expenses by charging compulsory pay deductions for food and accommodation. These circumstances are often compounded by exposure to harsh working and living conditions. In instances where pay and working conditions are unbearable, men – relatively uninhibited compared to domestic workers – sometimes break the terms of their visa by pursuing unauthorised and informal work with another employer. 'Outworking', as participants referred to it, allows men to walk away from mistreatment, overwork or underpay, but carries with it the additional challenges of private living expenses and a short but inevitable jail sentence when leaving the country.

The experiences of a young man from Polgahawela, who migrated to Qatar to work as a driver, illustrate typical practices of deception and hidden costs:

> Nothing promised happened there. They promised to give me free food, free accommodation and a basic salary of Rs1,000 per day. I was told that I could also do overtime. When I calculated all of these, my salary increased to approximately Rs65,000 per month. I was much convinced to go there. What happened there was the reverse. They deducted money from my salary and said they did not promise any offers as such. Someone convinced my mind to do the job for some time, saying that they would look into some possible changes with the passage of time. Believing their word, I signed the contract ... I could have illegally worked and earned quite a lot. Due to my children, I did not want to land up in any trouble. So, I did not choose that way.

Another young man, from Thavapuram, faced similar problems and resorted to outworking in order to save sufficient income to send home:

> I was sent to Saudi Arabia for a hospital cleaning job in 2007. At that time my agency agreed to pay 400 riyal to me in our money, Rs10,000. After I went there I got only 300 riyal for my monthly salary, and I couldn't save any money. I spent 200 riyal for my food there, so how could I save money? I worked there only two months, then I left my company and I worked illegally in a textile shop as salesman … I was arrested by the police and they handed me over to the Sri Lankan embassy, who made arrangements to send us home.

Similar to the experiences of domestic workers, the likelihood of male workers encountering employer malpractice appeared to be determined primarily by chance, as conveyed through the reflections of a successful Negombo migrant:

> I went as a driver, but I got a job as a company driver and that was a good opportunity. I was scared as to what would happen. I wondered if I would face many problems like others and whether I will not get my salary. But the place I got was very good.

However, as deception often stems from recruitment agents within Sri Lanka (ILO 2013), it was not surprising that the community in Thavapuram – where sub-agent malpractice is rife – experienced the greatest concentration of serious grievances amongst male workers.

The paradox of migrant agency

The degree of hardship and uncertainty observed in returnees' experiences of foreign employment, coupled with the limited and generally subsistent benefits of remittance income discussed in Chapter 3, poses an apparent paradox for conventional understandings of migrant agency. If temporary labour migration constitutes an expensive weighted gamble, involving a high likelihood of some form of personal suffering and little evidence of substantive or sustainable returns, why do individual men and women pursue such work? Such a decision hardly reflects what neoclassical economists would identify as rational, utility-maximising behaviour. As one woman from Negombo, who experienced great hardship during her time abroad, tellingly stated:

> What I say is that there's no use of going abroad, you can earn more here than going abroad. That is what I tell others also, who intend to go abroad. If they are younger, they can go to a garment factory, and here we can do dry-fish business, from which we can earn enough.

Structural-determinist and agency-centric perspectives each offer an intuitive explanation for this paradox. The first is that the macroeconomic structures of forced migration discussed in Chapter 3 are so overwhelming that migrants are unable to make empowered decisions and are led into temporary labour migration by virtue of their socio-economic marginalisation. The second contends that migrants' exercise of agency is constrained by an imperfect supply of information regarding the costs and benefits of temporary labour migration, distorting otherwise rational decision-making. Neither explanation is sufficient. According absolute sway to the economic structures of migration denies individual migrants' capacity to act meaningfully and entertains a determinism that discredits the important contributions of historical-structuralist analysis. Blaming information asymmetries is similarly unhelpful, as it effectively condemns social reality for trammelling the ideal abstraction of *homo economicus*, without scrutinising *why* or *how* knowledge becomes imperfect or whether human decision-making extends beyond a narrow economic rationality.

An observation by the SDC program officer touched incisively on an alternate explanation that had emerged from the interviews conducted with migrant returnees:

> People don't have much information and understanding about all of what is happening here because information at the workplace is from mouth to mouth, it is from the neighbours, and even if I have gone through a bitter experience, we have a culture in which I do not necessarily come back and share my bitter experience with the family.

This understanding suggests that enculturated notions of personal integrity are pivotal in determining what information, codified through personal experience and material signifiers, migrants choose to relay to others upon their return. It speaks to a fundamentally different conceptualisation of migrant agency, hinging not upon economic freedom (which is noticeably absent from many migrant realities) but the opportunity to re-author personal experiences and curate representations of self and identity that are consistent with cultural expectations.

This resonates with the deprivation of *status* experienced by the working poor within Sri Lanka, for whom labour migration plausibly offers a spatial vacuum in which personal experiences of exploitation and degradation can be endured outside the purview of peer scrutiny and later be reconstructed as narratives of success that align with prevailing gender norms. It suggests that migrants make decisions without possessing realistic insights into the economic realities of labour migration, but also that sheer economic calculation may play second fiddle to cultural impetuses for pursuing migration in the first place. As the following section details, the conspicuous expenditure of remittances on status goods is seen to complement the construction of gendered notions of success. For men, this often entailed the performance of masculinity through the medium of material wealth, while women were more likely to embody patriarchal expectations of chastity and care.

Through this lens, structure and agency are released from zero-sum antagonism, and the paradox dissolves. Processes of uneven development do structure forced migration through the degradation of local employment, but an inability to make decisions that yield positive economic outcomes does not negate the exercise of migrant agency, as agency can be more broadly interpreted as the motivation to reclaim personal *status* lost within those same processes of uneven development. Labour has been de-socialised under Sri Lankan neoliberalism, caught between the precarious realities of local underemployment and temporary labour migration; the crucial difference is that stigma abounds in the former, while the latter potentially offers sufficient privacy and remittances to construct *status* in lieu of substantially altering socio-economic circumstances. It should be noted, however, that those migrating under acute duress (as in Thavapuram) remain more likely to be impelled by sheer survival than personal considerations of *status* and that the motivations for migration cannot be unilaterally accounted for by any one factor.

Migrant agency: constructing success amidst exploitation

A prominent theme that emerged from interviews with returned migrants, sometimes explicitly but more often implicitly, was the degree of prestige associated with temporary labour migration. Many discussed experiencing a greater social standing within their community after returning home; almost all spent some portion of their remittances on status-enhancing goods – jewellery, fine clothing and a variety of home furnishings and consumer durables. This section examines the social and material construction of success observed amongst migrant returnees, before situating these experiences within overarching gendered norms and the perceived esteem attached to temporary labour migration. Recognising that discussions of personal success and *status* can be quite sensitive, interviews with migrant returnees did not press on these topics, instead asking broad questions about lifestyle changes that allowed participants to disclose opinions they felt comfortable airing. In light of the approach taken, this section of analysis supplements migrant insights by drawing extensively on researcher observations and secondary interviews with key stakeholders working with migrants and their communities.

Narrating and consuming success

From stigma to status

Consistent with an understanding of migrant agency rooted in *status*, the avoidance of stigma in existing lines of work was occasionally discussed by participants as a key motivation for pursuing temporary labour migration.

A middle-aged former fisherman from Negombo explained how the occupation he was born into compelled him to travel abroad for work as a young man:

> I wanted to get rid of the fishing lifestyle. I will not let my children be in this fishing society. I have been rejected so many times because of being a son of a fisherman. That is why I wanted to leave this society, anyhow, and have a better life.

Elsewhere a woman in Akmeemana, who had first internally migrated to Katunayake for a job in a garments factory, but then decided to migrate abroad with a group of co-workers, intimated a similar motivation for leaving, stating that she didn't leave for financial reasons, but because 'we felt like doing it'.

Poor social positioning was not only a direct motivation for foreign employment for some, but also presented itself as a barrier to respectable local employment for others, as such jobs are highly coveted and frequently tied to social class or political fealty.

A young man from Negombo explained his choice to migrate as emerging from his dissatisfaction with repeated attempts to find decent work in Sri Lanka:

> After leaving school, I wanted to do something good for my life. During that time, migration was the best option we saw at that age. I worked as a voluntary teacher, and I could not make the job permanent. After that I was fed up. I worked for two years. When they did not give us permanent jobs, I wanted to quit. After that there was an exam for security officers, I got the highest marks in Gampaha district from that, but I could not get the job at the harbour. Then I went for an interview at Lakspray. But I could not get both the jobs due to political reasons. At that time both these organisations were government organisations.

Another, a well-educated Muslim woman from Polgahawela, complained bitterly of how a lack of standing and political connections had prevented her from finding work as a teacher and convinced her to migrate:

> I wanted to work as a teacher, but didn't have the connections in my community. We could pay politicians for teaching jobs, but still wouldn't get any work.

With much of Sri Lanka's working poor unable to command acceptance and respect within the narrow confines of local employment, temporary labour migration offers reprieve as a form of employment that is socially perceived to carry esteem.

As explained by the SDC program officer, the social deficit between stigma and *status* is often a more compelling consideration than the convenience or remuneration attached to work:

> We hardly find willingness from our women to come and work somewhere in Colombo or other cities, whereas they might go for a similar job for a few thousand rupees more than they get here, or the same amount, or even a lesser amount, but they prefer to go anywhere else – to other countries – than finding a job in the country. Probably they think they will be seen at work by other people and they will also come to know about it. It has been difficult to understand why they do not want to accept jobs in Colombo, but rather prefer going abroad.

This observation was echoed by the project coordinator at the Colombo ILO office:

> I mean even if they're a carpenter or a labourer, there is still a minimum six or seven hundred rupees a day. If we need someone to come to our home, say to do some of the heavy-duty things, like polish the floors or whatever, we still give them food, plus 750 rupees minimum daily. That is not so much, but I mean some would prefer to get even slightly higher, but work overseas, rather than work here because it looks fancier, or sounds fancier … they choose overseas migration, and there's also this perception of going abroad, having the independence and freedom. Some people, they have money here, but you would find they still want to go abroad because they view people who have gone overseas in a different light. As in, okay, you have had the resources, you have had the freedom, you have seen the world and you have come back kind of thing. So it's kind of a trend or a fashion as well.

Some migrant returnees, too, mentioned how they were viewed differently before and after migration, noting that their social standing had changed after returning from abroad.

A woman from Akmeemana reflected on her family's social standing since returning from her job as a domestic worker in Kuwait:

> People look at us differently now. We don't look like beggars anymore. Even when my child goes to school, she used to wear the same clothes every day, but it's not like that now. We feel more respected. We used to be ignored at social gatherings, now people pay us more attention.

A woman from Polgahawela similarly ranked social acceptance amongst the changes to have come about from her migration:

> We have a stable life, no money problems, people are good with us now, we don't have much difficulties

Meanwhile, a male neighbour commented that:

> No one paid us any attention before, but now many people show respect to us.

The attachment of prestige to migration, irrespective of whether the trip had been successful in the eyes of the migrant themselves, was captured when an elderly man from Akmeemana quipped with annoyance:

> I didn't want social recognition. I wanted to buy a boat of my own. Now I use a friend's boat.

These admissions speak chiefly to the idea of gaining respect by way of improved material circumstances, for example, by using remittances to ameliorate prior experiences of stigma arising from dressing poorly and living in debt. The importance of these forms of status consumption is analysed shortly. It is first necessary, however, to address a complex attitudinal facet to the social standing of migrant returnees that takes shape around the tension between traditional Sri Lankan values (whether Sinhala-Buddhist, Sinhala-Catholic, Tamil-Hindu or Muslim) and foreign values adopted during migration. Broadly speaking, returnees sought social acceptance by reaffirming traditional gender norms yet pursued social distinction by asserting foreign (and often conflicting) values. While the majority of experiences reflected some combination of these ‘passive’ and ‘active’ strategies of migrant agency, the strain between reasserting and contesting established values was a defining feature of how most returnees framed their personal migration narratives and constructed integrity upon their reintegration in Sri Lanka.

Attitudinal change

When asked if her lifestyle had changed following migration, a middle-aged woman from Negombo bluntly proclaimed:

> No, it’s the same. Some people go abroad and change, but that is not good. We must stay the Sri Lankan way.

She had experienced modest success during her migration, earning enough money to fill in a plot of marshy land on which they would later build their house from income earned through her husband’s fishing and her own cooking and selling of Sri Lankan ‘short eats’.[4] In essence, by supporting her husband’s traditional livelihood and performing traditional feminine duties herself – that is, by cooking from home alongside carrying out other care duties – her reintegration into the local community involved a reaffirmation of established norms. Migration, and her remitted income, enabled a passive reclamation of *status* through an enhanced capacity to survive while adhering to local ways of life.

Her attitude stands in polar opposition to the previously mentioned former fisherman, living just two streets away, who left Sri Lanka on account of social persecution. His first migration, to Qatar, had resulted in illegal outworking and remittances sufficient only for his family to eat. He was, however, able to carry some money home in person after eventually working multiple jobs. When asked about the changes he experienced in his lifestyle following his return he explained:

> I changed a lot. Once I came back, I bought a bike, and that was the biggest thing to happen in my village. And I lost so many friends whom I used to have here before. Sometimes they came to hurt me, fight with me. That is when I changed a lot. It is not that I did not accept them, but I just did not

> want to live that life. I just lived alone, because I wanted to live a good life. I want to succeed in my life.

The value placed in his changing attitudes was clear, as rather than reintegrating in his home community, he restlessly used savings to pursue further migration, travelling to a range of countries as a ship-hand. Remarking on his life as a repeat migrant, he was particularly proud of the self-worth his experiences had afforded:

> I got so many experiences by going abroad. I told you that I have studied only up to Grade 8. But today, I feel like I have gained so many experiences by going to different countries and working, more than a person who has done even A Levels; even I have some knowledge of English which I can manage at certain times.

A third migrant from Negombo, a young man who had taken an atypical path by working as a welder on a US army base in Iraq, also spoke of experiencing a shift in values:

> I couldn't achieve what I wanted to, but I had a good exposure to a different social class. I didn't get to do any other kind of work, so I didn't get an exposure in that sense. But I learnt about a different lifestyle.... That exposure to a different culture has changed my life. I also felt that our lifestyle is very primitive and not developed.

Unlike the former fisherman, whose struggle to reintegrate pushed him abroad again, the younger man remained in his local community, where he continues to work as a welder with aspirations to run his own business. While migration had not been as financially rewarding as he had hoped, his impressions of people he had met abroad compelled him to emulate those values and carry himself differently in Sri Lanka.

Thus, within the same Sinhala-Catholic community in Negombo, these three migrants adopted varying degrees of attitudinal change that alternately upheld traditional values, rejected them forthright or represented an attempted reconciliation of local life with foreign values. All three can be understood as attempts to use the agency afforded by migration to achieve a sense of personal integrity: by conforming to pre-existing standards of worth; by emulating foreign values to stand apart; or – as was most often the case – by accommodating some combination of the two.

While exposure to foreign countries carries social esteem, the adoption of foreign attitudes can conflict with traditional ways of life. The ILO project coordinator described the challenge of reintegrating as a success:

> The thing is this: there are two things that happen. Sometimes you are noticed more and you're recognised better if you've been overseas and you

> come back. And if your family members run circles around you, that's one side of things. There's also another side of things where you find yourself not being able to fit back in with your family. You've modernised to a certain extent, but your husband is still chewing betel and wearing a sarong, and you know, there are certain issues where you can't reconcile and get back with the family. And also you find that you can't adjust to the social community structures that you were once part of. And that's a reason to also re-migrate.

Typically, then, those who have reintegrated well tend to have altered their social standing by embracing some aspects of traditional values while flouting others. Gendered differences are important as, outlined earlier in the chapter, men and women experience qualitatively different challenges to *status* under Sri Lanka's patriarchal framework as it confronts a crisis of masculinity. For women returnees seeking to reclaim integrity by reaffirming traditional feminine values, migration is often expressed as an extension of care roles, with remittances a way of adequately fulfilling motherly duties, such as providing education for the children and being a dutiful wife.

When asked whether she experienced any personal benefits from migration, a young mother from Polgahawela responded:

> Not really … I was able to complete certain tasks and I am happy. I raised my kids and the family has an improved status in the society.

It became immediately apparent that, in this case, her individual experience of migration had been reframed as care work for her family. This feeling was echoed by her neighbour, who answered:

> No, it was all for my family's life.

In Thavapuram, women expressed like sentiments. A middle-aged woman said:

> I feel proud to have looked after my kids and they are grownups now. I've never thought of my own benefits. I have the happiness that I earned and looked after my kids.

An older woman living nearby cast her experience, with noted pride, in light of preserving her marriage alongside the absence of migration:

> Our life is upgraded from my foreign employment. Some husbands have new marriages after sending off their first wife to foreign employment, but my husband is not like that.

Discussing the theme of fidelity, an officer within the Department of Labour expressed concern that women were frequently subject to sexual abuse in foreign employment but would rarely, if ever, discuss these experiences for fear of jeopardising their marriage by being perceived to be unchaste:

> In the Middle East they are using domestic workers for sex work within the household. For husbands, for sons, even for relatives. They believe it is better to keep adultery in the house, behind closed doors. When they come back, no one talks about it, they only mention the good things and never the bad experiences. There is also social stigma for women who have been sexually abused when they reintegrate into their home communities.

Meanwhile, some male returnees were also seen to re-socialise their labour through traditional notions of masculinity, converging in particular on the widespread desire to start a business or engage in autonomous self-employment as discussed in Chapter 3. Central to aspirations of self-employment is the social respectability attached to independence from debt and the ability to provide a stable income for the family: these are basic needs, but nevertheless hard for most men to satisfy amidst the conditions of local employment.

One man, a tuk driver from Negombo, expressed his happiness about being able to financially support his children and achieve independence from debt:

> Yes, we have benefitted. I put money into the children's accounts. We have a house to stay in so everything is OK. We used to live on rent, but now it's OK.

Another, from Thavapuram, had more modest achievements but discernible satisfaction in providing for his family:

> Yes, I am very happy about it. Our survival depended on my income. My family got healthy food.

Yet, alongside the influence of established gender roles, migrants almost ubiquitously sought to reintegrate beyond the scope of traditional values too. Having typically worked in conditions that afforded greater social and material freedoms than women, men often spoke about their exposure to – and desire to emulate – foreign attitudes and lifestyles. These interactions were typically discussed in terms of personal growth and cultural understanding, but tended to manifest materially through the purchase of foreign goods and clothing. Women too would often wear clothing gifted from their employers and, if able to travel freely in their spare time, purchase jewellery and goods from abroad.

As the senior director at IPS put it:

> They are like a frog in a well before going, but once they go there, they are open to broader horizons. They know more about the world, so they want to have better comforts and better facilities.

The ILO project officer explained how these broader horizons intersect with conspicuous expenditures:

> I mean, how can they face their community? They have sacrificed a lot of things and they have gone overseas, and they need to look like they've been overseas and come back. So yeah, the perfumes, the clothes, the handbags, I guess the big TV, the big fridge, you know, whatever. Some don't even have an electricity connection and they have big electrical items. They don't really think about that.

It is here, in the reification of foreign values as material possessions, that remittances begin to take on a different and distinctly social function as a means of constructing success through the consumption of status goods.

Jewellery, clothing and durables

The ostentatious display of status goods was perhaps the most consistent observation amongst the migrant returnees interviewed, with all but the most unsuccessful partaking in some form of conspicuous consumption. Migrants' houses were routinely larger than others in the community and sometimes featured patios adorned with Roman columns, or contained ornate lights and entertainment units that were only called into service when social visits trumped the cost of turning the electricity on. Participants themselves often wore prominent jewellery and unmistakeably foreign clothing, often in contrast to their non-migrant neighbours. Assessed quantifiably, 58 per cent of all migrants spent at least some of their remittances on jewellery, while 63 per cent spent at least some portion on consumer durables, second only to day-to-day consumption (at 86 per cent) in terms of sheer prevalence as a category of remittance expenditure.

Responding to this observation, the ILO project officer explained the importance of these status goods as means of being perceived as a success:

> They will also buy consumer and durable goods because it's a status symbol. If you've gone overseas to the Middle East for employment, and if you don't have a big fridge and a big TV and a big surround-sound system, then no one will take any notice of you. So their goal is to perhaps build a house, educate their children, but they end up getting distracted and then spending on these consumer durables.

The importance of being noticed in this manner was sometimes discussed quite frankly by migrants themselves.

One man from Negombo, who had travelled to Saudi Arabia as a gardener in 1986, recalled how he was unable to achieve much with the money he earned over three years of foreign employment, returning with only Rs11,000 after donating some to the church, supporting his sister's marriage and repaying loans.

But he also came back with a gold chain, two gold rings and a bracelet, which afforded him a sense of *status*:

> When I came back with all that jewellery, I came back with a different feeling than when I went. It was kind of to show off as a person who had come back from being abroad.

His friend, a fellow tuk driver in Negombo, reported similar feelings:

> You might change if you go to another country. But we have reached a certain standard, even our clothes are different. Everyone wants to stand out and show off a bit.

Elsewhere, a woman in Akmeemana spoke about her jewellery as the fruit of the hardship she endured as a domestic worker in Lebanon:

> I felt very happy. I felt that, I have earned all this by doing a lot of dirty work, washing toilets. I used to wear the jewellery to weddings, almsgivings, family gatherings. I felt very good, felt proud. I used to tell everyone how hard it was to work there, and that with great difficulty I earned all this.

To a great extent, these purchases can be characterised as a material expression of foreign values, consumed in tandem with attitudinal change; with certain consumer goods and styles of clothing hard to find or afford in Sri Lanka, goods brought back from abroad can signify worldly exposure and material affluence that sets migrants apart from their contemporaries.

A senior researcher at the Women and Media Collective (WMC), who has been working with migrant domestic workers for the past three decades, spoke about the enduring tendency to flaunt certain goods as an act of claiming *status*:

> When they come back from the Middle East, it's gold jewellery. And then, you know, different shoes, handbags, and definitely it is a social communication.... For them, the kind of designs and the bangles, and the necklaces and the earrings and all, you don't get it here. And also I think the gold they want is slightly yellowish, and it shines a lot, it's very simple and an investment in many ways because your status goes up, and you can bargain for a better husband or for your child or whatever.

However, there are parallel (and complementary) explanations for why so many status goods are purchased abroad, rather than within Sri Lanka's duty-free shops and jewellery markets.

One crucial observation is that gold jewellery is not a typical status good. As is reflected by the number of migrants who pawned jewellery in order to finance their recruitment fees, gold jewellery is treated – as elsewhere in South Asia – as an important form of currency that is both relatively immune to the vicissitudes of inflation and is highly portable relative to other assets. As Gamburd notes:

> Jewellery and expensive electrical goods act as a form of savings; worn, used, and displayed in times of prosperity, the items can be sold if needed and do not depreciate as quickly as the Sri Lankan rupee.... Not merely for show, these 'luxury' items provide a form of savings safer and more logical than money in the hand or in the bank.
>
> (2000, 43)

This is a particularly important recognition when gold jewellery is purchased abroad by women as it represents a highly personal form of wealth, if not inalienable from the individual then certainly more intimate than remittances sent home to be spent at the family's discretion. Furthermore, jewellery plays a vital role in dowry payments in Sri Lanka; having a lot of gold to offer can allow a family to realise upwards social mobility through arranging a 'good' marriage.

A second observation, emerging from interviews with key stakeholders, is that making foreign purchases is itself a highly socialised activity, influenced by peer pressure and what might be termed 'pecuniary emulation'.

The senior director at IPS commented on this tendency:

> When they see their colleagues wearing a good necklace or bracelet or whatever other jewellery their colleagues are wearing, they also come under pressure, they also feel like they should buy one ... that is one reason, so they can be on par with their colleagues. See, once the migrants go to the Middle Eastern countries they are in a foreign land and they become insecure. The only way they gain security is by developing connections with their Sri Lankan colleagues, so when they get into those networks, they find those with different lifestyles, jewellery, all that, so that influences them to buy it. Even though the same jewellery items are in the duty-free shop or the local street markets in Pettah....

This impression was echoed by the WMC researcher, who illustrated the convenience and recreational aspect of purchasing goods abroad while talking about her own research findings amongst migrant domestic workers in Jordan:

> When I was in Jordan, and that was the first time I actually worked with any type of migrant workers overseas, the women were talking about buying the refrigerator, and buying this and that, and I asked them, 'Why do you want to buy, when you can buy it there?' I think one of the reasons that some women gave was that 'No, but it is easier for me to buy it here' when they were out there. I think they feel that they have a choice ... because they're alone in the duty-free, they may not come home with their friends; over there they'll go shopping with their friends.

A high incidence of foreign purchases was borne out by survey data recorded during interviews, but not evenly across categories of expenditure. Fifty per cent of all migrants spent some income buying consumer durables from abroad, while only 29 per cent spent income on foreign-bought jewellery, suggesting that the tendency to purchase status goods during migration applied less readily to jewellery – perhaps because it is commonly and cheaply available within Sri Lanka. A number of women also reported receiving jewellery and clothing as gifts from their employers, possibly contributing to this discrepancy too.

In sum, it is possible to identify a variegated set of incentives that encourage migrants to spend their income, remitted or in person, on a variety of status goods. Whether consumed in the conspicuous emulation of foreign tastes, pragmatically as a personal asset easily redeemed in times of need or marriage, or simply by following the suit of other migrants, these displays of material wealth were widespread amongst the returnees interviewed and represent a fundamental signifier of successful migration. It is, perhaps, the principal means through which returnees and their families can claim *status* in the wake of their migration; the attitudinal navigation of traditional and imported social norms may form the deeper narrative of migrants' social standing within their home communities, but the conspicuous consumption of status goods provides a tangible means of constructing and projecting notions of self-worth, pride and integrity.

Re-socialising through consumption: between Veblen and Polanyi

The term 'conspicuous consumption' finds its origin in Veblen's *Theory of the Leisure Class* (2009 [1899]), where the concept is framed as a form of pecuniary emulation wherein lower social classes attempt to reproduce the standards of 'reputable and honorific consumption' set by the leisure class in any given society. Recognising that migrants' incomes facilitate such consumption is not, as has been suggested by neoclassical critiques (de Haas 2010), a value judgement that characterises such expenditures as wasteful or unproductive. Rather, Veblen's contribution was to identify that, cutting across the contextual specificities of different human societies, there is a general tendency to locate virtue in displays of material wealth or idle leisure, while ascribing subordinate social standing to those classes lumped with performing manual productive labour. Acts of conspicuous consumption, then, can be interpreted as efforts to overcome the general deficit of *status* experienced by the working poor, within the existing boundaries of societal worth. Under conditions of decent employment, with more equitable returns to labour, the working poor can have enough disposable income to partly socialise their labour through the consumption of status goods. This was noted, too, by T. H. Marshall (1992 [1950]) when he discussed the improving circumstances of Britain's (white and male) working poor at the end of the nineteenth century, identifying access to 'material civilisation' – afforded by larger incomes and cheaper goods – as a key foothold in winning social rights for the proletariat. And, as bell hooks remarks, this has perhaps become more pertinent still following the global consolidation of consumer capitalism:

> Tragically, the poor and well-off are often united in a capitalist culture by their shared obsession with consumption … the only way out of class shame is through conspicuous consumption.
>
> (hooks 2000, 46)

This observation takes on greater relevance in light of the social upheaval described in Karl Polanyi's *The Great Transformation* (2001), in which the invention and imposition of market society disembeds economic activity from its social, political and cultural context. These non-economic institutions are instead subsumed by the formal economic rationality of the market, which, in due process, de-socialises labour (along with land and money) as a *fictitious commodity* that is expected to respond to the law of the market. An emphasis on de-socialisation is important, as the defining feature of fictitious commodification is the erosion of decent work – resulting from the expectation that labour will be 'sold' as cheaply as 'the market' will bear – and with it the more equitable distribution of incomes and social rights. Played out in the context of Europe, Polanyi identifies a spontaneous social response to the de-socialisation caused by market society, taking shape as a protective countermovement to re-embed the economy (and, with it, labour, land and money) through social protection afforded by labour laws and the welfare state. Understood in Veblenian terms, the restitution of decent work granted the working classes sufficient income and standards of living to partake in pecuniary emulation and redress the deficit of *status* suffered under market society. Irrespective of the eventual trajectory of this 'double movement' between market society and social protectionism in Europe, there has been no broad protective countermovement following South Asia's exposure to market society and there appears little sign of one taking shape (Breman 2009).

Sri Lanka's 1977 neoliberal turn has been cited as a watershed moment for exacerbating processes of uneven development precisely because the reforms ushered in a localised vision of market society (Biyanwila 2011). Sri Lanka's working poor, already encumbered by a long history of accumulation by subordination rooted in colonialism, have not so much lost conditions of decent employment as had them stifled before their inception. Fictitious commodification has ensured that local employment does not offer enough disposable income for the working poor to socialise their labour, preserving a deficit of social standing that there has been no widespread social or political response to (aside from two failed Marxist insurrections or the civil war[5]). Participation in temporary labour migration fills this void by allowing all but the most disadvantaged migrants to re-socialise their labour through the conspicuous consumption of remittances. While remittances do not provide enough income for investment or sustainable economic benefit, they do often provide enough to construct a material edifice of wealth that connotes social and economic standing: be it through housing, jewellery and clothes, durables or whatever else.

This observation resonates ominously with Veblen's own description of the socio-economic realities belying conspicuous consumption by the lower classes:

> In any community where conspicuous consumption is an element of the scheme of life, an increase in an individual's ability to pay is likely to take the form of an expenditure for some accredited line of conspicuous consumption.... Through this discrimination in favour of visible consumption it has come about that the domestic life of most classes is relatively shabby, as compared with the éclat of that overt portion of their life that is carried on before the eyes of observers.
>
> (Veblen 2009 [1899], 76)

Thus, migrants' conspicuous consumption of remittances is not normatively condemned as wasteful or even arbitrary, but rather seen as a deceptively shallow facade of prosperity erected in the spirit of human dignity lost through the fictitious commodification of labour within Sri Lanka's uneven development.

Keeping up with the Jayasuriyas?

An elderly woman living in Negombo, formerly a domestic worker who had spent 15 years in Kuwait but now terminally ill with cancer, described in detail the changes to her family's lifestyle and social standing throughout the course of her time abroad:

> The way we lived before, we could not even buy any clothes, not even once a year. After I went, I sent money to buy new clothes. There was not much change in food because, either way, we eat. There was a slight change after I came back. The type of food changed after I came, because of what I brought. We had the feeling that we were much better now. We had an opportunity to wear new clothes and socialise, used to feel proud of all that. And we had the new equipment to use, so we felt good'. She then paused and added, 'But, now I feel that we are back in the same place.'

Living and working with her daughter, who had previously worked in a garment factory but was now pursuing self-employment by pickling fish in their small home near the fish market, it was indeed hard to discern any lasting traces of prosperity from such a long time spent abroad. Her story typifies the thin veneer of success that conspicuous consumption most often affords; an outwards construction of *status* that betrays the stubbornly difficult material realities that so often cause migrant families to pursue repeat or flow-on migration.

An underappreciated consequence of constructing a pretence of success, however, is that its social acknowledgement infers the transmission of unrealistic assumptions about migration. Just as women who remain silent about experiencing abuse for fear of social transgression communicate misleadingly positive impressions of domestic work, so too does the conspicuous projection of material prosperity convey inflated estimations of migrants' wealth and standards of living. When, as was the case in all four of the fieldwork locations, an entire community is heavily engaged in temporary labour migration the apparent wealth and success of returned migrants can create a strong incentive for others to migrate too. This was evident in the interviews with returnees, as many linked their pre-migration ambitions to 'living like others' or, as one young mother from Negombo remarked more candidly:

> Seeing other houses of those who have been abroad, I thought maybe I also will be able to have success in life like that.

Another, a middle-aged man also from Negombo, mentioned similar aspirations:

> When seeing their lives, their houses, I also wanted to have a life like that.

The senior director at IPS explained how this desire to emulate takes shape:

> So-and-so has been overseas and has gained experience, worked in different working environments, all those things do work in their minds before. And sometimes there can be peer pressure from other colleagues who have migrated, you know, in a village if the adjoining house the daughter has gone, even as a domestic, and comes back and boasts that she brings two TV sets and a washing machine the one next door feels that she should keep up with her peers.... Even if the employment overseas is not superior to the employment available in the local market the imagination is that it is going to be superior, so on that basis they expect higher wages plus better-quality employment, a combination of both.

Having experienced similar scenarios while working with migrant communities, the SDC program officer conveyed a similar understanding:

> The moment you come to Sri Lanka the little amount of money you bring you don't necessarily spend for good purposes, whereas you just lavishly spend them at the duty-free shops buying liquor boxes, cologne or perfume bottles and televisions and so on. Because that is the picture they want to show to society when they come, with big gold chains. But if you really go into the aspect of one-to-one discussion on their pain, their tears, their sweat is not known by the community. So when such a scenario exists, other women who are potential migrants do not understand the difficulties, whereas by looking at the things that are being expressed they also make the decision to go.

What emerges, then, is a self-reinforcing social consensus that signifies and interprets migration as a pathway to success, despite the extent of private hardships and unsustainable benefits experienced by a majority of migrants. In this sense, the use of migrant agency to construct *status* that is otherwise difficult to obtain under conditions of local employment also has the cumulatively causal effect of encouraging others to participate in the substantial risks of temporary labour migration.

Conclusion

This chapter, the last of the empirical section of the book, has offered a deeper understanding of migrants' social and economic realities by emphasising the exercise of individual agency alongside and within the structural and institutional constraints of temporary labour migration. An examination of gendered working realities at home and abroad reveals how a sexual division of labour in both contexts has produced gender-specific forms of exploitation that undermine the availability of decent work, challenge traditional gender roles and entail particular hardships for men and women. Considering the distinctly gendered means by which Sri Lanka's working poor has been de-socialised, it has then examined how migration presents individuals with opportunities to reclaim *status* within these same gendered parameters. By reinterpreting migrant agency through the concept of *status*, the importance of individual decision-making is neither disregarded nor overstated, but instead contextualised as a gendered negotiation of self-worth embedded within the widespread devaluation of labour throughout Sri Lanka and within avenues of foreign employment. It identifies both an ability to curate personal experiences in alignment with social expectations and, crucially, the possibility to conspicuously consume remittances to flaunt material signifiers of 'success'. Conspicuous remittance use is not interpreted as wasteful or 'unproductive', but an earnest response to the systematic deprivation of material and moral worth within a market-society that devalues labour but reveres consumerism. However, the very ostentation of such consumption amounts to a false pretence of 'success' that belies often meagre outcomes of temporary labour migration and misleads prospective migrants seeking to emulate a facade of prosperity. Independent of their social characteristics, these forms of conspicuous consumption also play an important role in influencing the macroeconomic implications of *remittance capital*, which is the topic of the final two chapters of the book.

Notes

1 'Juki' is a brand of sewing machine used extensively throughout the garments industry.
2 There is no systematic definition of 'skilled' or 'unskilled' work used by the SLBFE; distinctions are instead made arbitrarily according to particular forms of occupation. All of these occupations fit within what is here loosely termed 'low-skill' work.
3 In the case of Saudi Arabia – the largest recipient of Sri Lankan labour – domestic workers cannot leave the house independently of a male attendant, typically their employer.
4 A popular name for a variety of local snack foods.
5 The Janatha Vimukthi Peramuna (JVP) staged two armed insurrections, in 1971 and 1987, while the civil war took place between 1983 and 2009 – both can be understood as militant responses to social and economic pressures amongstmarginalised populations (see Samaranayake 1997; Bush 2003).

References

Biyanwila, Janaka. 2011. *The Labour Movement in the Global South: Trade Unions in Sri Lanka*. London: Routledge.

Breman, Jan. 2009. 'The Great Transformation in the Setting of Asia'. International Rotterdam: Institute of Social Studies.

Bush, Kenneth D. 2003. *The Intra-Group Dimensions of Ethnic Conflict in Sri Lanka: Learning to Read between the Lines*. New York: Palgrave Macmillan.

Gamburd, Michele Ruth. 2000. *The Kitchen Spoon's Handle: Transnationalism and Sri Lanka's Migrant Housemaids*. Ithaca, NY: Cornell University Press.

Gunatilaka, Ramani. 2013. *Women's Participation in Sri Lanka's Labour Force: Trends, Drivers and Constraints*. Colombo: International Labour Organisation.

Haas, Hein de. 2010. 'Migration and Development: A Theoretical Perspective'. *International Migration Review* 44 (1): 227–64.

hooks, bell. 2000. *Where We Stand: Class Matters*. New York: Routledge.

International Labour Organisation (ILO). 2013. *Recruitment Practices of Employment Agencies Recruiting Migrant Workers: A Review Aimed at Improving Recruitment Regulations and Drafting Recruitment Guidelines*. Colombo: ILO.

Khan, A., and H. Harroff-Tavel. 2011. 'Reforming the Kafala: Challenges and Opportunities in Moving Forward'. *Asian and Pacific Migration Journal* 20 (3–4): 293–313.

Kottegoda, Sepali. 2004. *Negotiating Household Politics: Women's Strategies in Urban Sri Lanka*. Colombo: Social Scientists' Association.

Lynch, Caitrin. 2007. *Juki Girls, Good Girls: Gender and Cultural Politics in Sri Lanka's Global Garment Industry*. Ithaca, NY: Cornell University Press.

Marshall, Thomas H. 1992. *Citizenship and Social Class*. London: Pluto Press. First published 1950.

Polanyi, Karl. 2001. *The Great Transformation: The Political and Economic Origins of Our Time*. Boston: Beacon Press. First published 1944.

Samaranayake, Gamini. 1997. 'Political Violence in Sri Lanka: A Diagnostic Approach'. *Terrorism and Political Violence* 9 (2): 99–119.

Sri Lanka Bureau of Foreign Employment (SLBFE). 2012. *Annual Statistical Report of Foreign Employment 2011*. Colombo: Sri Lanka Bureau of Foreign Employment.

Veblen, Thorstein. 2009. *The Theory of the Leisure Class*. Oxford: Oxford University Press. First published 1899.

6 Remittances and the financing of uneven development

Chapters 3, 4 and 5 have drawn on fieldwork findings to identify ways in which temporary labour migration in Sri Lanka has become a process with strong cumulatively causative characteristics at structural, institutional and personal levels. The dynamics of *forced migration* (Chapter 3), *place* (Chapter 4), and *status* (Chapter 5) collectively contribute to Sri Lanka's seemingly intractable path dependency on foreign employment, evidenced by steadily increasing ratios of foreign to local employment and by a similarly increasing ratio of remittance receipts to export earnings. In this chapter, the book develops an analysis of the most entrenched cumulatively causative mechanism – *remittance capital* – and its relationship with the financing of uneven development. It 'steps back' from the empirical study and places Sri Lanka's dependency on temporary labour migration into macroeconomic relief.

The chapter evaluates the orthodox framing of remittances as beneficial transfers of developmental capital by examining the macroeconomic implications of *remittance capital* in Sri Lanka. *Remittance capital* is distinct from other forms of developmental capital, as it is simultaneously comprised of private-income transfers and aggregate foreign-exchange inflows, both of which have important macroeconomic consequences. The chapter first explores the broader outcomes of household remittance expenditures, contending that what little 'investment' does occur is typically constrained within the informal sector, while consumption tends to redirect demand towards urban and international capital rather than generate local spillover effects. It then examines foreign-exchange inflows, identifying intrinsic constraints to inclusive development spending owing to correlative effects on structural unemployment and currency management. Sri Lanka's post-war development policy is scrutinised as evidence of these limitations. Lastly, it posits that the two sides of *remittance capital* – private income and public expenditure – together help Sri Lanka sustain an otherwise untenable path of uneven development characterised by continued accumulation by subordination.

Household remittance expenditure

The inwards flow of migrant workers' remittances has the potential to influence macroeconomic development in two overarching ways: directly, through the aggregate consumption and investment of remittance income, and indirectly, by amassing foreign exchange earnings in the current account. Of these, remittances are first and foremost transfers of private income that, when spent, carry important implications for sending economies. Although under-theorised, household remittance expenditure is a central aspect of migration-development for sending economies, as long-term growth prospects are likely to be influenced by the manner in which household remittances are saved and spent (Athukorala 1993). By examining the macroeconomic implications of household remittance expenditure in Sri Lanka, insights gained from fieldwork findings can be connected to broader patterns of consumption and investment throughout the economy.

Interviewing returned migrants can provide insight into the catalysts, constraints and cultures that shape individual migration narratives. By delving into the experiences of returnees, including the ways in which remittances have been used by the recipient household, it is possible to gauge whether and where migrants and their families feel to have benefited from the outcomes of foreign employment. Beyond assessing the development of individual households, detailed case studies are also a practical means of inferring the macroeconomic implications of household remittance expenditure in aggregate. In the absence of detailed census data on remittance expenditure, along with the inability of large quantitative surveys to shed light on the nuanced factors that shape household spending, triangulated case-study data offers the most detailed and pragmatic means of extrapolating a general pattern of household remittance expenditure. To date, the most comprehensive macroeconomic studies of remittance use in Sri Lanka have adopted this approach (Athukorala 1993; De Silva, Lakshman, and Ranasinghe 1993; Gunatilleke 1995; Gunatilleke, Colombage, and Perera 2010).

Prevailing assumptions on remittance expenditure

The 'rediscovery' of migration-development at the turn of the millennium was due in large part to the steady growth of global remittance transfers to developing economies, which in turn placed remittances themselves at the heart of an emerging developmental discourse encouraging temporary labour migration (de Haas 2012). A key aspect of this paradigm shift has been the belief that remittance expenditure automatically 'targets' poverty alleviation and the distribution of other economic benefits amongst those most in need, that is, migrants themselves. The World Bank, in its landmark report on the economic implications of remittances, claims that 'the bulk of the economic gains from migration accrue to migrants and their families, and these gains are often large' (2006, xii). The report goes on to specify that, beyond sheer poverty alleviation, remittances 'lead to increased household expenditures in areas considered to be important for development, particularly education, entrepreneurship, and health' (World Bank 2006, 117). While the report does concede a lack of evidence supporting a positive correlation between remittances and economic growth, a relationship that has come under sustained scrutiny (Barajas *et al.* 2009; Chami *et al.* 2018), it maintains that household remittance expenditure will entail poverty-alleviating consumption and development-catalysing investment in human and physical capital. These patterns of expenditure are presumed to have expansionary consequences for the sending economy, whose growth may nevertheless be held in check by counteracting losses of productive labour departing for foreign employment (World Bank 2006).

When considering remittance expenditure in isolation of labour supply issues, there is a clear expectation that migrants will consume and invest in a manner conducive to economic development:

> To the extent that they finance education and health and increase investment, remittances could have a positive effect on economic growth. Remittances may relieve credit constraints in the recipient community and spur entrepreneurial activity.... To the extent that they increase consumption, remittances may increase per capita income levels and reduce poverty and income inequality, even if they do not directly impact growth.
>
> (World Bank 2006, 104)

This resonates with other voices in migration-development policy, which typically suggest that remittances will either stimulate sending economies through consumption multipliers or investment in capital goods, both of which are deemed conducive to development (Ratha 2007; EMN 2010; Angenendt 2014; UNECE 2016). Concerning the effects of consumption, an OECD working paper, published the same year as the World Bank report, claims:

> there are a number of routes through which the macro-economic effects of remittance inflows can and do benefit the wider community and not just those families directly receiving the transfers. One such important route is through any multiplier effects of spending by the recipients. That is, the spending of remittances may generate incomes for those providing the goods and services purchased, and they in turn spend this income, setting off a chain reaction.
>
> (Katseli, Lucas, and Xenogiani 2006, 53)

These assumptions about remittance expenditure, though at the time newly embedded in a triple win migration-development policy doctrine, are reminiscent of earlier studies concerned with the impact of migrant incomes on patterns of consumption and investment in sending economies. For example, an ILO study of household remittance use in Sri Lanka produced a decision tree (see Figure 6.1) to demonstrate the various ways in which foreign incomes neatly flow into consumption or savings to be invested (De Silva, Lakshman, and Ranasinghe 1993). This decision tree reveals two 'dead ends' for migrant income (foreign expenditures and foreign investments), numerous pathways to consumption (of remittances, goods in kind and goods brought home) and an equivalent number

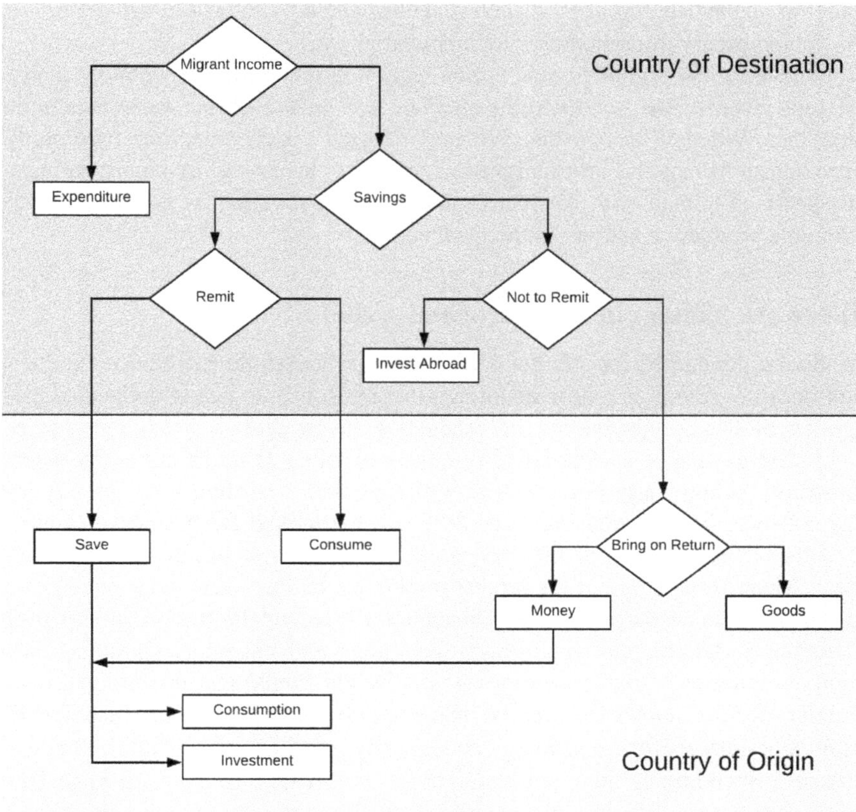

Figure 6.1 Remittance decision tree.

Source: De Silva, Lakshman, and Ranasinghe 1993.

of savings pathways (from remittances, sold goods in kind and money brought home) leading either to consumption or to investment in housing and formal/informal businesses. Contrary to most current research, the ILO study considers education and healthcare expenditures a factor of consumption rather than investment. This distinction not only illustrates the increasingly 'post-Washington' parameters of mainstream migration-development discourse (e.g. public services increasingly being framed as a private investments), but also the difficulty of categorising remittance expenditures that do not fit neatly into the binary of consumption and investment. In practice, there are *three* general categories of remittance expenditure identified in the literature: basic consumption, productive investments and a more contentious class of livelihood expenditures – including education, healthcare, housing, vehicles and consumer durables – that may or may not reflect or facilitate 'productive activity'. The degree to which livelihood expenses are considered factors of consumption or investment varies from one study to the next, but these expenditures are increasingly housed under an expanded definition of investment invoked by the triple win mantra of the contemporary migration-development paradigm.

In essence, the dominant assumption regarding remittance expenditure is that migrant incomes will, one way or another, lead to favourable macroeconomic outcomes. Whether by boosting domestic demand via consumption, by directly investing in formal and informal businesses or by 'investing' in a more ambiguous array of human and physical capital, migrant remittances are expected to stimulate productive activity in the local economy.

Fieldwork findings in macroeconomic relief

Fieldwork conducted for this book suggests that household remittance expenditure does not resemble a flow of foreign income split into neatly delineated categories of basic consumption or productive investment. Instead, remittances were seen to finance a wide range of expenses, often as much culturally determined as economically necessitated. While income was often spent on day-to-day consumption and housing, very little was earmarked for business ventures, let alone any entrepreneurship that could be considered formal-sector investment. Meanwhile, some of the largest remittance outlays were debt repayments to moneylenders – particularly in Thavapuram – or socially important expenses including jewellery, clothing, dowry payments and consumer durables. The complex realities of remittance use, bound by the spatial and institutional constraints of *place*, cloud the premise that migrant incomes have predictable and stimulatory effects for the sending economy. By using fieldwork findings to contextualise spending at the major junctures of De Silva, Lakshman and Ranasinghe's decision tree it is possible to conceive where and why the macroeconomic impacts of aggregate remittance expenditure might depart from the expectations of migration-development advocates.

The following subsections trace four key 'decisions' in the transfer and consumption of remittances by addressing: (i) the percentage of foreign income sent home as remittances; (ii) the prevalence and nature of goods brought home upon migrants' return; (iii) the ways in which remittances are directly consumed by recipient households; and (iv) the manner in which any eventual savings are used.

Remittance rates

An immediate consideration highlighted by the decision tree, though not in itself of consequence to remittance expenditure, is the percentage of migrant incomes that actually leave the foreign economy in the form of remittances. The average remittance rate amongst returnees I interviewed was 80 per cent of foreign income, a figure consistent with similar studies conducted in Sri Lanka (De Silva, Lakshman, and Ranasinghe 1993). For male migrants, a lesser proportion of income (an average of 70 per cent) was remitted because their employment was more likely to entail additional expenses: sometimes for transport, sometimes for food, sometimes for accommodation, but also for entertainment and socialising with other migrants in a manner that women domestic workers generally cannot. Conversely, women reported higher-than-average remittance rates as most of their day-to-day expenses were included in the terms of their employment while, as mentioned, opportunities to socialise and spend money are limited. Regardless of their eventual use, remittances represent only a percentage of the foreign income earned by migrant labour, the rest of which is retained by receiving economies and international firms – the macroeconomic implications of which are examined in the following chapter.

Goods brought on return

Foreign goods are frequently brought home by migrant returnees. Returnees cited two main reasons for this. First, for domestic workers in particular, employers would occasionally hand down clothes and consumer durables that were no longer needed, or gift jewellery and other small valuables. These acts of goodwill were sometimes discussed by returnees as the hallmark of a 'good' employer. Second, for others, spending income on foreign goods was a conscious decision tempered by personal or familial considerations of *status*. As discussed in Chapter 5, migrants face social pressure to return home as a visible 'success story', and bringing foreign goods in tow can be crucial in meeting this expectation. Although there are numerous duty-free shops catering to migrants at Bandaranaike International Airport, most of them selling 'big ticket' white goods and electrical items, a majority of the migrants interviewed purchased these items abroad instead. Fieldwork findings indicated that 50 per cent of all participants purchased consumer durables abroad, while 43 per cent purchased consumer durables within Sri Lanka after their return; some migrants bought goods while overseas and at home, while only a few (typically those cheated, abused or debt-burdened) bought no goods at all.

A combination of factors appears to make purchasing status goods from abroad more appealing than buying them locally. As suggested previously, the social and recreational aspects of shopping during days off (if applicable) offers an intuitive behavioural explanation for this preference for foreign goods, both because it is an opportunity to interact with other migrants and because it can also stir an element of peer pressure in spending decisions. Meanwhile, well-established shipping services offer to ferry goods at reasonable prices, reducing the logistical inconvenience of buying goods abroad.

One migrant, a woman from Akmeemana who had been working in Lebanon in the 1980s, explained that such a shopping trip had even been arranged by her employers:

> A few days before I came home to Sri Lanka, they took me to the shops and I have to spend my money and buy the things I wanted, such as jewellery and clothes. I bought a chain, a bangle, television, a fridge, some clothes to wear.

However, there is also an important qualitative difference between foreign goods and those available locally. Just as the social value of foreign jewellery is defined in part by colours and styles unavailable in Sri Lanka, so too do consumer durables brought from abroad appear to signify *status* beyond the more limited scope of brands and models that can be bought locally. Foreign goods, insofar as they are distinguishable from locally bought alternatives, broadcast a particular articulation of *status* by emulating foreign taste in a manner unobtainable except through the act of migration itself. As with the adoption of foreign clothes and mannerisms, the consumption of foreign goods creates a coveted point of social distinction that conveys adherence to the popular narrative of migrant success.

Thus, despite government attempts to incentivise local spending by issuing special duty-free permits to returning migrants, the social considerations bound up in the purchasing of foreign goods might be more meaningful to migrants. These same duty-free permits have created opportunities for returning migrants to make some extra money in transit, at the expense of forsaken government duties.

As the ILO project coordinator interviewed during fieldwork explained:

> Sometimes it's sold as well, while they're on the plane, to other people. Because I have myself been sitting at a departure gate, and overheard one girl tell the other girl, 'Look sister some people may approach you to buy your duty-free pass, you can say yes, you'll buy it for them, and at some point you can ask them for money and hand over the goods to them.' That kind of thing.

Returning to a macroeconomic perspective, goods bought on return amount to a further leakage of migrant incomes that would otherwise be remitted. As with foreign expenses, foreign purchases lay claim to a significant portion of migrant incomes before they even acquire the potential to stimulate the Sri Lankan economy. The countervailing inflow of purchased goods is no substitute for this lost income, as these are largely status goods that derive their social value by virtue of conspicuous ownership and are rarely sold on, with the exception of jewellery, which is frequently pawned as collateral for loans or the repayment of debt.

Direct consumption

The degree to which remittances are spent on day-to-day consumption is the first and often principal tier at which migrant incomes affect the sending economy. Fieldwork findings suggested that the direct consumption of remittances for basic needs of the recipient family was a common expenditure for 86 per cent of participants. Twelve per cent of returnees stated that these costs comprised the largest share of their remittance expenditure, with only housing and debt repayments more frequently identified as the largest expense; when considering second and third largest shares of expenditure (as shown in Table 6.1[1]), day-to-day consumption is clearly a prominent form of remittance use.

Table 6.1 Largest shares of remittance expenditure

Category	*Largest share* %	*Second-largest share* %	*Third-largest share* %
Business	4.0	8.0	6.0
Consumer durables	0.0	2.0	2.0
Consumption	12.0	28.0	16.0
Debt repayment	25.0	8.0	5.0
Education	7.0	13.0	17.0
Healthcare	2.0	3.0	3.0
Housing	35.0	9.0	2.0
Jewellery and clothing	4.0	4.0	14.0
Other	6.0	13.0	8.0
None	5.0	12.0	27.0
Total	100.0	100.0	100.0

Other studies of household remittance use in Sri Lanka corroborate a high concentration of day-to-day consumption costs relative to other categories of expenditure (Amjad 1989; Athukorala 1992; De Silva, Lakshman, and Ranasinghe 1993; Kottegoda 2004; Arunatilake *et al.* 2010; Gunatilleke, Colombage, and Perera 2010). Studies that have examined remittance expenditure in measurable detail estimate that Sri Lankan migrants spend as much as 35 per cent of their total remitted income on direct consumption (De Silva, Lakshman, and Ranasinghe 1993).

The Sri Lankan migration literature offers three dominant explanations for the degree of remitted income that finds its way into direct consumption, encompassing gendered decision-making structures, income displacement and the size and timing of remittance transfers. The first and perhaps most enduring interpretation is that Sri Lankan men, historically remittance-receivers owing to the feminisation of temporary labour migration, frequently squander their spouses' income on gambling and alcohol (Shaw 2010). Although such cases do happen, as borne out by contemporaneous anecdotal evidence (Kottegoda *et al.* 2013), the notoriety of men's 'wasteful' expenditure tends to outstrip the degree to which it occurs (Gamburd 2000). A second and related argument is that the presence of remittances acts to deter other family members from working, that is, as a moral hazard, so that while foreign income supports the household it also has to counteract a loss of local income, resulting in remittance-dependent consumption (Siddiqui and Perera 2000; Kottegoda 2004; Shaw 2010). A third contention is that remittances are sent as small, regular payments that are more easily consumed than saved, particularly under circumstances of inept remittance management (Shaw 2010).

Fieldwork findings from my study supported all of these considerations, to a certain extent. For example, three women spoke of having abusive partners who took advantage of them via foreign employment. One of these men in particular was able to coerce the respondent into migration, only to spend her remittances on alcohol, drugs and a relationship with another woman. Some spoke of their spouse's lack of economic activity during their absence, however this was most often the case where men had made a conscious effort to undertake the deficit of unpaid care work created by their wives' departure and was usually interpreted positively. Others expressed a clear exasperation with not understanding where the money had gone, although it is hard to attribute this frustration to the frequency of remittance transfers, mismanagement on behalf of the recipient, or a sheer insufficiency of income. What was most clear from the interviews, however, was the degree of economic hardship faced by migrant families and the material need to regularly commit remittances towards day-to-day consumption costs as a means of household survival. The acuteness of such circumstances differed according to place, but even the most successful migrant communities were seen to struggle to meet the rising cost of everyday life. In this sense, there is reason to attribute high remittance consumption to a state of underdevelopment itself, above and beyond financial mismanagement. This is supported by the finding that 84 per cent of returnees indicated that they were happy with the way their income was managed.

The day-to-day consumption of remittances has an immediate and widely recognised impact on poverty alleviation (Shaw 2010), although a lack of longitudinal survey data presents problems in assessing whether short-term improvements translate into lasting benefits for the household. Theoretical debates on the causality of migration and poverty remain unresolved (Skeldon 2005). Putting the potential for poverty alleviation aside, the extent to which remittances assume a subsistence function poses problems for the narrative of expansionary remittance use. The day-to-day consumption of migrant households, though stabilised by remittances, is unlikely to increase to the point of stimulating demand or generating spillovers in any substantial way.

Savings – consumption, housing and investment

The last and most theoretically contentious aspect of remittance expenditure is the use of income kept aside as savings. It is at this juncture of remittance use that foreign incomes are expected to crystallise as business investments and an array of livelihood expenditures that stimulate the local economy. However, insofar as 'savings' are taken to denote the use of income that is surplus to immediate consumption needs, it also pertains to the extensive debt repayments discussed in Chapter 4.

Of all the major categories of expenditure involving the use of savings, education costs emerge as the most frequent outlay, with 58 per cent of households spending at least some money on schooling. It is followed by housing, debt repayments, jewellery, healthcare, consumer durables and – lastly – business.[2] Perhaps more telling is the relative share of these expenditures, with housing the single largest remittance outlay for 35 per cent of migrants and debt repayment the largest for a further 25 per cent. In contrast, education was the foremost expense for 7 per cent of participants, with jewellery and business investment accounting for 4 per cent and healthcare just 2 per cent (see Table 6.1). These findings are broadly consistent with every major study concerning remittance use in Sri Lanka (Dias 1986; Gunatilleke 1986; Rodrigo and Jayatissa 1989; Amjad 1989; De Silva, Lakshman, and Ranasinghe 1993; Eversole and Shaw 2010; Gunatilleke, Colombage, and Perera 2010). Most notably, these studies affirm a pattern that appears to have changed very little since the early 1980s: concentrated remittance expenditure on housing and loan repayments, a dearth of business investments and various smaller outlays on education, consumer durables, personal effects and the amassing dowries (of which housing is often a key part). Such consistency in migrants' use of savings over time indicates that remittances have produced subsistence outcomes for migrants and their communities, rather than lasting development and accompanying shifts in patterns of expenditure.

The intricate ways in which *status* can be reconstructed through migration, amidst and often belying material hardship, offers an intuitive explanation for consumption trends. Home ownership, as a cultural expectation, is made increasingly difficult to fulfil under conditions of local employment, but as a symbol of personal independence and a platform from which to project the material edifice of success it is also the most immediate expression of *status*. It is the bedrock upon which consumer durables inherit their meaning; there is no use in acquiring televisions, fine crockery or leather settees without an appropriate room to house them in. Likewise, as with jewellery and other valuable assets, housing is often a key component in dowry payments and can be used to secure a 'good' marriage and in that way, too, reclaim a sense of social standing otherwise unobtainable.

These forms of expenditure are pivotal elements of conspicuous consumption that, far from being 'wasteful' as 'non-productive' spending, are an important form of resistance to a prevailing de-socialisation of labour. Investment in business, on the other hand, requires more savings, know-how and appetite for risk than most returned migrants are likely to possess. While some chalk up limited migrant investment as symptomatic of an inherent 'lack of entrepreneurial spirit' (De Silva, Lakshman, and Ranasinghe 1993, 44), it is important to consider that many return facing indebtedness or with insignificant savings. As discussed in Chapter 3, many migrants aspired to start a business or pursue self-employment in lieu of local employment opportunities, but were unable to do so with the money they sent home. In comparison, status goods are more affordable and confer immediate social benefits, the value of which might be greater than the pursuit of entrepreneurship and the risk entailed.

No migrants were observed to have made formal-sector business investments, a finding that reflects the status quo of a highly informal economy (Arunatilake 2012). Businesses uniformly involved informal self-employment, typically involving the ownership of a *kade* (corner shop), the purchase of a trishaw taxi, services such as repairs and tailoring, or home production of basic goods such as handicrafts and foodstuffs. The preponderance of such investments is echoed in other studies on remittance use in Sri Lanka. Athukorala, for example, notes that:

> According to disaggregated data on business investment ... such investment mostly takes place in trade, transport and other services, at the expense of 'productive' investment in manufacturing and agriculture.
>
> (1992, 517)

De Silva, Lakshman and Ranasinghe similarly find that:

> The so called 'productive' investment in the case of Middle East returnees tends to be concentrated in trade and service sectors. In Dias for example, only four of 150 returning male migrants invested in business – three in grocery shops and the fourth in a lathe workshop and battery recharging shop. This trend is noted in our survey as well.
>
> (1993, 47)

This undermines the prevalent assumption that remittances stimulate conventional 'productive investment' and highlights a lack of attention paid to the nature and limitations of investment in an informal economy, where business tends to reflect subsistence self-employment more than the accumulation and reinvestment of productive capital.

The essence of how migrants' savings are spent is succinctly captured by a returnee domestic worker interviewed by Gamburd, who advised:

> Money in the bank will vanish; if you start a business, it will go bankrupt. Invest in land and a house.
>
> (Gamburd 2004, 179)

This message distils the macroeconomic effects of remittance-use reported throughout the Sri Lankan literature: accumulated sums of migrant remittances are not saved or invested, but spent.

One key implication is that the expectation that remittance-use will increase productive or 'entrepreneurial' activity is poorly supported, particularly when the few business investments that do occur amount to a substitution of waged labour for informal self-employment. Yet there are two additional, though frequently overlooked, macroeconomic consequences of the patterns of remittance expenditure described above.

The first is that prominent forms of expenditure (i.e. education, housing, debt repayments, jewellery, healthcare and consumer durables) each effect a redistribution of income to the producers of those goods and services; the developmental impact of these spillovers is thus determined by the existing spatial distribution of capital ownership. The second is that expenditure on consumer durables is almost unanimously comprised of imported goods and these purchases together aggravate Sri Lanka's current account deficit by redistributing income out of the economy. Notably, lifestyle goods frequently classified as 'productive investments' within mainstream migration-development discourse feature heavily in this category. The findings of Eversole and Shaw indicate that:

> in Sri Lanka, 59 per cent of respondents reported a 'substantial' post-departure improvement in ownership of major household assets such as motorcycles, refrigerators, televisions and sewing machines, while 16 per cent reported a 'moderate' improvement.
>
> (Eversole and Shaw 2010, 190)

An earlier study by Gunatilleke (1986) offers a clear itemised comparison of such expenditures before and after migration (see Table 6.2). Although difficult to quantify, this study and others suggest migrants purchase a considerable amount of these consumer goods and it is reasonable to expect that remittance expenditure creates moderate import demand.

A critique of remittance-led development

Primary research indicates that the expected benefits arising from household remittance-use are overstated and oversimplify the remittance-transfer process. Elucidating the social and material pressures residing at key junctures in the flow of migrant incomes, from foreign wages to household savings, reveals a series of leakages and redirections that diminish the scope of remittances and associated multiplier effects to benefit the sending economy in any substantial way. Even before migrants are paid, deductions are often made for accommodation and food,[3] after which foreign expenses and purchases claim more income prior to remittance, which then largely augments household consumption (sometimes supplanting other incomes) and finances debt repayment, before residual savings can be allocated for more specific expenditures. Within the confines of established social expectations and limited means, these savings are seen to be spent more readily on housing, education, jewellery and consumer goods than on any form of business investments. Rather than fostering development amongst those

Table 6.2 Ownership of consumer durables

Item	*Pre-migration*	*Post-migration*
Sewing machine	108	178
Cookers	26	86
Refrigerators	11	78
Deep freezers	6	14
Radio	151	260
TV	16	191
Video player	2	38
Stereo	5	58
Washing machines	0	5
Dish washers	0	2
Vacuum cleaners	0	24
Fan	10	91
None of the above	315	145

Source: Gunatilleke (1986).

most in need, as the World Bank contends (2006), remittance expenditure appears to promote varying degrees of subsistence while generating spillovers that redirect income out of underdeveloped local communities and towards established loci of capital accumulation within Sri Lanka and – via imported goods – abroad.

This pattern of income redirection is partially anticipated by the authors of an OECD working paper otherwise optimistic about temporary labour migration. Their disclaimers about the general expectation of a remittance multiplier effect are worth quoting in full:

> Three general issues may be noted with respect to this potential multiplier effect. First, for additional domestic spending to result in added domestic production requires either idle capacity or fresh inputs to enable this production. Where production is effectively constrained by production capacity, additional spending is more likely to result in either rising prices or spending on imports.... Second, as already noted, migrants tend to originate from some, specific places and regions and not others. Local spending in these areas may not have much impact on other areas if the multiplier linkages remain largely local, which depends upon the extent of trade in goods and services beyond the specific community. Third, remittance transfers enter the economy through a select set of families. Their initial spending may or may not be similar to the national average. Nonetheless after one or two rounds in the spending-income chain, the multiplier effect of remittance spending is likely to resemble the multiplier effect of any other spending in this economy.
>
> (Katseli, Lucas, and Xenogiani 2006, 53)

Applying these general issues to empirical evidence from Sri Lanka suggests that: (i) spending on imports does occur in lieu of new or existing productive capacity (i.e. the general lack of a diversified manufacturing sector); (ii) with most of Sri Lanka's migrants originating from underdeveloped rural areas, spending promotes multiplier linkages with more developed regions instead of home communities; and (iii) spending does importantly differ from non-migrant households, insofar as remittances remain a crucial facilitator of status consumption. These outcomes portray a process that could be dubbed 'remittance-led uneven development'. Sri Lanka's case confirms the insights of more critical pockets of migration theory that invert the causality of 'migration-development' in emphasising development itself as a precondition for sustainable migration outcomes (Delgado Wise and Covarrubias 2009).

These findings have questioned the assumed macroeconomic implication of remittances as a form of private expenditure by highlighting various leakages of migrant income, patterns of household expenditures and the redistribution of demand this entails. The chapter now moves beyond primary research altogether in addressing the contradictions associated with the second and more indirect aspect of *remittance capital*, as a source of foreign-exchange earnings.

Remittances as foreign-exchange earnings

Remittance capital is framed by the mainstream migration literature as an important form of foreign-exchange earnings. In Sri Lanka, migrant worker remittances amounted to US$7.16 billion in foreign-exchange receipts during 2017, equivalent to 63 per cent of goods exports and 8.25 per cent of GDP for the same year (CBSL 2018).

Compared to other migrant-sending countries throughout Asia, Sri Lanka has a relatively regulated remittance infrastructure with high rates of formal transfers relative to unofficial remittances sent through informal channels (Gunatilleke, Colombage, and Perera 2010; Athukorala 1992). Formal transfers are those mediated by the 25 financial institutions[4] licensed by the Exchange Control Department of the CBSL and include money and postal orders, bank transfers and transactions conducted by money transfer businesses[5] (Lasagabaster, Maimbo, and Hulugalle 2005). While there is some discrepancy in attempts to gauge the magnitude of informal remittance transfers, Rodrigo and Jayatissa's (1989) widely cited findings suggest as little as 13 per cent of all transfers were informal during the mid-1980s, representing a prevalence of formal remittance capture second only to South Korea. More recent studies have inconclusively disputed these figures (Lasagabaster, Maimbo, and Hulugalle 2005; Page and Plaza 2006), but the weight of opinion suggests that informal remittances remain significantly lower than other major migrant-sending countries in the region, indicating the general efficacy of the formal transfer system.

The formality of remittances is an important consideration, as popular informal remittance channels such as the *Hundi* and *Hawala* systems leak potential foreign exchange receipts by exchanging *payment obligations* within an extensive international network of money brokers. Such transfers often involve no actual movement of money and, depending on the method of eventual settlement between money brokers, may elude banking channels altogether (El Qorchi, Maimbo, and Wilson 2003). By capturing a large share of remittances through formal channels, Sri Lanka streamlines the process by which migrant incomes contribute to the Balance of Payments as current transfers.

Throughout the migration-development literature there is a tendency to consider the foreign-exchange earnings provided by remittances as axiomatically beneficial to the sending economy. This assumption has been expressed by authors otherwise quite critical of temporary labour migration practices (Wucker 2004; Skeldon 2006; Faist 2008; Lenard and Straehle 2010; Martin 2012; Wickramasekara 2015). The Sri Lankan corner of the literature is no different, with several studies highlighting important constraints and challenges faced by migrant households while treating the macroeconomic benefit of aggregate foreign-exchange earnings as self-evident (Athukorala 1992; Kageyama 2008; Karunaratne 2008; Eversole and Shaw 2010; Gunatilleke, Colombage, and Perera 2010).

The implicit understanding is that remittances are vital in providing foreign-exchange earnings necessary to prop up the current account against countervailing trade deficits, thereby allowing the rupee to be kept strong and stable.

An overvalued rupee, in turn, keeps imports affordable while also facilitating international borrowing and easing the repayment of existing loans. With remittances comprising the single largest source of export earnings for Sri Lanka, and the principal cushion in the Balance of Payments since the early 1990s, it is easy to understand why this stability might be construed as positive (CBSL 2018). This sentiment is outlined concisely by the OECD working paper cited earlier in the chapter:

> For economies where imports are high relative to foreign exchange reserves, or for heavily indebted nations, any addition to foreign exchange availability can prove very valuable. Limited access to world financial markets inhibits production opportunities at home, by limiting availability of material imports and even of trade credit. In such instances, remittances can lower a critical barrier to production expansion and prove extremely valuable.
>
> (Katseli, Lucas, and Xenogiani 2006, 55)

The major problem with this reasoning is that any potential for developmental benefit is highly contingent on how the government utilises the money it borrows, which is itself constrained by incidental macroeconomic circumstances. An evaluation of remittances as a source of development finance requires consideration of two risks embedded in that macroeconomic scenario: 'Dutch Disease' and path dependency.

Dutch Disease

Dutch Disease is one of the more commonly acknowledged negative side-effects for small economies receiving significant remittance inflows relative to GDP, as is manifestly the case in Sri Lanka. Even outspoken advocates of remittance-led development acknowledge the likelihood of remittances leading to Dutch Disease under such circumstances (Ratha 2007). The term originates from a discussion of the Netherlands's rapid currency appreciation following the discovery of natural gas resources and the concomitant decline of manufacturing industries made uncompetitive by this adjustment. It applies equally to any situation where an isolated injection of capital in one area of the economy drives up the real exchange rate to the detriment of non-boom sectors, typically resulting in the reallocation of resources from tradeable to non-tradeable sectors of the economy (Corden 1984). In general, there have been several studies claiming a relationship between increasing remittances and an appreciation of the real exchange rate within emerging economies where such transfers make up a significant proportion of GDP (Lartey, Mandelman, and Acosta 2012; Hassan and Holmes 2013). The inflow of remittances into Sri Lanka has been shown to produce this effect (Roy and Dixon 2015; Rajakaruna 2017), with negative consequences for the tradeable sector suggested by the sharp decline of goods exports as a share of GDP alongside steady remittance growth between 2000 and 2017 (see Figure 6.2).

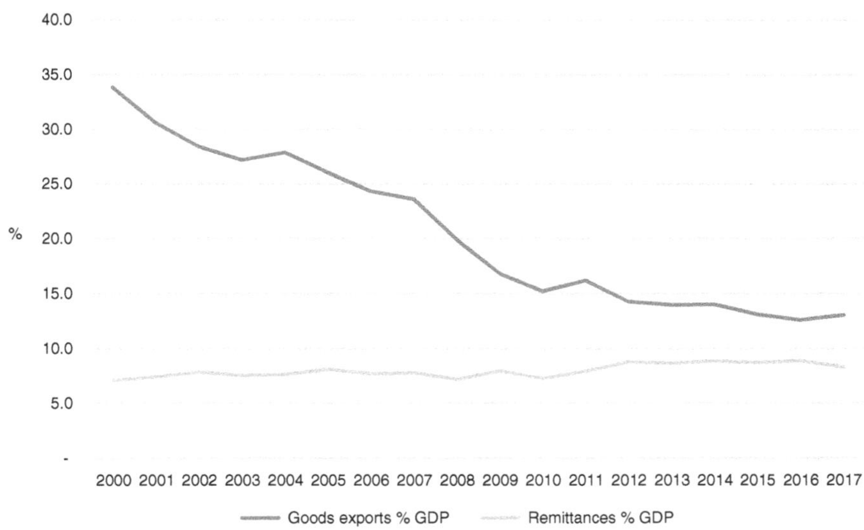

Figure 6.2 Goods exports vs. remittances (percentage of GDP), 2000–2017.
Sources: CBSL 2018; World Bank 2019.

The extent of Sri Lanka's experience of remittance-driven Dutch Disease and its ramifications for long-term development prospects were tellingly discussed by the senior director from the IPS during fieldwork interviews:

> If you look at the overall structure of the economy you see the services sector and accounts sector is 60 per cent of GDP, compared to manufacturing which is at 20 to 24 per cent of GDP. You see, all the services are very consumption driven. That is why the non-tradeable sector is the sector that is growing currently in Sri Lankan economy. And that is a very sad thing, because our growth is not sustainable. We are pursuing basically a debt-driven consumption and investment-led growth, rather than the traditional East Asian story of export-led industrialisation and FDI, a growth strategy which is much more sustainable. The productive non-tradeable sector is growing at a very high rate, but our productive tradeable sector is not at all growing satisfactorily. The exchange rate is also favourable for the non-tradeable sector because Sri Lanka is a highly indebted country. All these infrastructure projects the Rajapaksa government is doing are all debt-driven. To facilitate debt payment the government policy-makers are giving more importance to having an appreciated exchange rate, then debt payment becomes easier and that comes at a cost of export promotion.

The effects of Dutch Disease on remittance inflows appear to have been stronger under the Rajapaksa government, when foreign-currency reserves were more readily sold to defend an overvalued rupee. This made imports more affordable, and international loans more readily attainable and serviceable, but hampered the diversification of an already anaemic export sector. This in turn created a need for an increasing supply of remittances to continuing cushioning a worsening Balance of Payments scenario. In contrast, the incumbent government is more concerned about the vitality of the tradeable sector and the long-term macroeconomic implications of currency overvaluation. However, in allowing the rupee to depreciate, it has exposed the inverse dilemma, in which rising import prices create inflationary shocks and external debt swells to unsustainable levels. An IMF bailout of US$1.5 billion was necessitated in 2016 (Reuters 2016), and as of 2017 Sri Lanka's external debt was US$52 billion and equivalent to 59 per cent of GDP (CBSL 2018).

Beyond the immediate problems associated with the Dutch Disease effects of *remittance capital*, Sri Lanka's ensuing trade deficit and reliance upon foreign loans suggests a more deeply structured developmental limitation. Anwar Shaikh's critique of the law of comparative costs identifies precisely these characteristics as central to trade-driven underdevelopment, wherein trade disparities between developed and underdeveloped regions are not automatically resolved through comparative advantage, but instead become absolute advantages sustained by short-term capital flows (international loans) from surplus to deficit regions (Shaikh 1980). For Shaikh, a chronic inability to improve these terms of trade ensures that underdeveloped regions remain servicing external debt (along with interest incurred) to the advantage of more developed regions from which these capital flows originate. *Remittance capital*, by facilitating loan repayments while undermining domestic export industries, encourages further reliance on international loans while worsening the underlying trade imbalance. This, however, relates to uneven development between economies, a theme discussed in more detail in the following chapter.

Path dependency

A second consideration is the path dependency of a remittance-led development strategy. The presence of substantial remittances relative to exports indicates that temporary labour migration has already become something of a macroeconomic pillar, itself reliant on uneven development to ensure the continued need for the economically marginalised to pursue work abroad. As fieldwork findings indicated, *forced migration* is an overarching experience amongst Sri Lanka's working poor who would not leave for foreign employment if decent work (not necessarily equivalently remunerated) were available locally. Using *remittance capital* to finance an inclusive vision of development, including local employment generation, thus demands a counterintuitive break with path dependency because alleviating the structural pressure to migrate risks killing the cash cow of foreign-exchange receipts from migrant incomes. This path dependency towards uneven development is mutually reinforcing of Dutch Disease effects. On the one hand, a remittance-appreciated rupee helps finance development spending but inhibits the potential for mass employment in export production, while on the other hand, a structural disincentive to generate local employment further eschews industrial policy in favour of greater migration and more remittances. As migration also acts as a reflexive safety valve for latent political discontent arising from uneven development (Wickramasekara 2016), the marginalisation of Sri Lanka's poor can be sustained while developmental projects assuage the more obdurate interests of local capital.

Shaw discusses the symptoms of a path-dependent dynamic of uneven development when she notes:

> the sobering reality is that broad-based, poverty-clearing rural development has remained an elusive goal for most developing countries, and Sri Lanka's recent history gives little cause for optimism. The flow of remittances into Sri Lanka has created a vast new pool of potential investment capital and strengthened demand for locally produced goods and services. However, there has not been a commensurate expansion in local business activity, because the economic climate is highly unfavourable, due to civil conflict, high inflation, weak financial intermediation, and under-investment in infrastructure and human capital in the rural areas where three quarters of the population live.
>
> (Shaw 2010, 28)

However, in describing Sri Lanka's economic shortcomings through the lens of migrant entrepreneurship Shaw illustrates the superficiality of the concept, and the entire 'self-help' genre, in interpreting developmental processes. Far from being determined by an array of discrete market imperfections, the uneven returns accruing from *remittance capital* are embedded in larger historical structures and cannot be understood without attention to capitalist social relations and the state's mediation of these relations through developmental policy. An analysis of how Sri Lanka has used loans to finance developmental projects, and who has stood to gain from these policies, is therefore a useful means of demonstrating the path dependency of its remittance-driven economy.

Remittance-financed development spending

Following the end of the Sri Lankan civil war in 2009, the then-incumbent Rajapaksa government diverted large public spending from military operations to developmental projects. During this time, Sri Lanka spent an estimated US$8 billion on infrastructural projects, drawing heavily on loans provided by China's EXIM Bank and construction carried out in large part by the Chinese state-owned engineering firms (Safi 2018). These projects were predominantly concentrated in and around Colombo, with the notable exceptions of several infrastructural projects located in Rajapaksa's home district of Hambantota, in the majority-Sinhalese Southern Province (World Bank 2012; Gunasinghe 2012). Consistent with EXIM Bank's well-documented philosophy of combining development loans with economic self-interest (Bräutigam 2011), China has reaped conspicuous benefits from these projects. Construction of a highway from Colombo to Hambantota was partially contracted to the state-owned China Harbour Engineering Company (CHEC), as was the construction of a new shipping port and international airport near Hambantota (Safi 2018). Sri Lankan labour was substantially displaced by Chinese workers employed extensively throughout the construction process, greatly diminishing local employment spillovers (Gunasinghe 2012). Moreover, Hambantota port is itself geopolitically important to China, as it provides a strategic node in a 'string of pearls' allowing freighters to bypass Indian trading ports as part of the Belt and Road Initiative (Das 2017).

Despite deriving political power from a largely rural Sinhalese constituency, and sporting the popular image of representing the interests of that demographic, Rajapaksa's commitment to rural development hinged upon celebrating a tangible edifice of a progress that was – particularly for the poor – largely symbolic. Following Rajapaksa's loss of power, highway extensions to Hambantota remain incomplete, while its port operates at a fraction of capacity and Mahinda Rajapaksa International Airport is derided as the world's emptiest international airport (Safi and Perera 2018). As Gunasinghe notes:

> Hambantota, although having served as a commercial hub in ancient times, is no longer a critical nucleus or indeed even located close to one. The population is primarily dependent on agriculture and fishing and consists of the rural poor. Consequently, the area lacks both human and financial resources to develop as an industrial hub. Logical analysis fails to explain the focus on Hambantota for large scale infrastructure development and foreign investment promotion. Hambantota does however lay claim to being the ancestral home and electoral seat of the incumbent President and other members of his family who are actively engaged in politics. The scale and style of developments in Hambantota only makes sense when viewed as a long-term political investment strategy which spans generations.
>
> (2012, 2)

Research suggests Hambantota's development has induced forcible displacement and relocation of local populations leading to a loss of livelihoods, environmental degradation and psychological trauma (Gunasinghe 2012; Buthpitiya 2013). With Hambantota sitting idle, the incumbent Sirisena government accepted a Chinese proposal to establish a large, tax-exempt Special Economic Zone (SEZ) that can feed into the established trading route and service docked freighters at the Hambantota Port, which China now holds a 99-year lease for (Razak 2018). The new SEZ opened in January 2017, amidst protests from locals claiming that they had been dispossessed of their lands under the arrangement (Razak 2018). While job creation is intended, China has an 80 per cent stake in the SEZ and concerns have been raised about the ability for local workers to find employment in any but the most menial and exploitative of production roles conditioned by SEZ zoning, while foreign capital and skilled migrants stand to reap greater benefits (Buthpitiya 2013).

For the most part though, Sri Lanka's development policy has been emphatically urban in its concentration on Colombo. With Colombo having long held Singapore as a template for its idealised self, both the Rajapaksa and Sirisena governments have invested heavily in urban development that – through their respective 'port city' and 'megapolis' projects – aspire to 'modernise' in the image of the South-East Asian city-state. The US$1.4 billion port city project intends to create an offshore section of the city built on reclaimed land, providing more landmass for a new finance hub, luxury residencies, private hospitals, hotels and a theme park (Safi 2018). Meanwhile, the megapolis project is a US$40 billion public–private undertaking that entails a longer-term restructuring of Colombo into distinct zones – with dedicated shopping, entertainment and cultural districts – and rapid transit connections to outlying industrial, agricultural, coastal, IT, tourism and flight hubs (MMWD 2016). This blueprint for Colombo's urban transformation has foreseeable benefit to those with an interest in capital investments in the non-tradeable sector, whether local and international. There are clear wins, too, for China – both through the exporting of its own unemployment through contracts held by state-owned construction enterprises, and though the expansion of soft power and hard infrastructure necessary for the Belt and Road Initiative (Das 2017). There is less compelling evidence for the benefits that will emerge for Colombo's working poor.

Much of the redevelopment that has so far occurred in Colombo has taken place in areas that were, until recently, low-income settlements in central areas of the city (MMWD 2016). Described by the Urban Development Authority (UDA) as 'city beautification', development-induced displacement has resulted in involuntary urban resettlement that, although usually accompanied by upgraded facilities, often disrupts the lives of the poor as communities and livelihoods forged at the heart of the city are reassembled on its outskirts (Stenholm 2015). It is unlikely that Sri Lanka's service-led growth trajectory will provide decent work for these urban communities – let alone the majority of the population that lives outside Colombo and the Western Province. While agriculture makes up just 5 per cent of employment in the Western Province, it averages 35 per cent of employment across all other provinces and provides employment to over 2 million Sri Lankans, albeit at wages that are well below the average of industry and services (DCS 2017). Neither the port city nor the megapolis project details plans for supporting or transforming these livelihoods. That dredging from land reclamation is reportedly damaging nearby coastal environments and jeopardising the incomes of an estimated 8,000 people dependent on the local fishing trade is only the most immediate example of how urban development projects are manifestly non-inclusive to the interests of Sri Lanka's working poor (Safi 2018). As the former director of the UDA has remarked:

> the Port City will be a separate entity where only a certain class of people will live. Services may be provided by the local people, but the money coming to them is questionable.
>
> (Safi 2018)

This observation returns attention to the historical processes of accumulation by subordination that have shaped Sri Lanka's economy, repeatedly restructuring the relations of production by stoking existing class, gender and racial tensions in order to disempower labour and accumulate capital. Sri Lanka's otherwise unsustainable path of remittance-led development signals a more sophisticated embodiment of this same logic. By marginalising rural populations from development, Sri Lanka's current developmental policy subordinates migrants and would-be migrants, shifting the relations of production not by facilitating their involvement in local production, but by 'loaning' their labour to foreign employers. Remittances, representative of the wage component of that labour, represent the return on that loan: at once actual income sufficient to reproduce the migrant population in lieu of development and also an abstraction of that income in the form of foreign-exchange earnings. It represents, in essence, an exchange of unwanted poverty for much-needed loans. The use of those loans to finance development projects that cater to the interests of urban capital therein is, along with the redistributive effects of household remittance expenditure, the central mechanism through which accumulation is facilitated. Macroeconomically, this amounts to a fragile paradox, whereby local capital accumulation occurs independently of export growth and dependent upon migrant remittances, which can only occur insofar as uneven development persists. It partly accounts for the relative inaction of Sri Lanka, and other labour-sending countries, in addressing the rights and conditions of migrant workers in West Asia; the risk of disturbing the countervailing inflow of remittances poses too great a threat to a precariously balanced economy. As Gibson-Graham has argued, the degree of political control exerted by both migrant-sending and migrant-receiving countries to 'manage' migration is in this instance a manifestation of the close relationship between state and the interests of capital (Kottegoda 2004).

Conclusion

This chapter has argued that *remittance capital*, the sum of two constituent elements of household remittances and foreign-exchange earnings, allows for a process of uneven development that would otherwise be unsustainable. In practice, the use of remittances by migrant households falls short of the optimistic assumptions that are asserted in international policy discourse: contextualising the flow of foreign income reveals numerous remittance leakages, material hardships and social expectations that frustrate the 'investment' outcomes evoked by the language of entrepreneurship. Few productive investments are made, and nor should they be, as this effectively outsources the onus of development from the state to the poor themselves, in a manner that pathologises poverty and undermines the entitlement to decent local work. Significant expenditures that are made – be they on housing, education, debt repayments or status goods – have a tendency to redistribute income abroad (through imports) or towards local capital. The defunding and subsequent privatisation of Sri Lanka's education and healthcare, once the best public services in South Asia, only heightens this redistribution effect. While only providing subsistence for migrants themselves, remittances aggregate as a phenomenal injection of foreign capital for the economy. Rather than being a priori beneficial, a more nuanced consideration of the macroeconomic effects of a remittance-driven currency reveals inherent constraints to inclusive development arising from Dutch Disease and path dependency. Examination of Sri Lanka's post-war development policy corroborates this prognosis, as remittance-backed spending reinforces a path dependency on uneven and non-inclusive development that appears stable but harbours deep contradictions. Just as migrant returnees sometimes flaunt wealth they do not have, so too does Sri Lanka posture a development that is not really there.

Notes

1 'None' denotes a lack of primary or secondary remittance expenditures. In the case of primary expenditures, it reflects the failure to remit any income; in secondary expenditures, it reflects an absence of expenditure outside of previously denoted categories. For example, the large share of 'None' results amongst 'third-largest shares of remittance expenditure' indicates that all available remittances were spent on the first- and second-largest shares.
2 Business expenses were taken to include the purchase of vehicles, such as motorbikes and vans, which are otherwise hard to categorise as they may or may not be intended for business use.
3 For male workers; domestic workers receive board at no additional expense.
4 Twenty-two private banks, two national banks and the Sri Lanka Post Service.
5 Which are legally required to operate through a licensed financial institution

References

Amjad, R., ed. 1989. *To the Gulf and Back: Studies on the Economic Impact of Asian Labour Migration*. New Delhi: ILO.

Angenendt, Steffen. 2014. 'Creating a Triple-Win through Labor Migration Policy? Lessons from Germany'. Framework Paper. Migration Strategy Group. Washington, DC: The German Marshall Fund.

Arunatilake, Nisha. 2012. 'Precarious Work in Sri Lanka'. *American Behavioral Scientist* 57 (4): 488–506.

Arunatilake, Nisha, Suwendrani Jayaratne, Priyanka Jayawardena, Roshini Jayaweera, and Dushni Weerakoon. 2010. 'Impact of Remittances on the Household of the Emigrant and on the Economy of the Migrant's Country: Sri Lanka'. 10–13. South Asia Network of Economic Research Institutes. Colombo: Institute of Policy Studies of Sri Lanka.

Athukorala, Premachandra. 1992. 'The Use of Migrant Remittances in Development: Lessons from the Asian Experience'. *Journal of International Development* 4 (5): 511–29.

Athukorala, Premachandra. 1993. 'Improving the Contribution of Migrant Remittances to Development: The Experience of Asian Labour-Exporting Countries'. *International Migration* 31 (1): 103–22.

Barajas, Adolfo, Ralph Chami, Connel Fullenkamp, and Peter Montiel. 2009. 'Do Workers' Remittances Promote Economic Growth?' Working Paper WP/09/153. Washington, DC: International Monetary Fund (IMF).

Bräutigam, Deborah. 2011. *The Dragon's Gift: The Real Story of China in Africa*. Oxford: Oxford University Press.

Buthpitiya, Vindhya. 2013. 'Reconciling Rights, Responsibilities and Disjunctures: An Assessment of Sri Lanka's Post-War Development Drive'. Colombo: Law and Society Trust.

Central Bank of Sri Lanka (CBSL). 2018. 'Economic and Social Statistics of Sri Lanka 2018'. Colombo: Central Bank of Sri Lanka.

Chami, Ralph, Ekkehard Ernst, Connel Fullenkamp, and Anne Oeking. 2018. 'Is There a Remittance Trap?' Finance and Development. Washington, DC: International Monetary Fund (IMF).

Corden, W. M. 1984. 'Booming Sector and Dutch Disease Economics: Survey and Consolidation'. *Oxford Economic Papers* 36: 359–80.

Das, Khanindra Ch. 2017. 'The Making of One Belt, One Road and Dilemmas in South Asia'. *China Report* 53 (2): 125–42.

De Silva, Amala, W. D. Lakshman, and M. D. A. L. Ranasinghe. 1993. 'Migrant Remittances as a Source of Development Funding: A Study of Sri Lanka'. RAS/88/029. Sub-Regional Seminar on Migrant Remittances and Economic Development in South Asia. Colombo: UNDP/ILO.

Delgado Wise, Raúl, and Humberto Márquez Covarrubias. 2009. 'Understanding the Relationship between Migration and Development: Toward a New Theoretical Approach'. *Social Analysis* 53 (3): 85–105.

Department of Census and Statistics (DCS). 2017. *Sri Lanka Labour Force Survey: Annual Report – 2017*. Colombo: Department of Census and Statistics.

Dias, Malsiri. 1986. 'Sri Lanka'. In *Middle East Interlude: Asian Workers Abroad: A Comparative Study of Four Countries*, edited by Manolo Abella and Yogesh Atal, 177–246. Bangkok: UNESCO.

El Qorchi, Mohammed, Samuel Munzele Maimbo, and John F. Wilson. 2003. *Informal Funds Transfer Systems: An Analysis of the Informal Hawala System*. Occasional Paper/ International Monetary Fund 222. Washington, DC: International Monetary Fund.

European Migration Network (EMN). 2010. 'Specifications for EMN Study – Temporary and Circular Migration: Empirical Evidence, Current Policy Practice and Future Options in EU Member States'. Doc 192. Brussels: European Commission.

Eversole, Robyn, and Judith Shaw. 2010. 'Remittance Flows and Their Use in Households: A Comparative Study of Sri Lanka, Indonesia and the Philippines'. *Asian and Pacific Migration Journal* 19 (2): 175–202.

Faist, Thomas. 2008. 'Migrants as Transnational Development Agents: An Inquiry into the Newest Round of the Migration–Development Nexus'. *Population, Space and Place* 14 (1): 21–42.

Gamburd, Michele Ruth. 2000. *The Kitchen Spoon's Handle: Transnationalism and Sri Lanka's Migrant Housemaids*. Ithaca, NY: Cornell University Press.

Gamburd, Michele Ruth. 2004. 'Money That Burns Like Oil: A Sri Lankan Cultural Logic of Morality and Agency'. *Ethnology* 43 (2): 167–84.

Gunasinghe, Miyuru. 2012. 'Mega Development in Hambantota'. *Law and Society Trust Review* 23 (299): 1–21.

Gunatilleke, Godfrey. 1986. *Migration of Asian Workers to the Arab World*. Tokyo: United Nations University Press.

Gunatilleke, Godfrey. 1995. 'The Economic, Demographic, Sociocultural and Political Setting for Emigration from Sri Lanka'. *International Migration* 3 (4): 667–98.

Gunatilleke, Godfrey, S. S. Colombage, and Myrtle Perera. 2010. 'Macroeconomic Impact of International Migration: A Case Study of Sri Lanka'. 10-06. South Asia Network of Economic Research Institutes. Colombo: MARGA.

Haas, Hein de. 2012. 'The Migration and Development Pendulum: A Critical View on Research and Policy: The Migration and Development Pendulum'. *International Migration* 50 (3): 8–25.

Hassan, Gazi M., and Mark J. Holmes. 2013. 'Remittances and the Real Effective Exchange Rate'. *Applied Economics* 45 (35): 4959–70.

Kageyama, A. 2008. 'Extent of Poverty Alleviation by Migrant Remittances in Sri Lanka'. *South Asia Research* 28 (1): 89–108.

Karunaratne, Hettige Don. 2008. 'International Labour Migration, Remittances and Income Inequality in a Developing Country: The Case of Sri Lanka'. *Keizai-Shirin: Hosei Economic Review* 15 (3).

Katseli, Louka, Robert Lucas, and Theodora Xenogiani. 2006. 'Effects of Migration on Sending Countries: What Do We Know?' Working Paper 250. Working Paper Series. Paris: OECD Development Centre.

Kottegoda, Sepali. 2004. *Negotiating Household Politics: Women's Strategies in Urban Sri Lanka*. Colombo: Social Scientists' Association.

Kottegoda, Sepali, Ramani Jayasundere, Sumikā Perērā, and Padma Atapattu. 2013. *Transforming Lives: Listening to Sri Lankan Returnee Women Migrant Workers*. Colombo: Women and Media Collective.

Lartey, Emmanuel K. K., Federico S. Mandelman, and Pablo A. Acosta. 2012. 'Remittances, Exchange Rate Regimes and the Dutch Disease: A Panel Data Analysis'. *Review of International Economics* 20 (2): 377–95.

Lasagabaster, Esperanza, Samuel Munzele Maimbo, and Sriyani Hulugalle. 2005. *Sri Lanka's Migrant Labor Remittances: Enhancing the Quality and Outreach of the Rural Remittance Infrastructure*. Policy Research Working Papers. Washington, DC: The World Bank.

Lenard, Patti Tamara, and Christine Straehle. 2010. 'Temporary Labour Migration: Exploitation, Tool of Development, or Both?' *Policy and Society* 29 (4): 283–94.

Martin, Philip. 2012. 'Reducing Migration Costs and Maximizing Human Development'. In *Global Perspectives on Migration and Development: GFMD Puerto Vallarta and Beyond*, edited by Irena Omelaniuk, 27–52. Global Migration Issues 1. Dordrecht: Springer.

Ministry of Megapolis and Western Development (MMWD). 2016. 'The Megapolis: Western Region Master Plan'. Colombo: Ministry of Megapolis and Western Development.

Page, J., and S. Plaza. 2006. 'Migration Remittances and Development: A Review of Global Evidence'. *Journal of African Economies* 15 (Supplement 2): 245–336.

Rajakaruna, S. H. I. 2017. 'An Investigation on Factors Affecting Exchange Rate Fluctuations in Sri Lanka'. *Staff Studies* 47 (1): 69.

Ratha, Dilip. 2007. 'Leveraging Remittances for Development'. Washington, DC: Migration Policy Institute.

Razak, Azhar. 2018. 'Master Plan for Hambantota in the Works'. *Sunday Observer*. 9 June 2018. www.sundayobserver.lk/2018/06/10/news-features/master-plan-hambantota-works.

Reuters. 2016. 'IMF Agrees $1.5 Billion Bailout for Sri Lanka to Avert Balance Of …', 29 April 2016. www.reuters.com/article/us-imf-sri-lanka-idUSKCN0XQ063.

Rodrigo, C, and R. A. Jayatissa. 1989. 'Maximising Benefits from Labour Migration: Sri Lanka'. In *To the Gulf and Back: Studies on the Economic Impact of Asian Labour Migration*, edited by R Amjad, 255–96. New Delhi: ILO.

Roy, Ripon, and Robert Dixon. 2015. 'Workers' Remittances and the Dutch Disease in South Asian Countries'. *Applied Economics Letters*, August, 407–10.

Safi, Michael. 2018. 'Sri Lanka's "New Dubai": Will Chinese-Built City Suck the Life out of Colombo?' *Guardian*, 2 August 2018. www.theguardian.com/cities/2018/aug/02/sri-lanka-new-dubai-chinese-city-colombo.

Safi, Michael, and Amantha Perera. 2018. '"The Biggest Game Changer in 100 Years": Chinese Money Gushes into Sri Lanka'. *Guardian*, 26 March 2018. www.theguardian.com/world/2018/mar/26/the-biggest-game-changer-in-100-years-chinese-money-gushes-into-sri-lanka.

Shaikh, Anwar. 1980. 'Foreign Trade and the Law of Value: Part 2'. *Science and Society* XLIV: 27–57.

Shaw, Judith. 2010. 'Making Housemaid Remittances Work for Low-Income Families in Sri Lanka'. *Development in Practice* 20 (1): 18–30.

Siddiqui, Tasneem, and Myrtle Perera. 2000. *Temporary Labour Migration of Women: Case Studies of Bangladesh and Sri Lanka*. Santo Domingo, Dominican Republic: United Nations International Research and Training Institute for the Advancement of Women.

Skeldon, Ronald. 2005. 'Globalization, Skilled Migration and Poverty Alleviation: Brain Drains in Context'. Working Paper T15. Brighton: Sussex University Development Research Centre on Migration, Globalisation and Poverty.

Skeldon, Ronald. 2006. 'Interlinkages between Internal and International Migration and Development in the Asian Region'. *Population, Space and Place* 12 (1): 15–30.

Stenholm, Noora. 2015. 'Gendered Perspectives on Rehabilitation After Involuntary Resettlement in Urban Sri Lanka'. Masters Thesis, Helsinki: University of Helsinki.

United Nations Economic Commission for Europe (UNECE). 2016. 'Defining and Measuring Circular Migration: Final Report of the Task Force on Measuring Circular Migration'. Geneva: UNECE.

Wickramasekara, Piyasiri. 2015. 'Migration Regimes and Their Linkages for Family Unity, Integrity and Development'. In *The Palgrave Handbook of International Labour Migration: Law and Policy Perspectives*, edited by Marion Panizzon, Gottfried Zürcher, and Elisa Fornalé, 146–180. London: Palgrave Macmillan.

Wickramasekara, Piyasiri. 2016. 'South Asian Gulf Migration to the Gulf: A Safety Valve or a Development Strategy?' *Migration and Development* 5 (1): 99–129.

World Bank. 2006. *Global Economic Prospects: Economic Implications of Remittances and Migration*. Washington, DC: World Bank.

World Bank, ed. 2012. *Turning Sri Lanka's Urban Vision into Policy and Action*. Colombo: The World Bank Colombo Office.

World Bank. 2019. 'World Development Indicators'. Washington, DC: World Bank.

Wucker, Michele. 2004. 'Remittances: The Perpetual Migration Machine'. *World Policy Journal* 21 (2): 37–46.

7 The unequal 'wins' of temporary labour migration

The previous chapter analysed the macroeconomic characteristics of *remittance capital*, both as aggregate household consumption and net foreign-exchange earnings, to demonstrate its inherent tendency to aggravate uneven development in Sri Lanka. The structural contradictions of temporary labour migration, and the institutional apparatus that sustain them, are reinforced by workers' remittances that provide superficial relief to the poor while facilitating demand spillovers and developmental spending that primarily benefits a narrow segment of the urban economy. This finding not only belies one of the central claims of those advocating migration-development, that 'the bulk of the economic gains from migration accrue to migrants and their families' (World Bank 2006, xii), but stresses the importance of assessing the relative distribution of the gains heralded by the triple win rhetoric of policymakers. Disproportionate returns to capital relative to migrant workers themselves, manifest in uneven development, is a crucial part of this story. So too, however, are the disproportionate returns to developed and developing regions on a global scale. Broadening the scope of analysis beyond the local economy suggests that Sri Lanka is enmeshed in a more profound pattern of underdevelopment relative to centres of accumulation within receiving economies and across the globe. This chapter therefore turns attention to the global dimension of underdevelopment and the role temporary labour migration plays in anchoring Sri Lanka to the periphery of a world economy that is shifting from West to East, but leaving much of the South behind.

'Underdevelopment' is a relational concept. A comprehensive assessment of migration-development outcomes cannot limit its attention to local development alone, but must situate the entire dynamic within the encompassing structures of capital accumulation that shape the world economy. In doing so, this chapter rejects the notion of a mutually beneficial triple win scenario by drawing attention to the unequal gains arising from the formalisation of temporary labour migration as a prominent feature of a re-globalising world economy. The chapter is organised in three sections. It first contrasts the immediate economic benefits for migrant-sending and migrant-receiving economies by juxtaposing the impact of *remittance capital* in Sri Lanka with destination countries' access to a reserve army of migrant labour. Second, it extends this analysis by considering how the more indirect consequences of Sri Lanka's widespread migration – including the unequal costs of migration, reconfiguration of the care economy, foreign employment spillovers, import spillovers and demand volatility – constrains capital accumulation within the economy while encouraging it elsewhere. Finally, it identifies Sri Lanka as archetypal of a modern 'remittance economy', where an overdependence on foreign employment has underscored limited capital accumulation and poverty alleviation in lieu of development itself. Ultimately this has been to the disadvantage of the country as a whole, given the relatively much greater returns to foreign economies and the sheer precarity of remittances that are directly tied to demand from West Asia.

Unequal outcomes

The concept of a triple win outcome from temporary labour migration has been far-reaching and remarkably resilient in the face of sustained empirical uncertainty. In 2006, the World Bank declared that:

> International migration can generate substantial welfare gains for migrants, their countries of origin, and the countries to which they migrate.
>
> (2006, 25)

In 2010, the European Migration Network (EMN) reiterated this belief in the context of increasing policy attention to managed migration, stating that:

> Circular and temporary migration is reflecting globalisation, demographic change, new patterns of mobility and the growing demand for flexible labour markets. It also reflects a preference of many of the migrants themselves … it is viewed as a means to serve the labour market needs of countries of destination, promote development in countries of origin and benefit migrants themselves.
>
> (EMN 2010, 3)

In 2016, a report by the United Nations Economic Commission for Europe (UNECE) offered another paraphrasing, reiterating that:

> Circular migration is often seen as a win–win–win proposition, providing gains to countries of both origin and destination, as well as to the migrants themselves. In countries of destination, it can alleviate labour needs and increase economic production. In countries of origin, it can provide unemployment relief and both financial and human capital (in terms of skills and resources brought back to the country), as well as mitigate population loss due to emigration. Individual migrants also benefit via increased income, greater work experience, and the development of their human capital.
>
> (UNECE 2016, 1)

Although current policy interest in circular migration can be seen as an initiative of advanced capitalist economies to attain 'labour without people' (Wickramasekara 2011), the stringent enforcement of short-term employment that is central to the model has long been the norm in West Asia. As such, the corridor of temporary labour migration that exists between Sri Lanka and West Asia conforms to the idealised conditions under which the triple win is envisioned, that is, with the categorical inability for migrant workers to emigrate permanently. Sri Lankan labour migration to West Asia is therefore a suitable context through which to pit the expectations of a mutually beneficial triple win against actual economic outcomes, emphasising the relative distribution of the costs and benefits to sending and receiving economies. The following section focuses on the most immediate benefits produced by this corridor of temporary labour migration, while subsequent analysis draws attention to the indirect economic costs and consequences of sustaining these flows.

Relative 'wins'

Adherents of a triple win outcome generally proclaim: (i) that migrants gain from better income and skill acquisition; (ii) that sending economies gain from remittance inflows, unemployment fixes and a return on human capital ('brain circulation'); and (iii) that receiving economies gain by addressing their labour market 'needs' (World Bank 2006). These expectations are here counterposed against the experiences of Sri Lankan migrants, the Sri Lankan economy and the receiving economies of West Asia.

The win for migrants

Previous chapters have shown that empirical evidence, both from this study and others, challenges the assumption that migrants unequivocally benefit from earning foreign incomes. Even for the most successful migrants, remittances rarely translate into sustainable economic improvements for migrant families and more typically foster a reliance on foreign employment (by repeat or flow-on migration) to ensure economic subsistence. For those most disadvantaged prior to migration, the pursuit of foreign incomes often results in net indebtedness, due to the challenges of financing recruitment fees without existing assets and susceptibility to exploitation by local merchants of labour.

These outcomes reflect two important considerations belying the triple win narrative. First, a lack of sustainable employment upon return reflects the reality that low-waged workers, who comprise the vast bulk of temporary labour migrants, do not acquire skills that have meaningful application upon reintegration. For female domestic workers, foreign employment represents a marketisation of devalued and stigmatised reproductive work that has little social or economic footing within Sri Lanka, while low-waged male labourers often migrate precisely because there are insufficient local employment opportunities for the skills they possess. Moreover, given the extent of income differentials between Sri Lanka and the Gulf, skilled workers without decent work are often 'de-skilled' by migrating to take up low-skilled positions abroad (Skeldon 1992). As de Silva, Lakshman and Ranasinghe observe in Sri Lanka's case:

> The tendency for underemployment of skills overseas obviously lies in the income differential between home and host country for jobs requiring similar skills. This creates an incentive for migrants to seek work even at skill levels below what they possess.
>
> (1993, 16)

Second, with migrants themselves in large part shouldering the costs involved in facilitating their job placement, income gains are limited by recruitment fees and associated indebtedness. Even ardent advocates of temporary labour migration concede the negligible return on income for the poorest of migrant households, for whom migration-related loans can be crippling. Ratha's (2007) analysis of the short-term impact of remittances suggests that there is negligible income improvement for Sri Lankan households within the poorest three income deciles, indicating that whatever benefits arise from migration are contingent upon meeting a certain threshold of pre-existing means.

The plight of migrant returnees and their families has been explored extensively in previous chapters and discussion of this theme is here truncated to shift attention towards the relational aspect of macroeconomic gains accruing to Sri Lanka and the receiving economies of West Asia.

The win for sending economies

As with outcomes for migrants themselves, remittance-specific gains to the Sri Lankan economy have been thoroughly discussed already. Remittances are a mixed blessing at best, indirectly facilitating capital accumulation and development spending, but under intrinsic constraints that undermine export production and buttress an existing path dependency on uneven development. Factoring in the non-productive and import-stimulating character of household remittance use, the overall impact of *remittance capital* is modest and overwhelmingly aligned with the short-term interests of local factions of capital operating within the urban economy.

What, then, of the supposed 'wins' from unemployment relief and 'brain circulation'?

The argument that temporary labour migration provides unemployment relief is corroborated by Sri Lanka's historical and continued use of foreign employment as a 'safety valve' for unemployment and attendant political and economic pressures (Wickramasekara 2016). While reliable employment statistics only go back as far as 1991, it is clear that unemployment rates have declined in tandem with increasing foreign employment as a percentage of the labour force, illustrated below in Figure 7.1, lending weight to the general consensus that labour migration is the primary explanation for this trend (IPS 2013). More contentious is the construal of unemployment relief as beneficial to Sri Lanka's economy, as

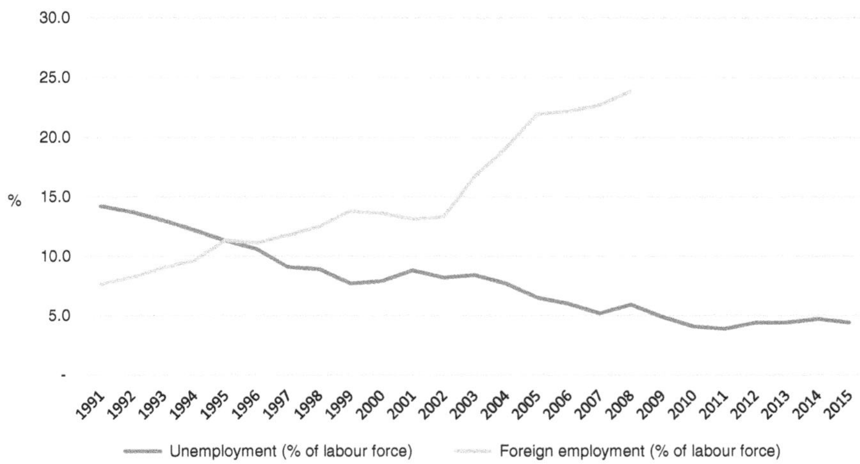

Figure 7.1 Unemployment vs. foreign employment, 1991–2015.
Sources; SLBFE 2012; World Bank 2019.

foreign employment effectively defers accountability for job creation. While unemployment rates have steadily fallen from 14.5 to 4.4 per cent between 1992 and 2014, the labour force participation rate has remained low and stagnant, decreasing from 56.6 to 53.1 per cent over the same period (World Bank 2019). That such minimal job creation has occurred in an economy characterised by growth in services alongside the preservation of a large agricultural sector is symptomatic of 'migration instead of development', where labour migration substitutes for the employment and foreign-exchange earnings typically achieved through export production. However, prolonged reliance on migration as a developmental stand-in can precariously reorient the economy. In addition to weakening export competitiveness through a remittance-strengthened currency, an overdependence on migration rewards a neglect of domestic unemployment and underemployment pressures with further remittances, irrevocably turning Sri Lanka's development strategy away from the model of scalable industrial mass employment that has driven economic development elsewhere in Asia.

Concerns about the relationship between unemployment, migration and economic development are shared by the IPS, who see the challenge of retaining skilled workers as an interrelated problem:

> Despite a persistent decline in Sri Lanka's rate of unemployment, questions remain of the productive nature of jobs that are being created in the current economic climate. Indeed, even as the numbers of Sri Lankan migrants seeking employment overseas is on the rise, a growing share of such migrants are skilled workers, indicative of less-than-favourable domestic labour market conditions for such workers.
>
> (IPS 2013, 18–19)

Although the SLBFE does not categorically record the education levels of departing migrant workers, occupational data from 2016 reveals that 89.4 per cent of foreign employment positions were accounted for by domestic work (26.8 per cent), 'low-skilled' (33.1 per cent) or 'unskilled' (29.5 per cent) (SLBFE 2016). Professional employment accounted for just 2.7 per cent of foreign positions, while ill-defined 'middle level' and 'clerical' positions account for the remaining 7.9 per cent of migrant departures (SLBFE 2016). Comparatively, 'low-skilled' and 'elementary' workers (i.e. excluding professional, high-skilled and service workers) accounted for 59.2 per cent of domestic employment for the same year (DCS 2017). While most foreign positions may reflect the employment of Sri Lankan migrants at their existing skill-levels, or the employment of migrants who would otherwise be economically inactive in Sri Lanka, some migrants are nevertheless working below their ability. With 'low-skilled' foreign employment often offering higher incomes than more skill-intensive domestic employment, it is easy to appreciate why deskilling might occur.

This observation confronts the anticipated benefit of a 'brain circulation' for migrant-sending countries and alludes to the practical realities of managing labour supply issues in an underdeveloped economy engaged in temporary labour migration. In the first instance, low-waged temporary labour migration involves employment in conditions that are not conducive to skill development tantamount to an inwards 'brain circulation'. Migrants frequently take up menial forms of foreign employment and without acquiring new skills abroad their labour remains underutilised within local production when they return, partly explaining the prevalence of repeat migration. At the same time, an increasing macroeconomic dependence on migration has overseen policy efforts to encourage the temporary migration of high-skilled workers as a means of maximising remittance inflows, creating tension with the competing need to retain high-skilled labour for the local economy (IPS 2012).

In offering a caveat to the anticipated 'brain circulation' for sending economies the World Bank notes:

> Some countries find it difficult to provide productive employment for many high-skilled workers because of their small economic scale or because misguided educational policies have resulted in a large supply of university graduates for whom no suitable jobs exist.
>
> (World Bank 2006, xiv)

In the context of migration-development this amounts to disingenuous reasoning. Naturally, a lack of productive capacity will hinder the ability to retain skilled labour, but this is a fundamental condition of underdevelopment arising from the historical structures of global capitalism and, more pointedly, colonialism. It is also a product of pedagogical mimicry within tertiary education throughout the Global South, where universities often share institutional lineage with their Global North counterparts and thus structure qualifications in accordance to mismatching labour needs (Potts 1990). Given that most migrant-sending countries reflect these circumstances, there is little point in hypothesising potential 'brain circulation' when skilled temporary labour migration takes place precisely because there is greater demand for skilled labour in relatively developed economies where the bulk of capital accumulation takes place.

With regard to low-waged migration, the World Bank is again unhelpful:

> low-skilled emigration can offer a valuable safety valve for insufficient employment at home. In the long run, however, developing country policies should aim to generate adequate employment and rapid growth, rather than relying on migration as an alternative to development opportunities.
>
> (World Bank 2006, xiv)

While migrant-sending countries' need for local development is obvious, the convenient oversight is that remittance-dependency is cumulatively causative and intrinsically undermines both the ability and incentive to create local employment opportunities for 'low-skilled' or skilled labour.

The win for receiving economies

Unlike the ostensible gains to be had by migrants and sending economies, the 'win' for receiving economies is more readily apparent. While the economic impact of remittances is largely indirect and constrained by a gamut of endogenous factors affecting household spending and developmental policies, the employment of migrant workers in migrant-receiving countries directly facilitates capital accumulation and social reproduction by provisioning a 'flexible' (i.e. cheap and exploitable) reserve army of labour and care.

The World Bank is less reserved in discussing the benefits that temporary labour migration produces for receiving economies:

> Destination countries can enjoy significant economic gains from migration. The increased availability of labor boosts returns to capital and reduces the cost of production. A model-based simulation performed for this study indicates that a rise in migration from developing countries sufficient to raise the labor force of high-income countries by 3 per cent could boost incomes of natives in high-income countries by 0.4 per cent. In addition, high-income countries may benefit from increased labor-market flexibility, an increased labor force due to lower prices for services such as child care, and perhaps economies of scale and increased diversity.
>
> (World Bank 2006, xii)

For the receiving economies of West Asia, whose own development has been anomalously independent of industrialisation due to the concentration of vast oil reserves amongst small populations, the ability to draw upon a reserve army of migrant labour has been an in-situ solution to domestic labour shortages. World Bank data estimates that in 1960, prior to the formation of OPEC and almost two decades before Sri Lanka commenced sending temporary labour migrants to the Gulf, there were 240,000 international migrant workers in Gulf Cooperation Council (GCC) countries. By 2015, the same dataset estimates there were 25 million international migrant workers in GCC countries that together accounted for anywhere between 32.3 per cent (Saudi Arabia) and 88.4 per cent (United Arab Emirates) of each country's total population (World Bank 2019).

More than simply redressing labour shortages, however, the GCC countries have systematically exploited migrant workers as cheap labour inputs to sustain development and catalyse economic diversification beyond oil production. As a region whose rapid amassing of wealth preceded the hallmarks of human and infrastructural development, West Asia has depended on migrant labour to build and service the rapidly changing contours of its oil economies. Migrant workers constitute the majority of the labour force in every GCC economy; the concentration of migrant labour varies between countries, but accounts for as much as 95 per cent of all workers in Qatar and the UAE (Baldwin-Edwards 2011). These workers are employed to construct physical infrastructure, undertake professional and domestic care work, and to provide low-cost labour to facilitate capital accumulation in an expanding non-tradeable sector that has become the largest engine of regional growth outside of oil exports (IMF 2013). By exercising a form of employer sovereignty derived from an ability to offer improved incomes, GCC countries have drawn on a segmented reserve army of migrant labour and care to target select aspects of their own development. Low-waged male labourers from a number of underdeveloped regions abstractly compete to provide cheap manual labour to complete infrastructural, commercial and residential construction projects; a glut of service workers without decent local employment similarly compete to work in non-tradeable sectors that diversify GCC economies; and domestic workers of various backgrounds are fetishised within an informal racial hierarchy that accords prestige to care workers from particular migrant-sending countries (Castles and Miller 2007; Haskins and Lowrie 2015).

In performing the dirty, dangerous and degrading work that affluent locals demand, but are unwilling to do (for similar pay) themselves, temporary migrants adhere to Cohen's (1987) depiction of migrant workers as 'the new helots': an underclass of quasi-free workers displaced by underdevelopment in the migrant-sending countries of the regional periphery and drawn into processes of core accumulation within receiving economies. However, unlike helots themselves – a homogenous body of subjugated workers – the very diversity of this reserve army of migrant labour is fundamental to its exploitation, as West Asian states are able to play one underdeveloped labour supply against others in order to reduce labour costs and maintain an absence of basic rights. In the case of the GCC countries, the 'win' from having access to this reserve army of migrant labour has been nothing short of foundational in underpinning the entire development of these economies.

Mutual benefits?

Comparing the outcomes of migrants, the countries they come from and the countries they work in reveals significant discrepancies in the relative distribution of anticipated 'wins' arising from temporary labour migration. Migrant workers are, perhaps unsurprisingly, the least assured of benefit, having to shoulder the burden of recruitment costs, endure labour-intensive foreign employment under precarious circumstances, and face a lack of suitable employment upon return. While most receive improved incomes, this outcome is tempered by the situational differences of *place* and existing socio-economic standing, and typically entails repeat migration that disrupts family life (as discussed in Chapters 3 and 4). The development of skills, meanwhile, is categorically limited by the nature of employment in West Asia. As a country of origin, Sri Lanka also reaps highly contingent benefits. *Remittance capital* is inherently fraught as a form of development capital, but these limitations are compounded by migration's tendency to reduce the impetus for local employment creation as foreign employment becomes an end in itself. The initial 'unemployment relief' of migration soon becomes entrenched as a structural barrier to industrialisation and, conversely to the expectations of 'brain circulation', an obstacle to the retention of skilled workers who are more readily utilised as remittance earners. Meanwhile, the receiving economies of West Asia make unequivocal gains by exploiting a diverse reserve army of migrant labour to build, service, grow and reproduce their own rapidly developed economies. While the GCC countries still face the challenge of creating jobs for local workers and further diversifying their economies, the absence of temporary labour migration would have made present levels of development unobtainable.

The uneven returns of temporary labour migration between Sri Lanka and West Asia undermines the notion of a triple win outcome by all but the coarsest of absolute measures. In relative terms, there is a clear stratification of beneficiaries, beginning with foreign employers and ending with migrant labour: put abstractly, the developed gain more than the developing, increasing relative disparities between the two. Nevertheless, temporary labour migration continues to receive support from countries of origin and destination alike. Certainly, for Sri Lanka, the promotion of foreign employment endures as a key developmental strategy. Although this would appear to infer a mutually beneficial arrangement between sending and receiving economies, any ostensible overlap in interests might more shrewdly be understood as the resonating preferences of influential factions of local and foreign capital. Embedded within Sri Lanka's path dependency on migration are the vested (and politically potent) short-term interests of those who directly benefit from the arrangement: the merchants of labour, urban service-sector businesses and the political elite itself. However, if temporary labour migration and remittance inflows were to persistently decline, the exchange rate and levels of local demand would fall in kind, harming those same factions of capital more rapidly than factor mobility permits profitable reinvestment in emerging industries. By continuing to adopt policies that promote migration and sustain an accompanying regime of accumulation by subordination, Sri Lanka is safeguarding the short-term interests of particular actors at the cost of inclusive development. The long-term interests of capital *in general* are equally compromised by this pursuit, as a lack of inclusive development will ultimately undermine the growth of local wages and demand to the detriment of the entire economy.

The indirect implications of temporary labour migration

The short-term consequences of temporary labour migration tend to be framed in terms of simple economic metrics: gross income for migrants, aggregate remittances for sending economies and labour supply for receiving economies. This analysis is supplemented by attention to 'human capital' formation, although – as the previous section has argued – in a manner that is unhelpfully abstracted from the economic reality of countries of origin like Sri Lanka. However, beyond the narrowly defined gains proclaimed by the triple win doctrine, there are various indirect implications of temporary labour migration that have, by and large, been neglected by conventional economic analysis. These secondary implications warrant greater attention, as they can potentially intensify the underdevelopment of migrant-sending countries relative to more developed regions of the world economy. The following section discusses five prominent themes in reference to Sri Lanka's relationship with temporary labour migration: the unequal costs of migration, reconfigurations to the care economy, foreign employment spillovers, import spillovers and demand volatility.

Unequal costs of migration

The relative costs of migration incurred by sending and receiving economies is an important consideration that is often overlooked when assessing the economic outcomes of foreign employment.

In light of the obvious disparity of means between foreign employers and migrant workers, international conventions have called for employers to bear the entirety of recruitment costs (Martin 2012). These efforts have been met with little success. The direct costs associated with facilitating labour migration pays dividend to the merchants of labour in both migrant-sending and migrant-receiving countries. In this regard, it mostly represents an internal redistribution of income to capital in both economies. Individual or corporate employers pay for the services of recruitment companies in West Asia, while associated agents and sub-agents in Sri Lanka charge substantial recruitment fees to prospective migrants. Sri Lankan agents additionally receive commission from foreign recruiters, though predominantly for domestic-worker job orders, as domestic workers are in increasingly high demand due to restrictions placed on women's migration by other migrant-sending countries (ILO 2013). The direct costs of arranging foreign employment thus entails a small net transfer from migrant-receiving to migrant-sending countries, although the potential benefit of this is overshadowed by the inflated cut taken by Sri Lankan 'middle men' who exploit the abundance of prospective male migrants by forwarding their business liabilities as recruitment fees. As argued in Chapter 4, this is a manifestation of accumulation by subordination arising from (and reinforcing) uneven development.

Beyond recruitment costs, foreign employment represents a significant indirect expense for the migrant-sending country, expressed as the sum of public investment in the education and welfare of labour power to be employed abroad (Delgado Wise 2009). These outlays may be targeted investments in migrant labour, as with the costs associated with Sri Lanka's cursory pre-departure training for migrant domestic workers, but primarily reflect the more general social reproduction costs associated with the upbringing of any working-age citizen: the provision of public healthcare, basic schooling and food or income benefits. Abstractly, Sri Lanka subsidises the cost of production in West Asia, not only by 'lending' cheaper labour but by relieving receiving economies of the long-term expenses involved in reproducing labour power. It is difficult to gauge the extent of these expenses, as they reflect a fluctuating portion of overall public investment across time, but it suffices to assume that with an active migrant population equivalent to approximately 25 per cent of the total workforce as of the last available estimate (SLBFE 2012), it is not a trivial outlay.

This effect is furthered by GCC countries' obstinate refusal to grant basic social and welfare services to migrant workers, ensuring that they must reproduce their labour power independently of state investment. In instances where this is not possible – through injury, sickness or loss of employment – migrant workers must return to Sri Lanka. With Sri Lanka also attempting to minimise public expenditure on reproducing labour power, the onus of welfare then shifts, guided by the ethos of 'self-help development', to become a private burden borne by migrants and their families. Nonetheless, even the limited amount of public investment Sri Lanka makes in reproducing migrant labour power represents an expense footed by Sri Lanka and not the countries of destination that actually employ and profit from the workers in question. These lopsided costs might be more understandable if migration truly were temporary, and migrant labour power predominantly employed in Sri Lanka, possibly with newly acquired skills from working abroad. However, with skill-stagnant migrant returnees frequently disengaging from the workforce or pursing repeat migration, this is not the dominant reality of temporary labour migration from Sri Lanka to West Asia.

Reconfiguration of the care economy

Closely associated with the hidden expenses of reproducing labour power are temporary labour migration's profound implications for Sri Lanka's informal care economy.

Sri Lanka's declining commitment to public expenditure in the reproduction of labour power has been possible, in large part, to patriarchal gender norms that ascribe the burden of reproductive labour almost exclusively to women, whether in paid employment or not (Jayaweera 2002). Limited public health provisioning, along with an absence of institutional support for child and elderly care, is made possible on account of the social expectation that women are duty-bound to informal care provision (Withers 2016). For women participating in paid employment in Sri Lanka this often produces the 'double burden' of being both breadwinner and housekeeper, as gendered labour market institutions exploit, rather than acknowledge or compensate for, the onus of reproductive work (Elson 1999). There is, for example, no evidence that women's participation in paid employment produces a decline in unpaid care work. A study of time-use between married couples in Colombo found that when women entered paid employment their average working day lengthened to 16 hours, while the length of the average man's working day was largely unaffected (Satharasinghe 1999). The typically young and unmarried women who work in Sri Lanka's garment factories may serve as an exception to this double burden, but only insofar as their employment – itself a commodification of erstwhile reproductive tasks – entails internal migration that spatially disrupts their ability to perform care work. Once married or returned home, these workers, too, are embedded in an informal care regime that allots women a disproportionate share of the productive and reproductive labour that household survival often depends upon.

The widespread participation of Sri Lankan women in domestic work has placed further strain upon this care regime. The commodification of reproductive work as a 'labour export' has created a care deficit throughout Sri Lanka that, owing to the exceptionally gendered division of reproductive labour, is not readily filled by husbands or male relatives (Withers and Piper 2018). Instead, the care vacuum is most often filled by female relatives and neighbours. A recent study into the familial composition of primary caregivers in the absence of migrant mothers suggests that grandmothers assume primary care duties in 34 per cent of cases, followed by aunts in 26 per cent of cases, fathers in 23 per cent of cases and elder children 11 per cent of cases (Cooray 2017). This corroborates a more extensive household survey by Jayaweera and Dias (2009) that demonstrated that male spouses of migrant domestic workers rarely, if ever, took over care roles and household duties while their partners worked abroad. An earlier study instead suggested that communal ties often play a prominent role in resolving the question of care work, with children left behind often cared for by female neighbours (Kottegoda 2004). On the basis of these findings, the care deficit of migrant domestic workers will likely contribute to the 'double burden' of other working women, create intergenerational pressures that turn typical care-receivers (children and the elderly) into care-givers, or – where men do commit to performing reproductive labour – substitute for productive labour.[1] Given that temporary labour migration from Sri Lanka has historically been highly feminised, this presents a major disruption to the normal functioning of the care economy and the pressure placed on it to reproduce labour power with minimal support from the state.

While the migration of domestic workers places strain on Sri Lanka's care economy, it simultaneously relieves the burden of reproductive labour from women in the receiving economies of West Asia. Although female labour-force participation rates for most GCC countries remains lower than the global average, individual country rates have all steadily increased since reliable data became available in 1990 (World Bank 2019), suggesting that women are increasingly pursuing employment (predominantly in the public sector). A majority of households in GCC countries employ at least one domestic worker, who generally performs upwards of 80 per cent of the care work for the family (Forstenlechner and Rutledge 2011). This care relief allows foreign women to commit more time to productive activity, skill acquisition or what Veblen (2009 [1899]) terms 'the conspicuous consumption' of leisure. Just as the productive labour of migrant workers subsidises the cost of production in receiving economies, so too do domestic workers subsidise the reproductive capacity required to produce workers, skills and *status*. Ironically it is often the flip side of *status*, the stigma associated with performing socially degraded work, that compels Sri Lankan domestic workers to migrate internationally and relieve foreign care regimes in preference to migrating internally in response to demand for care within more affluent Colombo households. This contrasts with the experiences of temporary labour migrants from the Philippines, for example, where the prevalence of poorly paid care work is such that the households of migrant domestic workers can afford to employ local domestic workers in their stead (Lindio-McGovern 2016). It is difficult to discern which substitute for reproductive labour is more detrimental, Sri Lanka's reliance on informal familial care or the Philippines' exploitation of subordinated paid care, but it is clear that both systems create local care deficits while generating a care surplus for foreign economies.

Foreign employment spillovers

Another indirect implication to consider is the extent of migrant incomes that remain within, and thus stimulate demand for, the receiving economy. Chapter 6 examined this issue from the perspective of remittance transfers, where fieldwork findings were triangulated with other studies to suggest that Sri Lankan migrants remit approximately 80 per cent of their income, with male workers remitting less than female domestic workers on account of additional living costs associated with the conditions of their employment. From the perspective of migrant-sending countries, the portion of migrant income that is not remitted constitutes a 'leakage' that diminishes the magnitude of aggregate remittance inflows. From the perspective of migrant-receiving countries of the GCC, the basic needs of migrant workers – access to food, shelter, hygiene and socialisation – become a means through which wages are reappropriated as demand spillovers.

An explicit example of this appropriation is the malpractice of charging migrant construction workers a mandatory income deduction for food and/or accommodation that is meant to be provided as a condition of employment (ILO 2013). This tactic invariably involves the deception of migrant labourers, who are routinely assured by recruitment agents that the salaries they agree to are inclusive of these living costs, only to be charged for poor food and overcrowded accommodation once their visa status is tied to the employer. These employers, by passing their own costs on to workers, are essentially undercutting already low wages for male migrant workers to extract greater surplus value from their labour; vulnerable migrants are jostled into losing income to forcible 'spillovers' that suppress remittances and directly facilitate increased capital accumulation. Yet foreign capital benefits from less orchestrated spillovers too, insofar as the everyday personal expenses of migrants contribute to demand for local goods and services. Such expenses are typically modest: fieldwork findings indicated that domestic workers would generally spend money on phone calls, letters and personal hygiene items, whereas male workers were likely to spend additional money on food and socialising. Nonetheless, these incidental purchases were seen to account for at least 10 per cent of migrant incomes that then become demand spillovers for the receiving economy. Given the heavy concentration of migrant workers throughout the GCC countries, these incidental expenditures represent a considerable recirculation of wage payments as general consumption throughout those economies.

Import spillovers

As with foreign employment spillovers, the issue of import consumption was introduced in Chapter 6, but only discussed insofar as demand for foreign goods represents another form of remittance leakage. However, the extent to which remittance usage creates effective demand that redirects outside of countries of origin is one of the more neglected macroeconomic side-effects of remittances. In lieu of empirical support for the direct investment of remittances, migration-development adherents generally contend that the consumption of remittances has a positive impact on productive investment in the migrant-sending country by generating increased demand for local goods (Mallick 2010). While overall levels of consumption may well increase, the assumption is muddied by the potential for remittance usage to increase demand for imported foreign goods. Remittance-driven spillovers for local production must therefore be contextualised alongside other spillovers for foreign production, not only with regard to the relative volume of demand created but also in relation to compositional differences between local and foreign industries that stand to benefit.

In Sri Lanka's case, 'development' emerged from the uneven spread of capitalist relations under colonialism and took shape through various permutations of low value-added, demand-inelastic production ordered through strategies of accumulation by subordination (discussed in Chapter 2). Current production echoes this circumscriptive strategy of accumulation and retains its limitations, being largely split between a plantation economy mired by declining terms of trade and an increasingly hollowed-out garment industry dependent on subordinated female labour. It is this non-inclusive pattern of development that has conditioned the degradation of work and deprivation of *status* that engenders *forced migration* and its macroeconomic corollary of remittance inflows. Yet, having delimited most local production to niches filled by subordinated labour, Sri Lanka lacks the industrial capacity to capture the portion of household remittance expenditure that is directed towards vehicles, consumer durables and other manufactured wares. Remittances spent on these manufactures, often imbued with heightened socio-cultural importance as status-affirming goods, become import spillovers that boost effective demand for production elsewhere in the world economy. 'Elsewhere', following pronounced geographic shifts to the core of global production during the 1970s, refers not only to Europe and North America but increasingly the industrialised economies of East and Southeast Asia.

Using protectionist trade measures and state-driven industrial policy to guide export-oriented industrialisation, the likes of Japan, South Korea, Taiwan, Hong Kong and Singapore have achieved rapid and reasonably inclusive economic development (Chang 2006). Meanwhile 'market communism' has overseen massive export-driven growth in China and, to a significantly lesser extent, Vietnam. These emerging economies, along with traditional regions of core production throughout the Global North, benefit from the effective demand created by remittance consumption in underdeveloped economies such as Sri Lanka. For economies that employ migrant workers as labour power for export industries – such as Malaysia and South Korea – some remittances spent on imports may even reverberate within an enclosed effective demand loop between underdeveloped and developing regions. However, in general terms it is not particularly important whether import spillovers direct towards migrant-receiving economies or not (as is patently not the case in the oil-economies of West Asia); conceptualising the 'wins' of temporary labour migration as restricted to a tripartite relationship between migrants and their countries of work and residence is itself a narrow abstraction of economic reality. Greater significance lies in recognising: (i) that *forced migration* results from underdevelopment; (ii) that underdevelopment is accompanied by a lack of industrial production; (iii) that the macroeconomic impact of *remittance capital* stymies industrialisation; and (iv) that in the continuing absence of industrialisation, remittance consumption will create import spillovers for developed and developing economies that have industrialised. The increased effective demand created by remittances may indeed produce some spillovers for basic local production and services, but it may also widen the developmental gap by increasing demand for the value-added, demand-elastic manufactures of industrial economies of scale.

Demand volatility

The final indirect implication of temporary labour migration that demands greater attention is the issue of demand volatility for migrant labour, arising from potential political and economic crises within receiving economies. Remittances are praised for typically being counter-cyclical,[2] in that migrants tend to retain employment better than local workers during downturns and remit more in response to economic adversity at home (Ratha 2007). Comparatively little attention has been paid to the potential for major disturbances in migrant-receiving economies to effect reduced demand for migrant labour and so disrupt remittance flows. For Sri Lanka, along with other migrant-sending economies of South Asia, demand for temporary migrant labour overwhelmingly originates from the oil-rich GCC countries of West Asia. In this context, migrant remittances are therefore principally tied to the strength of a single commodity and the economies it sustains. This 'pegging' was a concern to Sri Lankan economists observing a decline in demand for migrant labour as global demand for oil, having driven up prices during the oil shocks of the 1970s, petered out amidst the 'oil glut' of the 1980s (Rodrigo and Jayatissa 1989; Athukorala 1993; De Silva, Lakshman, and Ranasinghe 1993). Ultimately, falling demand for migrant workers did not last, as oil prices stabilised throughout the 1990s and began increasing sharply after the turn of the millennium (SLBFE 2012). Sri Lanka was further insulated by the predominance of migrant domestic workers, whose jobs in private households were not susceptible to the same vicissitudes affecting construction work (Rodrigo and Jayatissa 1989). Nonetheless, the flow of all migrants – including domestic workers – can also be affected by restrictions imposed on foreign employment by migrant-sending countries in response to volatile conflicts or abusive employment, such as Sri Lanka's repatriation of workers during the Kuwait War (Perera 1992) and a number of bans to domestic worker migration issued at various times by a number of South Asian countries (Eelens, Mook, and Schampers 1992).

While demand volatility has not yet been seriously disruptive to remittance flows, previous downturns were enough to provoke concern about the sustainability of Sri Lanka's dependence on a fairly homogenous pattern of mass migration closely tied to West Asia's oil-economies. Addressing this concern, de Silva, Lakshman and Ranasinghe advise that Sri Lanka diversify its migration flows:

> In assessing sustainability of migration and remittance inflows, we need to consider skill composition and migrant destinations since these determine Sri Lanka's ability to make use of increased labour demand, and the wages migrant workers are able to earn abroad.
>
> (1993, 14)

Yet the skill composition of Sri Lanka's temporary labour migrants remains virtually unchanged since the time these concerns were aired. Furthermore, and despite limited efforts to bilaterally promote skilled migration to countries such as South Korea, there has been very little change to the countries receiving Sri Lankan workers – labour migration to West Asia still accounts for the vast majority of foreign employment, with Saudi Arabia, Qatar, the UAE and Kuwait making up 80 per cent of placements as of 2016 (SLBFE 2016).

However, between 1994 and 2016, remittances have increased from US$715 million to US$7.16 billion (World Bank 2019), while also expanding as a percentage of goods export earnings from approximately 25 per cent to 63 per cent in (CBSL 2018). Thus, while a lack of diversification has ensured that vulnerability to volatile demand remains, the magnitude of potential disruptions to remittance flows has greatly increased. Given the historical instability of oil prices, of which tumbling values throughout 2014 and 2015 are a reminder, the emergent role of remittances as Sri Lanka's macroeconomic linchpin seems precariously poised lest recession, crisis or war takes root in GCC economies.

Sri Lanka, remittance economy

Temporary labour migration – considered within the parochial scope of the benefits forecasted by triple win prognoses and applied to Sri Lanka as an archetypal migrant-sending country – produces economic outcomes that are disproportionately advantageous for migrant-receiving countries. Considering the indirect implications of these movements of labour and income in the context of existing productive disparities throughout the world economy highlights further developmental hurdles borne from this arrangement. Infrastructural development, economic diversification and the provision of care in West Asia is derived from the strategic exploitation of different sub-groups of foreign workers. Together these workers comprise a diverse reserve army of migrant labour employed without the traditional costs of producing or maintaining a workforce, as migrant welfare remains the onus of countries of origin and informal care regimes within migrant households.

For Sri Lanka, whose uneven development has been shaped by a resilient logic of accumulation by subordination, the 'loaning' of labour power in exchange for *remittance capital* has proven easier and more lucrative than the break with path dependency that would be necessary to employ the same labour locally. More than just reallocating labour to subsidise foreign production and services, migration has also transformed social reproduction by commodifying care work to subsidise the daily and intergenerational reproduction of foreign households at the expense of care deficits created within migrant households and communities in Sri Lanka. Meanwhile, the inflow of migrant incomes is partially siphoned off as basic demand for receiving economies before being redistributed via household remittance consumption, the spillovers from which cannot be fully absorbed by Sri Lanka due to the same conditions of underdevelopment that encourage migration in the first place. Demand for imports contributes to global demand propelling the growth of industrial economies that are often removed from the flow of temporary labour migration altogether. With the ladder of industrial development receding from view, Sri Lanka is left to confront a vulnerable overdependence on remittances, as an entirely exogenous source of developmental capital that is precariously tied to the continued good fortune of West Asia's oil-economies.

Sri Lanka typifies what can be understood as a *remittance economy*, where an overdependence on foreign employment has underscored limited capital accumulation and poverty alleviation in lieu of development itself. The fragmented expenditure of remittances at the household level reinforces existing macroeconomic imbalances – with non-subsistence expenditures generally spilling over into centralised processes of accumulation or foreign imports. At the same time, the overvaluation of the currency through remittance receipts undercuts competitive manufacturing and the potential to achieve a more sustainable and inclusive growth trajectory through export diversification. From this perspective, it is not the short-term distribution of 'wins' between sending and receiving economies that is of particular importance, but the long-term developmental limitations of temporary labour migration for economies that are – relative to regions of intensive capital accumulation in value-added production and services – already underdeveloped. While *remittance capital* drives limited and uneven patterns of development (as discussed in Chapter 6), Sri Lanka's path dependency on migration fosters structural economic limitations that are ultimately to the detriment of the economy as a whole. Meanwhile, the emergence of *remittance economies* like Sri Lanka widens developmental disparities by displacing degrees of labour and effective demand to the benefit of already-developed economies. In this sense, the direct exploitation of migrant labour by the oil-economies of West Asia is only the most immediate facet of a more complex movement of labour and capital throughout the world economy.

Trade and production are essential features of the migration-underdevelopment story. Temporary labour migrants, and the economies they originate from, are embedded within a transnational division of labour that is as much defined by in-situ demand for workers as it is the outsourcing of industrial production (Cohen 1987). Importantly, movements of capital (inflows of FDI) and movements of labour (outflows of migrant workers) seldom overlap to a significant extent within the same developing economy. While some countries are locked into a 'race to the bottom' of labour standards for industrial production within their own borders, other countries have emerged as 'labour exporters'. These *remittance economies* tend to share common characteristics of trade and production, typically involving a relative absence of value-added industry alongside declining terms of trade for a range of low-value, inelastic exports. As Petras observes:

> overseas migration deprives the nation of its most innovative, skillful and ambitious workers who provide the basis for creating a diversified economy based on industry and services.... What remains is a client state dependent on agro-mineral exports, tourism and of course immigrant remittances.
>
> (Petras 2007, 49)

Although referring to Mexico's experience with temporary labour migration to the US, Petras's description applies equally well to Sri Lanka, as it does too for the Philippines, Nepal, Pakistan, the state of Kerala in India, Indonesia, and a number of small Caribbean and Pacific Island economies, all of which readily conform to the characteristics of *remittance economies*. It is similarly conspicuous that economies positioned as migration-development 'success stories', such as South Korea, Spain, Taiwan and Turkey (de Haas 2010) have experienced smaller and qualitatively different migration outflows in tandem with state-driven industrialisation and inwards migration, representing an entirely different economic reality.

Conclusion

This chapter has critically examined the broad developmental implications of temporary labour migration for Sri Lanka, as a migrant-sending country, *relative to* the migrant-receiving countries of West Asia and other developed or developing regions of the world economy that are altogether estranged from this particular flow of labour. Addressed from this comparative view of development, the assumptions behind the promotion of temporary labour migration as a triple win scenario amount to an unequal distribution of 'wins' that benefit the developed before the developing, and migrant workers least of all. The immediate outcomes of temporary labour migration thereby constitute an arrangement that exacerbates existing developmental disparities between Sri Lanka and the GCC countries that exploit its workers as part of a diverse reserve army of migrant labour. However, the full extent of Sri Lanka's experience of migration-underdevelopment is only appreciable once the indirect implications of its systemic reliance on temporary labour migration are considered. The uneven costs, care burdens, demand spillovers and overall precarity inherent to widespread temporary labour migration leads to the assessment that Sri Lanka represents one of a handful of emerging remittance economies whose dependency on migration substitutes for development in the short-term while entrenching long-term underdevelopment. Importantly, the indirect implications of temporary labour migration are not constrained to sending and receiving economies, but instead overlap with established patterns of trade and production to generate potentially significant windfalls for developed and developing regions of the world economy.

Notes

1 Parreñas (2005) finds that Sri Lankan men left behind struggle to perform productive and reproductive roles at once, whereas women left behind frequently adopt this 'double burden'.

2 Although studies have shown remittance flows to be loosely pro-cyclical in Sri Lanka (Gunatilleke, Colombage, and Perera 2010).

References

Athukorala, Premachandra. 1993. 'Improving the Contribution of Migrant Remittances to Development: The Experience of Asian Labour-Exporting Countries'. *International Migration* 31 (1): 103–22.

Baldwin-Edwards, Martin. 2011. 'Labour Immigration and Labour Markets in the GCC Countries: National Patterns and Trends'. Research Paper 15. London: Kuwait Programme on Development, Governance, and Globalisation in the Gulf States.

Castles, Stephen, and Mark J. Miller. 2007. *The Age of Migration: International Population Movements in the Modern World*. 3rd edition. Houndmills: Palgrave Macmillan.

Central Bank of Sri Lanka (CBSL). 2018. 'Economic and Social Statistics of Sri Lanka 2018'. Colombo: Central Bank of Sri Lanka.

Chang, Ha-Joon. 2006. *The East Asian Development Experience: The Miracle, the Crisis and the Future*. London: Zed Books.

Cohen, Robin. 1987. *The New Helots: Migrants in the International Division of Labour*. Research in Ethnic Relations Series. Aldershot: Gower.

Cooray, Devoushi. 2017. 'The Care Drain and Its Effects on the Families Left Behind: A Case Study of Sri Lanka'. *Comparative Sociology* 16 (3): 369–92.

De Silva, Amala, W. D. Lakshman, and M. D. A. L. Ranasinghe. 1993. 'Migrant Remittances as a Source of Development Funding: A Study of Sri Lanka'. RAS/88/029. Sub-Regional Seminar on Migrant Remittances and Economic Development in South Asia. Colombo: UNDP/ILO.

Delgado Wise, Raúl. 2009. 'Forced Migration and US Imperialism: The Dialectic of Migration and Development'. *Critical Sociology* 35 (6): 767–84.

Department of Census and Statistics (DCS). 2017. *Sri Lanka Labour Force Survey: Annual Report – 2017*. Colombo: Department of Census and Statistics.

Eelens, Frank, T. Mook, and Toon Schampers. 1992. 'Introduction'. In *Labour Migration to the Middle East: From Sri Lanka to the Gulf*, 1–27. London: Kegan Paul International.

Elson, Diane. 1999. 'Labour Markets as Gendered Institutions: Equality, Efficiency and Empowerment Issues'. *World Development* 27 (3): 611–27.

European Migration Network (EMN). 2010. 'Specifications for EMN Study – Temporary and Circular Migration: Empirical Evidence, Current Policy Practice and Future Options in EU Member States'. Doc 192. Brussels: European Commission.

Forstenlechner, Ingo, and Emilie Jane Rutledge. 2011. 'The GCC's "Demographic Imbalance": Perceptions, Realities and Policy Options'. *Middle East Policy* 25 (30).

Gunatilleke, Godfrey, S. S. Colombage, and Myrtle Perera. 2010. 'Macroeconomic Impact of International Migration: A Case Study of Sri Lanka'. 10-06. South Asia Network of Economic Research Institutes. Colombo: MARGA.

Haas, Hein de. 2010. 'Migration and Development: A Theoretical Perspective'. *International Migration Review* 44 (1): 227–64.

Haskins, Victoria K., and Claire Lowrie, eds. 2015. *Colonization and Domestic Service: Historical and Contemporary Perspectives*. Routledge International Studies of Women and Place 14. New York: Routledge.

Institute of Policy Studies (IPS). 2012. *Sri Lanka: State of the Economy 2012*. Colombo, Sri Lanka: Institute of Policy Studies of Sri Lanka.

Institute of Policy Studies (IPS). 2013. *Sri Lanka: State of the Economy 2013*. Colombo, Sri Lanka: Institute of Policy Studies of Sri Lanka.

International Labour Organisation (ILO). 2013. *Recruitment Practices of Employment Agencies Recruiting Migrant Workers: A Review Aimed at Improving Recruitment Regulations and Drafting Recruitment Guidelines*. Colombo: ILO.

International Monetary Fund (IMF). 2013. 'Labor Market Reforms to Boost Employment and Productivity in the GCC'. Riyadh: International Monetary Fund.

Jayaweera, Swarna, ed. 2002. *Women in Post-Independence Sri Lanka*. New Delhi: Sage Publications.

Jayaweera, Swarna, and Malsiri Dias. 2009. 'Gender Roles and Support Networks of Spouses of Migrant Workers'. In *Gender and Labour Migration in Asia*, 43–115. Geneva: International Organization for Migration (IOM).

Kottegoda, Sepali. 2004. *Negotiating Household Politics: Women's Strategies in Urban Sri Lanka*. Colombo: Social Scientists' Association.

Lindio-McGovern, Ligaya. 2016. 'The Philippines: Pressures for Change in the Work/Care Regime'. In *Women, Work and Care in the Asia-Pacific*, edited by Marian Baird, Michele Ford, and Elizabeth Hill. London: Routledge.

Mallick, Hrushikesh. 2010. 'Remittances, Consumption, Investment and Economic Growth'. In *India Migration Report 2010: Governance and Labour Migration*, edited by S. Irudaya Rajan, 30–67. New Delhi: Routledge.

Martin, Philip. 2012. 'Reducing Migration Costs and Maximizing Human Development'. In *Global Perspectives on Migration and Development: GFMD Puerto Vallarta and Beyond*, edited by Irena Omelaniuk, 27–52. Global Migration Issues 1. Dordrecht: Springer.

Parreñas, Rhacel Salazar. 2005. *Children of Global Migration: Transnational Families and Gendered Woes*. Stanford, CA: Stanford University Press.

Perera, P. D. A. 1992. 'Needs of Kuwait Returnees of Sri Lanka: An Assessment'. SLBFE Commissioned Study. Colombo: MARGA Institute.

Petras, James F. 2007. *Rulers and Ruled in the US Empire: Bankers, Zionists, Militants*. Atlanta, GA: Clarity Press.

Potts, Lydia. 1990. *The World Labour Market: A History of Migration*. London: Zed Books.

Ratha, Dilip. 2007. 'Leveraging Remittances for Development'. Washington, DC: Migration Policy Institute.

Rodrigo, C., and R. A. Jayatissa. 1989. 'Maximising Benefits from Labour Migration: Sri Lanka'. In *To the Gulf and Back: Studies on the Economic Impact of Asian Labour Migration*, edited by R. Amjad, 255–96. New Delhi: ILO.

Satharasinghe, A. J. 1999. 'Time-Use Analysis of Husbands and Wives'. *Sri Lanka Journal of Population Studies* 2: 11–24.

Skeldon, Ronald. 1992. 'International Migration Within and From the East and South-East Asian Region: A Review Essay'. *Asian and Pacific Migration Journal* 1 (1): 19–63.

Sri Lanka Bureau of Foreign Employment (SLBFE). 2012. *Annual Statistical Report of Foreign Employment 2011*. Colombo: Sri Lanka Bureau of Foreign Employment.

Sri Lanka Bureau of Foreign Employment (SLBFE). 2016. 'Different Perspectives of Departure Details'. Colombo: Sri Lanka Bureau of Foreign Employment.

United Nations Economic Commission for Europe (UNECE). 2016. 'Defining and Measuring Circular Migration: Final Report of the Task Force on Measuring Circular Migration'. Geneva: UNECE.

Veblen, Thorstein. 2009. *The Theory of the Leisure Class*. Oxford: Oxford University Press. First published 1899.

Wickramasekara, Piyasiri. 2016. 'South Asian Gulf Migration to the Gulf: A Safety Valve or a Development Strategy?' *Migration and Development* 5 (1): 99–129.

Wickramasekara, Piyasiri, International Labour Office, and Bureau for Workers' Activities. 2011. *Circular Migration: A Triple Win or a Dead End?* Geneva: ILO.

Withers, Matt. 2016. 'Sri Lanka: Working Realities and Gendered Fictions'. In *Women, Work and Care in the Asia-Pacific*, edited by Marian Baird, Michele Ford, and Elizabeth Hill, 148–64. London: Routledge.

Withers, Matt, and Nicola Piper. 2018. 'Uneven Development and Displaced Care in Sri Lanka'. *Current Sociology* 66 (4): 590–601.

World Bank. 2006. *Global Economic Prospects: Economic Implications of Remittances and Migration*. Washington, DC: World Bank.

World Bank. 2019. 'World Development Indicators'. Washington, DC: World Bank.

Conclusion

Migration-underdevelopment

The evidence and analysis marshalled throughout this book demonstrates that Sri Lanka's growing dependency on temporary labour migration and *remittance capital* has not yielded an economic panacea but ingrained a complex process of migration-underdevelopment.

The benefits anticipated by the dominant triple win policy rhetoric are conspicuously absent within this dynamic: migrant households struggle to achieve subsistence outcomes without recourse to cyclical foreign employment, while aggregate remittance inflows produce a set of macroeconomic constraints that stifle inclusive economic development. Sri Lanka's remittance economy is not sufficiently explained by existing historical-structuralist critiques of migration-development either, as scant attention to the institutional features of migrant-sending countries and an under-theorisation of remittances has proven analytically limiting. This research has addressed both oversights by returning to the Marxian root of historical-structuralist theories, where the contextually specific spread and shaping of capitalist social relations is identified as a defining characteristic of uneven development (Brenner 1977). By drawing upon the multiscalarity inherent in this approach, I have emphasised how existing uneven development has created diverse migration practices across Sri Lanka and enabled *remittance capital* to reproduce otherwise unsustainable patterns of non-inclusive development. I argue that temporary labour migration operates as a logical continuation of 'accumulation-by-subordination' strategies that have defined Sri Lanka's colonial and postcolonial economic development by systematically exploiting marginalised populations in degraded forms of work. Whereas this was earlier achieved by deriving rents from semi-feudal production, temporary labour migration represents a more sophisticated abstraction of the same relationship by 'loaning' Sri Lanka's working poor as indentured migrant labourers whose remittances indirectly sustain urban development projects to the benefit of a wealthy minority. Despite extending the short-term viability of uneven development and keeping poor households above the poverty line, Sri Lanka's dependency on temporary labour migration and *remittance capital* is entrenching long-term underdevelopment by neglecting local industrialisation in favour of routing labour power and effective demand to other regions of the world economy.

This analysis has been guided by three important departures from prevailing migration-development discourse.

Multiscalar migration theory

The theoretical framing of temporary labour migration as a multiscalar process is the first of these contributions. The migration-development debate has been popularly construed as a pendulum oscillating over time between 'pessimistic' and 'optimistic' appraisals of migration's developmental potential, respectively couched in structure-centric and agency-centric theories but equally deterministic in their conclusions (de Haas 2012). Yet the supposed rigidity of historical-structuralist perspectives, and moreover the entire structure–agency dichotomy permeating the migration-development literature, has been overstated. Historical-structuralist contributions to migration theory have been far less deterministic than their detractors imply, insofar as emphasising the structural constraints of capitalist development is not tantamount to denying the exercise of individual agency *within* those structures. Instead, I argue that the Marxian root of historical-structuralist perspectives offers a coherent framework in which to reconcile individual realities with the economic structures they are grounded in.

Constricting the migration-development debate to a structure–agency binary has also entailed a tendency to neglect a middle tier of institutional factors that shape migration decisions, processes and outcomes, along with the potential for multiscalar research to draw meaningful linkages between overlapping levels of analysis. My use of a multiscalar migration theory has instead emphasised these interconnections. By examining the intersections of global patterns of capital, countrywide structures of uneven development, local institutions and individual agency it has tried to provide a holistic but contextually sensitive assessment of the varying causes for, experiences during and outcomes of temporary labour migration from Sri Lanka to the oil-economies of West Asia. Each scale of analysis has been explored through corresponding conceptual tools – *status, place, forced migration* and *remittance capital* – that describe overlapping cumulatively causal tendencies, together coalescing to produce a deep-seated path dependency on temporary labour migration.

This multiscalar approach also informed a distinct approach to fieldwork, in which *place* is positioned as a means of probing the interplay of structures, institutions and agency. An empirical emphasis on the diversity of migration experiences within countries of origin like Sri Lanka is a second way in which the research has deviated from mainstream approaches to migration-development.

Diverse migration experiences

Conducting fieldwork across four geographically and demographically distinct locations has enabled my research to capture contextually sensitive impressions of how migration practices and experiences vary throughout Sri Lanka. Clear differences between migrant communities throughout Sri Lanka were uncovered in the course of research. These differences demonstrate how developmental marginalisation can compound migration problems, but also reveal the importance of more subtle interactions involving gender norms, religious affinity, cultural practices and community knowledge. Recognising disparate migration experiences both reaffirms the importance of multiscalar research and rejects prevalent generalisations of migrant workers as uniformly empowered by rational decision-making or disempowered by structural underdevelopment. Instead, this approach contends that historically and geographically specific subordination of gender, ethnicity and class differentiates the circumstances of migration while also revealing complex migration cultures with path dependencies of their own.

Three themes – *forced migration, place* and *status* – have been introduced to identify key differences and cumulatively causal features at structural, institutional and agency levels. The interweaving of gendered analysis throughout the discussion of each of these prominent empirical themes represents a further contribution made by the book, as existing research has tended to focus specifically on the experiences of women (particularly in Sri Lanka, where female migration has been unusually dominant) or overlooked considerations of gender entirely by homogenising experiences of the migrant individual. By distinguishing between the specific conditions, experiences and outcomes of women's *and* men's migration – and by exploring the patriarchal framework and gendered tensions that bind and mediate these differing realities – the research has allowed for a more sophisticated understanding of how gender permeates the relationship between migration and development in Sri Lanka.

Forced migration describes how Sri Lanka's uneven development has, with varying degrees of severity, displaced economically marginalised communities into foreign employment and constrained migrants' ability to successfully reintegrate upon their return. Sri Lanka's neoliberal turn has concentrated feminised productive activity in narrow and exploitative avenues of accumulation in the urban economy while undermining the viability of traditional male livelihoods that households have historically depended on. Returnees interviewed overwhelmingly indicated that they would not have migrated if decent local employment were available, a sentiment supported by migrants' yearning for a 'good life' amounting to little more than the desire for a sustainable livelihood. The outcomes of migration, meanwhile, were substantially tempered by the limitations of prevailing underdevelopment; indebtedness and household expenses claimed a significant portion of remittances and left little income for 'investment' beyond basic assets. While less marginalised and better prepared communities could make greater use of migration, households were typically seen to subsist off remittance incomes and engage in repeat or 'flow-on' migration to sustain these income streams.

The circumstances under which migration occurred varied appreciably from one community to another, reflecting prevailing developmental disparities but also locationally specific migration strategies and cultures. An analysis of *place* complements structural understandings of the causes and outcomes of temporary labour migration by addressing the particular institutional factors that give rise to heterogenous migration practices and influence the expenses associated with foreign employment. Recruitment practices of the 'merchants of labour' adapt to the landscape of uneven development by using the relative mobility of capital to exploit the material conditions, communal knowledge and cultural practices fixed in *place* while strategically responding to fluctuating foreign demand for male and female migrant workers. In Thavapuram especially, acute developmental adversity and recent exposure to foreign employment conspired to allow a network of sub-agents and labour brokers to exact inflated recruitment fees for poorly paid jobs. An existing lack of wealth and assets conditioned a particularly high dependence on local moneylenders as a source of financing and, as a result, instances of severe indebtedness amongst returnees. However, other local migration practices were observed to afford a means of resisting exploitation by the 'merchants of labour' by facilitating alternative recruitment and financing strategies. The Muslim community in Polgahawela was particularly successful in this regard, as religious affinity with West Asian employers allowed encouraged private recruitment via friends and family, while principles of Islamic banking and strong communal bonds engendered a system of collectively financing the individual costs of migration. Nevertheless, loosely regulated recruitment practices are seen to exploit the geographic and demographic contours of uneven development to produce conditions of 'uneven migration' within which vested business interests entrench temporary labour migration as a developmental strategy.

Migrant agency, too, is a crucial aspect of migration outcomes, but not when understood in the parochial terms of rational utility-maximisation put forward by neoclassical migration theories. The concept of *status* offers an intuitive means of reframing agency with greater sensitivity to migrants' expressed frustrations with, and aspirations for, life in Sri Lanka. Exercised within the structural and institutional constraints of temporary labour migration and social expectations aligned with prevailing gender norms, *status* entails the use of migration to negotiate self-worth amidst the widespread devaluation of labour throughout Sri Lanka and within avenues of foreign employment. Paradoxically, the very 'invisibility' of foreign employment shields migrants from the stigma attributed to degraded local work, while also offering the ability to 'reinvent' personal narratives that satisfy social expectations. Remittances, along with gifts from employers, meanwhile enable the conspicuous consumption of status goods as a form of social currency: housing, consumer durables, jewellery and clothing can all be potent signifiers of *status*. Conspicuous remittance use is therefore an earnest reclamation of *status* derived in lieu of decent local work and, for many, an important factor of successful migration. However, conspicuous consumption often obfuscates the hardships and shortcomings of migration as a survival strategy, projecting a facade of prosperity that encourages other members of a community to migrate in pursuit of their neighbour's apparent wealth.

Incapable of being sufficiently explained by singular explanations of migrant agency or structural underdevelopment, empirical analysis of Sri Lanka's diverse migration experiences reveals a series of cumulatively causal pressures conditioning a reliance on temporary labour migration at structural, institutional and agency levels. The resultant path dependence is expressed macroeconomically by a growing dependency on *remittance capital* as a means of sustaining uneven development.

Remittance capital

The book's final contribution has been to offer a systematic conceptualisation of *remittance capital* and its macroeconomic implications for Sri Lanka. Remittance transfers reside at the crux of recent migration-development optimism, both as private-income transfers to stimulate household consumption and investment and as aggregate foreign-exchange inflows to improve access to developmental loans. In practice, this 'duality' of *remittance capital* has perpetuated the contradiction of Sri Lanka's uneven development: private remittances act as subsistence for the economically marginalised, while aggregate remittances strengthen the currency to cheapen imports and enable developmental loans for the benefit of the urban service sector. Inherent 'Dutch Disease' effects that undermine export diversification, along with inevitable debt-servicing from the associated trade deficit, instils a path dependence on temporary labour migration as a solution to mass employment and macroeconomic stability. This dependence in turn conditions an inherent structural constraint to inclusive development, as the availability of decent and decentralised local employment threatens to 'kill the goose that laid the golden egg'. It is in this sense that Sri Lanka has, through temporary labour migration, revitalised the logic of accumulation by subordination that has produced and reproduced structures of uneven development.

However, situating Sri Lanka's dependency on *remittance capital* in international relief reveals a deeper process of underdevelopment, wherein an unequal distribution of the 'wins' supposedly accruing from temporary labour migration exacerbates economic disparity between the developed and developing. The employment of productive and reproductive forces abroad, rather than at home, entails the relative development of migrant-receiving economies at the expense of migrant-sending countries. The indirect consequences of temporary labour migration – including the cost of reproducing labour power, care deficits, import spillovers and demand volatility – create further risks and burdens for sending economies. In the case of import spillovers, made likely by a strong currency and the comparative absence of local industry, the potential benefits of migration are no longer limited to receiving economies but extend to manufacturing regions throughout the world economy. That these outcomes are observable in a number of predominantly agricultural and unevenly developed migrant-sending countries points to the emergence of a new genre of 'remittance economies' whose path dependence on *remittance capital* is conditioning their long-term underdevelopment.

A triple win?

These three analytical directions shine a critical light on aspects of migration-development that have been readily overlooked by the conventional wisdom of the triple win thesis. Applied to Sri Lanka, the conclusions drawn from this approach comprehensively reject the notion that temporary labour migration yields mutually beneficial outcomes, or that remittances form a valuable source of developmental capital. In light of these findings, serious questions must be asked of the dominant migration-development policy discourse, particularly the continued espousal of migrant entrepreneurship and remittance-driven development without a quantum of evidence to lend veracity to such expectations. The triple win is essentially an argument that the ends of temporary labour migration justify its means; in the context of the South Asia to West Asia migration corridor, in which the most egregious violations of human and labour rights are entirely commonplace, this justification falls alarmingly short.

Mainstream migration-development theory and research has lagged behind the triple win agenda, allowing influential international organisations to uncritically promote temporary labour migration strategies that have permeated development policy and practice. In this manner, the idea of a triple win has gained discursive power and given safe haven to exploitative labour practices that form around fissures in the world economy that run deep into the historical structures of capitalism and imperialism. Temporary labour migration has produced disproportionate, rather than mutually beneficial, outcomes: migrant workers do not often accrue sustainable wealth or well-being from the 'weighted gamble' of foreign employment; migrant-sending countries become locked into contradictory patterns of remittance-driven uneven development; but migrant-receiving economies and their citizens unequivocally gain from access to cheap and pliable labour. It is a development strategy through which the burden of risk and personal hardship is squared on the vulnerable, while the benefits accrue most evidently to those already empowered.

It is not only across South Asia that temporary labour migration is playing out in this manner. As the global locus of industrial production has shifted towards East and Southeast Asia, so too has productive and reproductive labour been systematically sourced through the internal and international migration of temporary workers from regions and countries bereft of substantive development. As non-inclusive growth continues throughout this expanding semi-periphery of the world economy, economic and political crises loom on the horizon of the sluggish post-industrial core of Europe and North America. Here the 'global race for talent' remains in full swing, but low-waged migrant workers are increasingly limited to temporary work visas that mimic the stringent circularity of labour migration schemes found across Asia. The prognosis is the proliferation of low-wage temporary labour migration as a global norm, with potentially dire developmental implications for a swelling global reserve army of labour and care, along with those countries of origin grappling with structural impediments to more proven development strategies.

The continued promotion of migration-development by policymaking institutions of the Global North may not convey a wilful neglect of migration outcomes so much as reflect the embrace of a parochial vision of development itself. Much akin to the concept of microfinance, remittance-led development is a popular narrative in the genre of 'self-help development', in which credit constraints form the principal impediment to a latent groundswell of entrepreneurship that, unfettered, would spearhead generalised prosperity. It represents the quintessence of 'post-Washington' neoliberalism: a capitalist rendering of development that locates poverty in ahistorical market imperfections, made more palatable by celebrating the poor themselves as individual 'agents of development'. There is conspicuous disregard for state-driven development and the accompanying rungs of public services, welfare, job creation, protectionism and industrial policy that have historically comprised the 'ladder' to capitalist development (Chang 2003). Instead, cast as individual agents of development, migrants are held accountable for improving their own circumstances by 'selling' their labour power abroad and subsequently 'investing' their remitted wages. Yet remittance expenditures on housing, vehicles, consumer durables, education and healthcare do not qualify as 'investments' in any conventional sense; these are a mix of basic assets and erstwhile public goods that should be affordable without recourse to intensely exploitative foreign employment.

The emergence of remittance economies geared towards the mass provision of migrant labour as a substitute for local development should be recognised as a problematic symptom of temporary labour migration's relationship with underdevelopment. For Sri Lanka, as with other remittance economies, the pertinent problem is therefore not 'how to leverage migration for development' but 'how to prevent migration as a form of underdevelopment'. The most pressing need within these countries is to create locally available decent work, so that temporary labour migration is a genuine choice and not a necessity (Piper and Withers 2018). The practical challenges to achieving this are overwhelming. Wickramasekara (2016) asserts the need for South Asian economies to disentangle themselves from temporary labour migration in the long term, but cites the sheer magnitude of prevailing underdevelopment and the symbiotic nature of migration to the Gulf as fundamental barriers to breaking the 'perpetual migration cycle'. The cumulatively causal processes I have identified in this book only add to the scale of this dilemma. I therefore offer no discrete policy recommendations, nor identify any quick solutions; not for a lack of want, but precisely because the central contradiction of migration-underdevelopment tightens with a structural and institutional momentum that cannot be readily unwound. Reversing this scenario will require a jarring break with path dependency, an alternative and inclusive development strategy that is viable within the parameters of a shifting world economy, and the fulcrum of political will. This is a tall order, by any measure, but one that may prove enduringly detrimental to ignore.

References

Brenner, Robert. 1977. 'The Origins of Capitalist Development: A Critique of Neo-Smithian Marxism'. *New Left Review* I (104): 25–92.

Chang, Ha-joon. 2003. *Kicking Away the Ladder Development Strategy in Historical Perspective*. London: Anthem Press.

Haas, Hein de. 2012. 'The Migration and Development Pendulum: A Critical View on Research and Policy: The Migration and Development Pendulum'. *International Migration* 50 (3): 8–25.

Piper, Nicola, and Matt Withers. 2018. 'Forced Transnationalism and Temporary Labour Migration: Implications for Understanding Migrant Rights'. *Identities* 25 (5): 558–75.

Wickramasekara, Piyasiri. 2016. 'South Asian Gulf Migration to the Gulf: A Safety Valve or a Development Strategy?' *Migration and Development* 5 (1): 99–129.

Index

Page numbers in **bold** denote tables, those in *italics* denote figures.

Abella, Manolo 45
accumulation by dispossession 34, 37, 38
accumulation by subordination 34–5, 36, 56, 87, 140
agency, of migrants 102–4, 170
agricultural economy 51, 139
Agunias, Dovelyn 21
Akmeemana, migrants from 51, 52–4, *53*; business investments 66, **66**, 67; debt 83, **83**; housing 57; methods of financing recruitment costs 82, **82**; motivation for migration 104; recruitment methods **76**, 77–8, 79; remittance expenditure 66, **66**, 67, 68, **68**, 125; and status 105, 106, 112
armed forces 38
Association of Licensed Foreign Employment Agents (ALFEA) 90
Athukorala, Premachandra 129–30

Bandaranaike, Sirimavo 35
Baran, Paul 34
Berenger, Leon 90
brain circulation 4, 150–1, 153
breadwinner employment, feminisation of 7, 39–40, 62, 97, 156
Brenner, Robert 23
British imperialism 34
business investments (by migrants): as pre-migration ambition 60–1, 62–3, 64; remittance expenditure on 65, **65**, 66–9, **66**, **127**, 129–30; and underdevelopment 64

capitalism: capitalist development 20, 23; capitalist social relations 23–5; and civil war 38–9; and economic reforms 63; imperial capitalism 34; and labour market 16–17; and neoliberalism 35–7; *see also* remittance capital
care deficit 156
care economy 96, **96**, 97, 155–7
Castles, Stephen 20
Catholics 42, 54–5, 108
Centre for Migration Research and Development (CMRD) 60, 69
Ceylon Today 91
China, and development projects 137–8, 139
circular migration 21, 146–7
civil war: causes of 37–9; and forced migration 51, 55–6; impact on economy 7, 38; post-war reconstruction 38–9; and recruitment networks 87–8; and Thavapuram 55–6
class 23, 26, 34, 36, 38, 64, 69, 152; *see also* status
closed economy model 34–5
Cohen, Robin 152
Colombo, and development projects 139
Colombo Process 90
colonialism 33–5
conspicuous consumption 25, 26, 114–16, 129; *see also* status
construction work 5, 42
consumption: conspicuous consumption 25, 26, 114–16, 129; consumer durables 131, **131**; day-to-day consumption 61, 63, 126–8, **127**; direct consumption 126–8, **127**; and displays of status 111–18, 125–6, 129; and pre-migration ambitions 61, 62–3; re-socialising through 114–16; remittance expenditure on 65, **65**, 66, 67–8, 131, **131**; *see also* remittance capital

costs of migration 74–93, 169–70; demographics of debt 75–81; and media coverage 91–3; merchants of labour 85–9; methods of financing recruitment 82, **82**; migrant indebtedness 81–5; policy responses 90–1; recruitment costs 76–81, *76–7*; regulation and representation 90–1; unequal costs of 154–5
cultural subjugation 34–5

Daily Mirror 92
day-to-day consumption *see* consumption
De Silva, Amala 122, *123*, 124, 129, 130, 148, 160
De Silva, S.B.D. 34
de-socialisation of labour 96, 104, 115, 129
debt: demographics of 75–81; migrant indebtedness 81–5; prevalence and severity of 83–4, **83**; as reason for migration 84; and recruitment expenditure 56, 75–82; remittance expenditure on **65**, 66, **127**, 128
Delgado Wise, Raúl 25, 26, 50
dependency theory 17, 23–4
destination countries *see* receiving economies
development: concept of 10, 23–4; remittance spending on 137–40
Dias, Malsiri 156
domestic workers 6–7; as absent mothers 92–3, 156; abuse of 5, 91–2, 99–100, 109–10; and care economy 155–7; and consumption of goods 113; demand for 42; gendered division of 97–8, **98**; government policy 91–3; recruitment costs 75, 76–7, *76–7*, 80–1; training programme 44; working conditions 98–101
dowry payments 58, 113
dual labour market theory 16–17, 25, 50
Ducanes, Jeffrey 45
Dutch Disease 134–6, *135*
duty-free permits 126

education: lack of government investment in 60; and pre-migration ambitions 59–60, 62–4; privatisation 63–4; quality of public education 63–4; remittance expenditure on 65, **65**, **127**, 128
Eelens, Frank 41
electrical goods 111, 113, 125, 131, **131**
Emmanuel, Arghiri 23–4
ethnic discrimination 39
ethnic subordination 34–5
ethnic violence 37–9
European Migration Network (EMN) 146
Eversole, Robyn 130–1
exploitation: gendered economy of export production 39–40; and historical-structuralism 14, 16, 17, 18–19, 20, 21, 22, 23–4, 25, 168; working conditions 40, 43, 44, 98–102, **99**; *see also* costs of migration
Export Processing Zones (EPZs) 6–7, 36, 39–40, 54, 97

Family Background Report (FBR) 7, 42, 92
fieldwork 5; and diverse migration experiences 168–71; locations 52–7, *53*
fishing industry 54, 104
flow-on migration 70
forced migration and uneven development 49–72, 169; aspirations of migrants 57–64; challenge of reintegration 65–71; concept of 25, 26–7; decline of traditional livelihoods 50–2; the 'good life' 57–64; locational difference 52–7; number of trips 69; reasons for migration 50–2, 54–7, 57–61; remittance dependency 69–71; remittance expenditure **65**, 65–71; repeat migration 69–71, **69**
foreign-exchange earnings 8–9, 133–7, *135*
foreign goods 125–6, 158–9; *see also* consumption
formal remittance transfer 133

Gamburd, Michele Ruth 113, 130
garment industry 37, 39, 40, 54, 58–9
Gulf Cooperation Council (GCC) 152, 155, 157–8, 160
gender: allocation of reproductive labour 62–3; and breadwinner employment 7, 39–40, 62, 97, 156; and care economy 155–7; composition of migrants 7; and direct consumption 127–8; division of labour 6–7, 35, 37, 39–40, 92; gendered subordination 34–5, 39–40, 92; and gendered working realities 96–102, **96**, **98**, **99**; and pre-migration ambitions 62–3, **62**; and reintegration 109–11; remittance expenditure **65**, 65–6; remittance rates 98, 124–5; repeat migration 70, **70**; *see also* women

gender pay gap 98
gendered subordination 34–5, 39–40, 92
Gibson-Graham, J.K. 140
Giddens, Anthony 19
Gunasinghe, Miyuru 138
Gunder Frank, Andre 16
Gunatilleke , Godfrey 131

Haas, Hein de 14–17, 18–19, 20
Hambantota 137–8
handloom industry 36, 39
Harris, J. 15
Harroff-Tavel, H. 99
Harvey, David 34
healthcare: privatisation 64; remittance expenditure on **65**, **127**
historical-structuralism 14, 16, 17, 18–19, 20, 21, 22, 23–4, 25, 168
hooks, bell 114–15
household strategy 19–20
housing: and pre-migration ambitions 54, 57–9, 62–3; remittance expenditure on 65, **65**, 70, **127**, 128, 129; and status 129

imperialism 33–5
industrialisation 37
informal care economy 155–7
informal remittance transfer 133
infrastructural projects 137–40
Institute of Policy Studies (IPS) 45, 58, 64, 110, 113, 117, 135, 149
international labour migration *see* temporary labour migration
International Labour Organisation (ILO) 5; and housing 58; and national labour migration policy 43; and recruitment process 85, 86, 88; and remittance capital 122–3, 126; and repeat migration 69, 70; and status 106, 108–9, 111

Jayatissa, R.A. 133
Jayawardena, Kumari 34
Jayawardene government 35, 36, 40
Jayaweera, Swarna 156
jewellery 111, 112–13, 114
Jordan 113

kafala system 98
Kapur, Devish 20
Katseli, Louka 122, 132, 134
Katunayake EPZ 39, 54
Kelegama, Saman 37
Khan, A. 99
Kottegoda, Sepali 97

labour brokers 86, *86*, 87, 88
labour market: and colonialism 33–5; decentralised employment 63; demand for labour 50–1, 159–61; dual labour market theory 16–17, 50; and gender 62–3, 96–102, **96**, **98**, **99**; local employment 36, 37, 50–2, 96–7; and neoliberalism 63; unemployment 148–9
labour migration *see* temporary labour migration
labour power reproduction 155
Lakshman, W.D. 122, *123*, 124, 129, 130, 148, 160
Lebanon 100, 112, 125
loans 55, 56, 82, **82**, 83–4
local employment: lack of 36, 37, 50–2; and gendered working realities 96–7
low-skilled workers: abuse of 43, 44; demographics of 42, **96**, 150; gendered division of 97–8, **98**; government policy 43, 44, 151; impact of migration on 147–8
LTTE (Liberation Tigers of Tamil Eelam) 55–6
Lucas, Robert 122, 132, 134
Lynch, Caitrin 97

Mackeen, Faizar 90
Mahinda Rajapaksa International Airport 138
marriage, dowry payments 58, 113
Marshall, T.H. 114
Marxism 14, 16, 17, 23, 25, 26
masculinity, crisis in 97; *see also* gender
media, and migrant welfare 91–3
merchants of labour 27, 40–1; exploitation by 56, 170; mapping 85–9, *86*; labour brokers 86, *86*, 87, 88; methods of financing recruitment 82, **82**; moneylenders 55, 56, 82, **82**, *86*; and Muslims 55, 170; personal contacts 75, **76**, 78, 79, 80, 81, 100; recruitment agencies 40–1, 56, 75–82, 85–9, 90–1, 154–5; recruitment costs 76–81, *76–7*; regulation of 90–1, 170; sub-agents 86–7, 88–9, 90–1, 93; SLBFE 75, **76**; and unequal costs of migration 154–5
methodology 28–9
migrant agency paradox 102–4, 170
migrant hero 44
migration-development, history of 3, 14–29; dual labour market theory 16–17; historical-structuralism 14, 16, 17, 18–19, 20, 21, 22, 23–4, 25, 168;

migration-development *continued*
methodology 28–9; and middle ground 14, 18, 19, 20; multiscalar migration theory 24–8, 168; neoclassical theory of 15–16, 18–20, 50; new theoretical approach 23–4; and optimism 14, 18–19; and pessimism 14, 18–19; post-Washington 21–2; structural determinants of migration 16; as swinging pendulum 14, 18–20; triple win thesis 4–5, 21–2; and unequal exchange 17
Migration Employment Authority 91
migration-underdevelopment 23–8, 167–73
Ministry for Foreign Employment Promotion and Welfare (MFEPW) 43–4, 90
Ministry of Labour and Labour Relations 88
moneylenders 55, 56, 82, **82**, *86*
Mook, T. 41
motivation for migration *see* forced migration and uneven development; status
multiscalar migration theory 24–8, 56, 168; methodology 28–9
Muslim communities 7, 38, 40; demand for migrants from 42, 55, 80; favourable migration practices 55; recruitment methods 79–80; working conditions 100–1; *see also* Polgahawela, migrants from

Nafeek, Rizana 5, 91–2
Nation, The 9
National Labour Migration Policy 43
National Vocational Qualification (NVQ) 44
Negembo, migrants from 51, *53*, 54–5; business investments 60, 66, **66**; debt 83, **83**; education 59; housing 58–9; methods of financing recruitment costs 82, **82**; and migrant agency 102; motivation for migration 104, 105; recruitment methods **76**, 78–9; remittance expenditure 66, **66**, **68**; and status 104, 107–8, 110, 111–12, 116, 117; working conditions 100, 102
neo-Marxism 14, 16, 17
neoclassical theory of migration 15–16, 18–20, 50
neoliberalism 14, 19, 20, 21; and civil war 38; and forced migration 26; in Sri Lanka 35–7, 115

New Economics of Labour Migration (NELM) 14, 19–20, 50

occupations, and gendered working realities 96–102
oil industry 35, 40, 160
outworking 101–2

path dependency 69–71, 136–7
patriarchy: patriarchal ethno-nationalism 34–5, 92; *see also* gender; women
pecuniary emulation 26; *see also* status
Petras, James F. 162
Piore, Michael J. 16–17, 25, 50
Piper, Nicola 21–2
place: concept of 25, 27; fieldwork locations 52–7; *see also* costs of migration
plantation economy 34, 51
Polanyi, Karl 115
Polgahawela, migrants from *53*, 55; business investments 61, 66, **66**, 67; debt 83, **83**; methods of financing recruitment costs 82, **82**; motivation for migration 105; recruitment methods **76**, 79–80; remittance expenditure 66, **66**, 67, 68, **68**; and status 105, 106, 109; working conditions 101
policies to promote labour migration 43–5
political economy of uneven development in Sri Lanka 33–46; and colonialism 33–5; demographics of migration 41–2; and ethnic violence 37–9; gendered economy of export production 39–40; managing migration 41–5; and neoliberalism 35–7; temporary labour migration 40–1
poverty alleviation 121–2, 128; *see also* remittance capital
privatisation 36, 63–4
Purkayastha, Bandana 1

Qatar 81, 101, 107
qualifications 44

Rajapaksa government 7–8, 44–5, 135–6, 137–8, 139
Ranasinghe, M.D.A.L. 122, *123*, 124, 129, 130, 148, 160
Ratha, Dilip 148
rational choice theory 3, 18, 20
rativiru 44
Razak, Azhar 9
receiving economies: benefits for 4, 16,

21–2, 146, 151–2, 153; and demand for labour 16, 50; and demand volatility 159–61; foreign employment spillovers 157–8; status of migrants 25; and unequal outcomes 146–7; and unequal costs of migration 154–5; working conditions in 98–102; *see also* triple win thesis
recruitment agencies 75–81, **76**; exploitation by 56, 170; fees 75, 77–9, 80–1, 82; mapping 85–9, *86*; proliferation of 40–1, 75; regulation of 90–1, 93; sub-agents 86–7, 88–9, 90–1, 93; and unequal costs of migration 154–5; *see also* merchants of labour
recruitment methods/costs *see* merchants of labour
reintegration: challenge of 65–71; and lifestyle change 107–11
remittance capital 4–5, 120–41, 171; amount of 3–4, 6, 8, 9; categories of expenditure 123–4; concept of 25, 27–8, 120; and consumption of goods 111–16, 120–1, 125–6, 129–31, **131**; critique of remittance-led development 131–2; and development spending 137–40; direct consumption 126–8; and distribution of capital ownership 130, 132; Dutch Disease 134–6; and expenditure out of the economy 130, 132; fieldwork findings on expenditure 124–32, **127**, **131**; foreign employment spillovers 157–8; as foreign-exchange earnings 133–7, *135*; and foreign goods brought home 125–6; government's reliance on 8–9; import spillovers 158–9; and leakages 126, 131, 132; macroeconomics impacts of 124–32; migrant dependency on 69–71; migrant expenditure of 62–3, **62**, **65**, 65–9; and multiplier effect 122, 131–2; and path dependency 136–7; prevailing assumptions on remittance expenditure 121–4, *123*; remittance rates 98, 124–5; and savings **127**, 128–31; spending decision tree 122–3, *123*; and triple win thesis 4, 21; as win for sending economy 148–51; *see also* status
remittance economy, Sri Lanka as 161–3, 173
remittance expenditure *see* remittance capital; status
remittance rates 98, 124–5
repeat migration 69–71, **69**
research methodology 28–9
Rodrigo, C. 133
rural areas 36, 37, 97; and development projects 138, 140

Safi, Michael 139
Sassen, Saskia 17
Saudi Arabia 5, 68, 78, 81, 91–2, 100, 102, 111
savings **127**, 128–31
Schampers, Toon 41
self-employment 60–1, 64, 66, 67, 129
self-help development 20, 137, 155, 173
service industries 63
sexual abuse 109–10
Shaikh, Anwar 136
Shaw, Judith 130–1, 137
shipping industry 54
Sinhala Only Act 1956 35
Sirisena government 8, 45, 138, 139
skill composition of migrants, and demand volatility 160; *see also* low-skilled workers; skilled workers
skilled workers: demographics of **96**, 150; development of 43–4, 45; gendered division of 98, **98**; importance of 43–4; paucity of 44–5; retention of 45, 149; underemployment of 147–8, 150–1; upskilling 44
Sri Lankan Bureau of Foreign Employment (SLBFE) 43–4, 56, 75, 85, 89, 90–1, 92
social relations of production 23–5, 34
social theory of consumption 26
socialisation of labour 114–15; *see also* status
socially transformative development 23
Special Economic Zone (SEZ) 138
Sri Lanka Foreign Employment Agency (SLFEA) 43
Sri Lanka Freedom Party (SLFP) 35
Sri Lanka Migration Employment Authority Act 91
Stark, Oded 19
status 95–118, 170; concept of 25–6; and consumption of goods 111–16, 125–6, 129–31, **131**; display of 111–16, 116–18; emulating other migrants 116–18; and foreign goods brought home 125–6; and gendered working realities 96–102, **96**, **98**, **99**; and home ownership 129; inflated estimations of migrants' wealth 116–18; lifestyle change 107–11, 116–18; and migrant agency 102–4; narrating and consuming

status *continued*
success 104–16; and pre-migration ambitions 116–18; reintegration and gender 109–11; transient nature of 116; working conditions 98–102, **99**; *see also* remittance capital
stigma 26, 96, 97; as motivation for migration 104–7; *see also* status
sub-agents 86–7, 88–9, 90–1, 93
Sunday Times, *The* 90
Swiss Development Corporation (SDC) 70, 87–9, 97, 103, 105, 117

Tamils: and civil war 38; cultural subjugation of 34; exclusion of 35, 37; and forced migration 55–6; garment industry 39; migration trends 41, 42; *see also* Thavapuram, migrants from
tea industry 40, 51
temporary labour migration (general): in the Asian century 1–6; demographics of 7, 41–2, 152; as foundations of the remittance economy 40–1; policies to promote 43–5; and Sri Lanka 6–9; triple win thesis 4–5, 21–2, 146–53, 172–3; *see also* forced migration and uneven development; migration-development, history of; temporary labour migration and unequal wins
temporary labour migration, and unequal wins 145–63; and care economy 155–7; and demand volatility 159–61; foreign employment spillovers 157–8; import spillovers 158–9; indirect implications of 154–61; mutual benefits 153–4; relative wins 147–52; Sri Lanka as archetypal remittance economy 161–3; unequal costs of migration 154–5; unequal outcomes 146–7; win for migrants 147–8; win for receiving economies 151–2; win for sending economies 148–51; *see also* forced migration and uneven development
Thavapuram, migrants from 51, *53*, 55–6; business investments 61, 66, **66**; civil war 87–8; debt 83–5, **83**; education 59; housing 58; migration as new phenomenon 87–8, 89; recruitment costs 76–7, *76–7*, 82, **82**; recruitment methods **76**, 80–1, 170; remittance expenditure 66, **66**, **68**; and status 109, 110; working conditions 100, 101–2
Todaro, M. 15
traditional livelihoods 52, 53, 54, 55
training programmes, skills development 44
triple win thesis 4–5, 21–2; impact of 172–3; unpicking of 146–53

underdevelopment 23–8, 167–73
underemployment 51, 97, 148
unemployment 51, 148–9, *149*
uneven development *see* costs of migration; forced migration and uneven development; migration development, history of; political economy of uneven development; remittance capital
United National Party (UNP) 35, 35–6, 40–1
United Nations Economic Commission for Europe (UNECE) 146
upskilling 44
urban areas: concentration of capital in 17; and development projects 139; and export production 37, 39–40; and recruitment agencies 85–6
Urban Development Authority (UDA) 139

Van Hear, Nicholas 22
Veblen, Thorstein 26, 114, 115, 116, 157
visas 67, 79, 81, 98, 101

wages 16–17; gender pay gap 98; income of migrants 98; underpayment of **99**, 101–2; *see also* remittance capital
Wallerstein, Immanuel Maurice 17
Wamanan, Arthur 9
Washington Consensus 19, 21–2
Weeraratne, Bilesha 92
Wickramasekara, Piyasiri 147, 173
women: as absent mothers 92–3, 156; as cheap labour 6–7; demographics of migration 42; gendered subordination 34–5, 39–40, 92; and media coverage 91–3; and neoliberalism 36; stigma 97; *see also* domestic workers; gender
Women and Media Collective (WMC) 112, 113
working conditions 40, 43, 44, 91–2, 98–102, **99**, 109–10
World Bank 4, 121–2, 132, 145, 146, 150, 151
world-systems theory 17, 23–4

Xenogiani, Theodora 122, 132, 134

Yahampath, Sita 91

zakat 55, 80

www.ingramcontent.com/pod-product-compliance
Ingram Content Group UK Ltd.
Pitfield, Milton Keynes, MK11 3LW, UK
UKHW011015180926
475701UK00004B/754
* 9 7 8 1 0 3 2 4 0 1 5 0 8 *